Negotiating Identities: Education for Empowerment in a Diverse Society

by Jim Cummins

"Our classroom was full of human knowledge. We had a teacher who believed in us...he didn't hide our power, he advertised it."

— Adriana and Rosalba Jasso (1995)

Ontario Institute for Studies in Education
Published by

**California Association
for Bilingual Education**
320 West G Street, Suite 203
Ontario, CA 91762

First Edition: 1996

Text and cover design by Carole M. Aldrich

Library of Congress Catalog Card Number: 96-084344

ISBN 1-889094-00-5

This book is dedicated to Antonia López, Marilyn Prosser, and teachers in the Foundation Center preschools whose educational vision transformed the lives of countless preschool children and their families

Table of Contents

Acknowledgements

When *Empowering Minority Students* was published by the California Association for Bilingual Education (CABE) in February 1989, my expectation was that I would revise and update it within about two years. In fact, it has taken seven years for the ideas in this book to gel sufficiently to come to print. Many people have contributed to this process. My greatest debt is to educators throughout North America and elsewhere whose practice has informed and elaborated the theory in the book. In an important sense the book represents a stage in a continuing dialogue about how to create contexts of empowerment in schools. The practice of many educators illustrates far more eloquently than any theory how power can be generated collaboratively in the interactions between educators, students, and communities and how these interactions can simultaneously challenge structures of injustice in schools and other institutions of society. Thus, I see the book as a collaborative effort that draws on the energy, insights, and dedication of many educators.

Discussions with academic colleagues regarding the education of culturally diverse students during a period of almost 20 years have also contributed greatly to my understanding of the issues. I would particularly like to thank Alma Flor Ada, Stephen Krashen, Tove Skutnabb-Kangas, Merrill Swain, and Lily Wong Fillmore for their support, constructive criticism and insights from the earliest germinations of these ideas. More recently, discussions with David Corson on language policies and bilingual education in the international sphere and with Sonia Nieto on the intersections between multicultural education and critical pedagogy have exerted a significant influence on my work. I would also like to thank Dennis Sayers, co-author of *Brave New Schools: Challenging Cultural Illiteracy through Global Learning Networks* for many discussions of issues concerning the education of bilingual students and the potential impact of technology in improving educational outcomes. Ideas developed collaboratively with Dennis are particularly reflected in Chapter 6.

During the past four years I have been involved in the development of a grades 1–8 language development program, *ScottForesman ESL: Accelerating English Language Learning.* My co-authors of that program, Anna Uhl Chamot, Carolyn Kessler, J. Michael O'Malley, and Lily Wong Fillmore, have greatly increased my understanding of the teaching/learning process and their ideas as much as mine are reflected in the framework outlined in Chapter 4.

Others who have contributed in a variety of ways to the development of these ideas are: Margarita Calderón who first invited me to dialogue with educators in California in the late 1970s; David Dolson, Norm Gold, Dennis Parker, Fred Tempes and their colleagues in the Office of Bilingual Education of the California State Department of Education in the early 1980s who helped forge and implement a theoretical framework that has had immense impact on the education of bilingual students in that state and elsewhere; Margo Okazawa-Rey whose editorial feedback helped refine the initial expression of the "empowerment framework" published in the Harvard Educational Review in 1986; Naomi Silverman who first expressed an interest in publishing *Empowering Minority Students;* Nanci Goldman and Fiona O'Donoghue who, in very different Canadian contexts, demonstrated how a transformative perspective could fuel the change process in culturally diverse schools; and Antonia López who showed me what could be achieved in bilingual preschool programs oriented to empowerment of teachers, children, parents, and communities and also why such programs are so threatening to those who wish to preserve a coercive power structure.

I am also extremely grateful to those who provided suggestions or "corrective feedback" on draft chapters of this volume: David Corson, Bonnie Freeman, John Gibbons, Pauline Gibbons, Mary Ann Larsen-Pusey, Lois Meyer, and many students in both Fresno Pacific College and the Ontario Institute for Studies in Education. Others who have provided feedback and encouragement at various stages are: Marcel Danesi, Robert DeVillar, Chris Faltis, Fred Genesee, Kazuko Nakajima, Alistair Pennycook, and Joan Wink. For permission to quote their insightful suggestions about schooling (p. 171-172), I would like to thank Jessica and Julia Rosciglione (ages 9 and 7) and their mother Jane O'Hare.

Finally, I would like to express my appreciation to Ellen Jeske-Lieto for assistance in preparing the manuscript, to Carole Aldrich of The Design Group for the design and layout of this volume, and to Mitch Geriador of CABE for his patience and good humor as deadline after deadline passed with no final manuscript in sight.

Preface

This is a revised and expanded version of *Empowering Minority Students* published by the California Association for Bilingual Education (CABE) in 1989. The themes and overall structure are similar to those of the earlier book. In particular, both books focus on how power relations operating in the broader society influence the interactions that occur between teachers and students in the classroom. These interactions can be empowering or disempowering for both teachers and students. The basic argument in both books is similar: culturally diverse students are disempowered educationally in very much the same way that their communities have been disempowered historically in their interactions with societal institutions. The logical implication is that these students will succeed academically to the extent that the patterns of interaction in school reverse those that prevail in the society at large. In other words, a genuine commitment to helping all students succeed academically requires a willingness on the part of educators, individually and collectively, to challenge aspects of the power structure in the wider society.

Thus, the term *empowerment* entails both sociological and psychological dimensions: to create contexts of empowerment in classroom interactions involves not only establishing the respect, trust, and affirmation required for students (and educators) to reflect critically on their own experience and identities; it also challenges explicitly the devaluation of identity that many culturally diverse students and communities still experience in the society as a whole. In concrete terms, when the school affirms the value of students' primary language and encourages them to take pride in their cultural background, it repudiates the escalating societal discourse proclaiming that bilingualism "shuts doors" (Arthur Schlesinger Jr.) and disadvantages both the individual and the wider society (Newt Gingrich).

The most immediate difference between the two books is in their titles. I felt the original title needed to be changed because two of its three words are problematic. As several investigators have pointed out (e.g. Clarke, 1990; Macedo, 1994; Ruiz, 1991), use of the verb "empower" in a transitive sense ("to empower someone") suggests that educators are giving the gift of "empowerment" to their students who are thereby consigned to the role of passive recipients rather than agents of their own empowerment. This was certainly not the intent of the original analysis but it made sense in rewriting the book to avoid this type of connotation and its potential for misunderstanding.

The term "minority" has also become problematic. To an increasing number of educators and communities, the term has assumed pejorative connotations and is also seen as inaccurate in view of demographic realities and projections. So-called "minority" students (e.g. Latino/Latina, African American, Asian American, Native American, and other groups) currently constitute the "majority" school population in California and in the nation's largest cities. [1] I have thus tried to avoid using the term, preferring instead terms such as "bilingual," "culturally diverse," and sometimes "English Language Learning" (ELL), depending on the context.

The title of this volume reflects the fact that relationships between educators and students are at the heart of student learning. The interactions between educators and students always entail a process of negotiating identities. The concept of *negotiating identities* recognizes the agency of culturally diverse students and communities in resisting devaluation and in affirming their basic human rights, but it also focuses on the fact that identities develop in a social context. As articulated by R.D. Laing, the late Scottish psychiatrist: "No one acts or experiences in a vacuum... all 'identities' require an other" (1969, pp. 81-82). The ways in which student-teacher identities are negotiated in classroom and school interactions play a major role in determining students' orientation to self and their orientation to academic effort, as illustrated by the words of Adriana and Rosalba Jasso on the cover of this volume.

As educators, we are constantly sketching an image not only of our own identities and those we envisage for our students, but also of the society we hope our students will form. Students who have been failed by schools predominantly come from communities whose languages, cultures and identities have been distorted and devalued in the wider society. In the past, schools have reinforced this pattern of disempowerment by punishing students for speaking their home language in the school and ignoring or dismissing the knowledge and values of particular communities. Schools viewed culturally diverse students as inherently inferior, a judgement frequently legitimated by culturally-biased IQ tests. Not surprisingly, students usually disengaged themselves from school learning under these conditions.

The central argument of the book is that if schools and society are genuinely committed to reversing this pattern of school failure, with its massive human and social costs to the nation, the interactions between educators and students in schools must actively challenge historical patterns of disempowerment. This requires that schools respect students' language and culture, encourage community participation, promote critical literacy, and institute forms of assessment that contribute to the school as a learning community rather than pathologize culturally diverse students as scapegoats for the failure of schools and society.

The collaborative creation of power by students and teachers within the classroom frequently is resisted by the power structure of the school and the wider society. This is one of the major reasons why almost 15 years of intense focus on educational restructuring in schools across North America has had minimal impact on the achievement levels of culturally diverse students. Most of the reforms have focused on cosmetic modifications to surface structures, leaving intact the deep structures that reflect patterns of disempowerment in the wider society.

As I reflect back on the seven years since the original volume was published and look forward to the turn of the millennium, I am struck by a conflictual mixture of optimism and pessimism. The increasing recognition in states such as California that educators require specialized knowledge and skills to teach effectively in multilingual contexts is shadowed by the extreme shortage of bilingual teachers which limits the extent to which genuine bilingual programs can be instituted. The clear demonstration of the importance of promoting first language literacy, provided by the Ramírez report (Ramírez, 1992) and by the work of Wayne Thomas and Ginger Collier (1995), among others, is largely obliterated in the public mind by the increasingly strident media denunciation of cultural diversity as a threat to the fabric of nationhood. The demonization of bilingual education and cultural diversity as the "enemy within" in this orchestrated discourse echoes in a very scary way the extreme forms of scapegoating of difference that have preceded spasms of ethnic conflict in various countries throughout this century.

The discourse related to diversity of all kinds (gender, linguistic, cultural, religious, sexual orientation etc.) is still ruled by the imperatives of *Us versus Them* — what I call in this volume, *coercive relations of power*. Yet, we cannot turn on a television or open a newspaper without seeing the appalling consequences of this way of relating to each other. [2]

Coercive relations of power are not inevitable. In fact, virtually all of us are familiar with an alternative way of relating among people, communities and nations. We have all experienced how power can be generated in interpersonal relationships — how the empowerment of one partner augments rather than diminishes the power of the other. This book is about how to institute these *collaborative relations of power* in the classroom and school.

The book is hopeful because it is based explicitly on the premise that individual educators have a considerable degree of control over how they structure their interactions with culturally diverse students. Although there are usually many constraints and influences on how educators define their roles, ultimately they have choices in the messages they communicate regarding students' language and culture, in the forms of parent and community participation they encourage, and in the extent to which they promote collaborative critical inquiry as a dominant form of learning in their classrooms. There are many examples in the book of how communities, educators and students have collaborated to generate power.

The book is also realistic because it acknowledges the enormous pressures that constrict the options available to educators, students, and communities. The portraits of collaborative empowerment in the book are still very much the exceptions. In many schools that serve culturally diverse communities across North America, the "savage inequalities" identified by Jonathan Kozol (1992) are still very much in evidence, despite the best efforts of committed educators.

My own frustration in this volume will probably be evident; my frustration with the hypocrisy of documents such as *America 2000* or its Clinton era reincarnation as *Goals 2000* which proclaim that by the year 2000 all American children will start school ready to learn, while ignoring the fact that an additional one million children under the age of 6 have fallen into poverty between 1987 and 1992. The link between poverty, educational failure, and incarceration has been demonstrated repeatedly (e.g. Hodgkinson, 1991). The fact that many of these impoverished preschool children are destined for prison seems to bother those in power very little, despite the fact that the costs to the taxpayer for incarceration are many times more than what would have been required to prevent poverty, school failure, and incarceration.

We have alternatives to the current directions. These alternatives require educators to recognize that relations of power are at the core of schooling and also to recognize that, as educators, we have choices regarding how power is negotiated in our classroom interactions. This volume attempts to sketch how educators and students together can create, through their classroom interactions, a microcosm of the kind of society where everybody feels a strong sense of belonging regardless of race, gender, language, culture, creed or sexual orientation. The creation of these interpersonal and collective spaces represents an act of resistance to those elements within the societal power structure that are intolerant of difference and are motivated to maximize individual profit at the expense of the common good.

Endnotes to Preface

1. It is worth noting that the term "minority" is not generally viewed as pejorative in European and Canadian contexts where certain officially-designated minorities have legal and constitutional rights as a result of their status (e.g. official language minorities in Canada, namely francophones outside of Quebec and anglophones within Quebec).

2. Anybody who doubts the existence of coercive relations of power should read Marilyn French's (1992) book *The War Against Women* which documents the universal oppression of women in countries throughout the world. For example, although women do between 65 and 75 percent of the world's work and produce 45 percent of the world's food, they hold only ten percent of the world's income and one percent of the world's property.

Chapter 1
Identity and Empowerment

Relationships dominated all participant discussions about issues of schooling in the U.S. No group inside the schools felt adequately respected, connected or affirmed. Students, over and over again, raised the issue of care. What they liked best about school was when people, particularly teachers, cared about them or did special things for them. Dominating their complaints were being ignored, not being cared for and receiving negative treatment. (Mary Poplin and Joseph Weeres, *Voices from the Inside: A Report on Schooling from Inside the Classroom*, 1992, p. 19).

Although Poplin and Weeres' study focused only on four schools, it represents one of the most in-depth examinations of schooling ever carried out in North America. Their conclusion is based on 24,000 pages of interview transcriptions, essays, drawings, journal entries, and notes. The multicultural urban Californian schools they studied exhibited "a pervasive sense of despair" well summed up by one student who said: "This place hurts my spirit." Teachers in these schools reported that their best experiences were when they connected with students and were able to help them in some way. However, they also reported that they did not always understand students who are culturally different from themselves. They also felt isolated and unappreciated inside schools by students, administrators, and parents as well as within the larger society.

The voices of students, teachers, administrators and parents that line the pages of this report communicate clearly that **human relationships are at the heart of schooling**. The interactions that take place between students and teachers and among students are more central to student success than any method for teaching literacy, or science or math. When powerful relationships are established between teachers and students, these relationships frequently can transcend the economic and social disadvantages that afflict communities and schools alike in inner city and rural areas. Many of us can vividly remember inspiring teachers who, because they believed in us, generated far greater academic effort on our part than did teachers who just taught their subject.

However, the history of education in North America demonstrates equally clearly that relationships established in school can be disempowering for students and communities. Negative messages can be overt or covert, intentional or, more frequently, unintentional. For example, prior to the 1970s, it was extremely common for educators to reprimand bilingual students for speaking their home language (L1) in the school. The message to be internalized was that students' language, culture, and previous experience have no place within this school or, by extension, within this society. To be accepted within the mainstream society, represented by the school, required that students become invisible and inaudible; culture and language should be left at home. [1]

More subtle forms of unintentional rejection were also common. For example, a large-scale study conducted by the U.S. Commission on Civil Rights (1973) in the American southwest reported that Euro-American students were praised or encouraged 36% more often than Mexican-American students and their classroom contributions were used or built upon 40% more frequently than those of Mexican-American students. It is not hard to see how, under these conditions, many students might come to see themselves as not very bright academically. This is particularly the case when their command of the language of instruction is still at an early stage of development.

The title of this volume points to these interactions, these ways of *negotiating identities*, as fundamental to the academic success of culturally diverse students. When students' developing sense of self is affirmed and extended through their interactions with teachers, they are more likely to apply themselves to academic effort and participate actively in instruction. The consequent learning is the fuel that generates further academic effort. The more we learn, the more we want to learn, and the more effort we are prepared to put into that learning.

By contrast, when students' language, culture and experience are ignored or excluded in classroom interactions, students are immediately starting from a disadvantage. Everything they have learned about life and the world up to this point is being dismissed as irrelevant to school learning; there are few points of connection to curriculum materials or instruction and so students are expected to learn in an experiential vacuum. Students' silence and non-participation under these conditions have frequently been interpreted as lack of academic ability or effort, and teachers' interactions with students have reflected a pattern of low expectations which become self-fulfilling.

In the past, the school's rejection of students' language and culture tended to reflect the broader society's subordination of cultures and languages other than those of the dominant group. In many societies throughout the world, students who experience the most persistent and severe educational difficulties tend to come from communities that, over generations, have been discriminated against and viewed as inherently inferior by the dominant societal group (Ogbu, 1978, 1992). This pattern of relationships between dominant and subordinated groups in the wider society is typical of colonial situations in which the indigenous population is widely disparaged by the colonial power. This is illustrated historically by the attitudes of the British in Africa, India, or Ireland during the heyday of the British empire. The current attitudes of ruling elites in many Latin American countries towards indigenous peoples similarly illustrate this pattern.

The historical experience of subordinated groups in many parts of Europe (e.g. Catalans and Basques in Spain) and in the North American context reflects their status as *internal colonies* (Blauner, 1969). Schools reflect the values and attitudes of the broader society that supports them and so it is hardly surprising that in the United States students from African American, Latino/Latina, and Native American communities have experienced extensive devaluation of their cultures and languages within the school context. In some cases, students perceive that their identity is endangered by this process of devaluation and consequently drop out of school in order to preserve their sense of self.

A central argument of the present volume is that this devaluation of identity played out in the interactions between educators and students convinces many students that academic effort is futile. They resist further devaluation of their identities by mentally withdrawing from participation in the life of the school. In inner city areas, they frequently find family and affirmation of identity in the streets as members of gangs. [2]

To turn this scenario around and reverse the pattern of academic failure inevitably requires that educators, students, and communities challenge the historical pattern of subordination that has characterized relations in the broader society. When educators encourage culturally diverse students to develop the language and culture they bring from home and build on their prior experiences, they, together with their students, challenge the perception in the broader society that these attributes are inferior or worthless. When educators and culturally diverse parents become genuine partners in children's education, this partnership repudiates the myth that culturally diverse parents are apathetic and don't care about their children's education. When classroom instruction encourages students to inquire critically into social issues that affect their lives (e.g. racism, environmental deterioration, omissions of groups other than "dead white men" from official histories, etc.), students' intelligence is activated in ways that potentially challenge the societal status quo.

It is important to note at the outset that affirmation of identity is not an uncritical process. It does not imply that educators or students should accept all cultural manifestations in a "liberal" non-evaluative way. Many cultural practices and social structures violate the United Nations Declaration of Human Rights and other United Nations charters (see Skutnabb-Kangas & Phillipson, 1994). Students should be encouraged to reflect critically on both their own cultural background and on the culture of the host society in order to identify and resolve contradictions. This process will bring alternative perspectives into the open for both the teacher and students and enable them to understand their world and their identities more coherently than if only one perspective were presented as valid. Affirmation of identity thus refers to the establishment of the respect and trust between educators and students that is crucial for each to reflect critically on their own experience and beliefs. Respect and trust imply that educators listen carefully to their students' perspectives and learn from their students. If teachers are not learning much from their students, it is probable that their students are not learning much from them.

The ways in which negotiation of identity is related to the empowerment or disempowerment of students and communities can be illustrated by contrasting two sets of school-community interactions. The example of a family literacy project in the Pajaro Valley school district in California shows how interactions between educators and parents that affirm student and community identity can result in empowerment of educators, students and parents. The second example draws on the historical experience of First Nations (Native) students in residential schools in the Canadian context; it illustrates in an extreme way how colonial orientations to schooling have shattered the fragile identities of young children and destroyed communities. [3]

Empowerment through Negotiation of Identity: The Pajaro Valley Family Literacy Project

The Pajaro Valley School district serves a mostly rural population in the area surrounding Watsonville, California. More than half the students in the district are Spanish-speaking and in the past more than half of these have dropped out before completing high school. This compares to a dropout rate of about 35% in the general student population (Ada, 1988a). During 1986, a group of Spanish-speaking parents varying in size between 60 and 100 met once a month to discuss (among themselves and with Alma Flor Ada) children's literature and to read stories and poems written both by their children, and, increasingly, by themselves. Ada points out that most of these parents had very little schooling and many had never read a book before, much less thought about writing one.

Alma Flor Ada's involvement with the district arose out of an invitation from the school librarian to participate in a "meet the author" program during which she read some of her (Spanish) stories to the children and discussed aspects of what is involved in the process of writing. Children's enthusiasm was enormous and it was decided to follow up the interest that had been stimulated in the children by involving their parents in a similar literacy experience.

The planning of the project (by Alma Flor Ada, Alfonso Anaya, director of the bilingual program, and teachers) was carried out carefully in order to encourage parental participation. For example, meetings were carried out in the library rather than the school itself because of frequent negative associations that culturally diverse parents have with schools; the subject of the meetings was non-threatening, namely children's literature; parents were respectfully invited to participate (through written invitations in Spanish and follow-up personal phone calls); a parallel program for children was offered in a nearby room (films, storytelling, etc.); and several teachers' aides offered to give rides to parents who lacked transportation. In addition, all the bilingual teachers participated in the meetings, which were conducted entirely in Spanish.

The initial discussion at the first meeting covered the purpose of the program and issues such as the importance of promoting children's proficiency in their home language and pride in their cultural heritage. In addition, parents' crucial role as their children's first and best teachers was stressed. According to Ada (1988a):

> The results of this initial discussion were overwhelming. It was obvious that the parents were deeply moved. One mother stood up and

explained: 'What is happening to us is that no one has ever told us that our children are worth something, and no one has ever told us that we are worth something.' (p. 227)

The dialogue on these general themes was followed by a presentation of five children's story books, chosen primarily for their appeal in terms of literary content and presentation. Alma Flor Ada read each of the books aloud to the whole group of parents, dramatizing the action and showing the illustrations. Then parents were invited to select the book they wanted to take home and to join a small group for discussion of that particular book. These discussions were facilitated by the bilingual teachers who were careful to accept and validate everyone's participation while guiding the discussion to more reflective levels of analysis.

In addition to a copy of the book they had chosen, each parent was given a list of questions as a general guide for home discussions with their children. These questions were based on Ada's (1988b) *Creative Reading* methodology (see Chapter 6) and were intended to extend children's and parents' under-standing of the story by relating it to their prior experience, critically analyzing aspects of the story, and applying their understandings to real-life situations. In addition, participants were given a list of suggested activities related to the book and a blank book in which children might be encouraged to write their own sto-ries or dictate them for the parents to write. All sessions were videotaped.

From the second session, the parents met first in small groups according to which book they had selected the previous month in order to talk about their experiences in discussing the books with their children. Then in a whole group format they read and listened to some of the stories the children wrote or dictated. Finally, the new books were presented and small groups formed to discuss them.

Ada sums up the major results of the project as follows:

parents have begun to read aloud to their children, the children have begun to bring home books from the school library, and parents and children have gone to the public library in search of books. At the first meeting we had a show of hands to find out how many parents had public library cards. None did. At a meeting nine months later almost everyone reported several visits to the library to check out books. (1988a, p. 223)

In addition, the teachers' aides borrowed the videotapes and showed them in the community, thereby giving the children the opportunity of seeing their parents on television reading aloud the stories created by the children. According to Ada, "the children have felt double pride, both in seeing their parents on the screen, and in hearing their own stories being read aloud." This experience greatly increased children's motivation to write.

Other consequences were an increase in self-confidence and self-expression on the part of the parents, indicated by parents taking over the roles of small-group facilitators, giving presentations on the use of children's literature at the Regional Migrant Education Conference, and requesting the opportunity to purchase books in Spanish for their children, since the one book a month that they took home was insufficient. At the parents' suggestion, a book of stories their children wrote was compiled.

Ada quotes extensively from the parents themselves about their reaction to the program. Two examples will illustrate the empowerment process that took place over the course of these meetings:

> Another mother said: 'Ever since I know I have no need to feel ashamed of speaking Spanish I have become strong. Now I feel I can speak with the teachers about my children's education and I can tell them I want my children to know Spanish. I have gained courage'…

> One of the fathers said: 'I have discovered that my children can write. And I bring another story [written by his child]. But I have also discovered something personal. I have discovered that by reading books one can find out many things. Since my children want me to read them the stories over and over again, I took them to the public library to look for more books. There I discovered books about our own culture. I borrowed them and I am reading, and now I am finding out things I never knew about our roots and what has happened to them and I have discovered that I can read in Spanish about the history of this country [the U.S.A.] and of other countries.' (1988a, p. 235-236) [4]

It is clear that these parents are gaining the internal resources, confidence and motivation to exert greater control over the forces that affect their lives. The community's language, culture, and experiences have been acknowledged and validated, a genuine partnership has been established with the school, and the potential of literacy to transform their lives and the lives of their children has been understood. [5] This experience can be described as *empowering*, not because it made the parents or children feel good, but because it challenged and transformed the power relations that are embedded in more typical modes of school-community interactions.

The ways in which these power relations operate can be seen in the discourse surrounding "parental involvement" that has arisen in the North American context during the past 30 years. Despite the fact that this term lines the pages of the many manuals of school effectiveness that have been produced during this period, one can search in vain through most of this literature to find examples of genuine partnerships between schools and parents from culturally diverse backgrounds. [6] Because parents fail to show up to meetings designed to teach them "parenting skills" or other strategies for overcoming their children's "deficits," educators have assumed that they are just not interested in their children's education. This perspective is illustrated by Lloyd Dunn (1987), the author of the widely-used *Peabody Picture Vocabulary Test*, who explicitly blames Spanish-speaking parents for their children's academic difficulties when he argues that "teachers are not miracle workers" (p. 65) and "Hispanic pupils and their parents have also failed the schools and society, because they have not been motivated and dedicated enough to make the system work for them" (p. 78). In other words, his argument is that educators are powerless to reverse the debilitating effects of apathetic and incompetent Latino/Latina parents (whom Dunn also regards as genetically inferior [p. 64]).

This form of discourse defines culturally diverse students and parents as inferior in various ways and therefore responsible for their own school failure and poverty. It also takes the focus of critical scrutiny away from the schools and society, thereby legitimating the educational and social status quo and deflecting pressures for change.

Projects such as the Pajaro Valley example and others (e.g. Balderas, 1995; Delgado-Gaitan, 1994, McCaleb, 1994; Torres-Guzman, 1995; Weinstein-Shr & Quintero, 1995) show that culturally diverse parents strongly desire to contribute to their children's education. The parental involvement manifested in these projects exposes the structures of disempowerment that masquerade as "normal" patterns of interaction between schools and culturally diverse communities. Parents who have survived brutal oppression in their home countries and are experiencing poverty and hardship as they struggle to raise their children care passionately about their children's education. However, if ability to speak English and knowledge of North American cultural conventions are made prerequisites for "parental involvement," then many of these parents will be defined as apathetic and incompetent and will play out their pre-ordained role of "uninvolvement."

In contrast to the affirmation of identity and empowerment that are reflected in the interactions between educators and parents in the Pajaro Valley example, the second example describes the disempowerment that indigenous peoples experienced historically in the educational system. Although the primary example is from Canada, equally disturbing accounts could have been drawn from countries such as Australia, New Zealand or the United States.

Disempowerment through Negotiation of Identity: The First Nations Residential School Experience

Residential schools in Canada operated in similar ways to boarding schools in the United States insofar as students were taken from their communities, often against their parents' will, and permitted to return to their communities only sporadically. Some of these schools were still operating up to about 20 years ago. The story of what happened in these schools for more than one hundred years has begun to emerge in the Canadian context from the first-hand accounts of survivors. Physical, sexual, and psychological abuse were rampant and federal, provincial and Church authorities simply turned a blind eye to what they knew was going on. Eradication of Native identity was seen as a prerequisite to making students into low-level productive citizens.

As expressed more than one hundred years ago by the General Secretary of the Methodist Church of Canada, removal of children from the influence of their homes (for at least five years) was a necessary condition for both salvation and civilization:

> Experience convinces us that the only way in which the Indians of the Country can be permanently elevated and thoroughly civilized, is by removing the children from the surroundings of Indian home life, and keeping them separate long enough to form those habits of order, industry, and systematic effort, which they will never learn at home. ... The return of children to their houses, even temporarily, has a bad effect, while their permanent removal [back home] after one or two years residence results in the loss of all that they have gained. (Letter dated April 2, 1886, from A. Sutherland, General Secretary of

the Methodist Church of Canada, Missionary Department to Laurence Vankoughnet, Deputy Superintendent of Indian Affairs. Quoted in Tschantz, 1980, p. 7)

Tschantz goes on to document the extreme violence used in these schools to dissuade children from using their mother tongue, the key to their identity:

Dolphus Shae's testimony to the Berger Inquiry (1977:90) of his experiences at the Aklavik Residential School describes not only the terrifying experiences which he and many other children endured, but also the resentment which lasted all his life: 'Before I went to school the only English I knew was 'hello' and when we got there we were told that if we spoke Indian they would whip us until our hands were blue on both sides. And also we were told that the Indian religion was superstitious and pagan. It made you feel inferior to whites…We all felt lost and wanted to go home…Today I think back on the hostel life and I feel furious.' (Tschantz, 1980, p. 10)

Platero has described similar realities for Navajo students in the United States:

For nearly a hundred years the policy of the United States government was to acculturate the Navajo, so that the Navajo could be assimilated into the White society. To effect this assimilation Navajo children were taken from the shelter of the family and sent to boarding school. Almost every child who entered the boarding school spoke only Navajo, and most of the people employed at the boarding schools spoke only English. When a Navajo child spoke the language of his family at school, he was punished. …Kee was sent to boarding school as a child where — as was the practice — he was punished for speaking Navajo. Since he was only allowed to return home during Christmas and summer, he lost contact with his family. Kee withdrew both from the White and Navajo worlds as he grew older, because he could not comfortably communicate in either language.…By the time he was 16, Kee was an alcoholic, uneducated and despondent — without identity. Kee's story is more the rule than the exception. (Platero, 1975, p. 57-58)

The process of identity negotiation in schools is a reciprocal one between educators and students. For example, in the case of First Nations students in residential schools, educators defined their role as dispensers of salvation, civilization and education to students who necessarily had to be defined as lacking all of these qualities. In other words, the self-definition of educators required that students and their communities be defined as heathen, savage and without any valid form of cultural transmission (education). This devaluation of identity was communicated to students in all of the interactions they experienced in schools, ranging from brutal punishment if they were caught speaking their languages to widespread sexual abuse of both boys and girls, as illustrated in the following newspaper account of a conference focused on the residential school experience in British Columbia:

> A representative of four British Columbia native bands said yesterday that they intend to call churches and governments to account — morally and financially — for the damage done to their communities through the religious residential school system. ...the council of four Shuswap Indian bands decided to mount the conference after the community started to conquer widespread alcoholism and social problems in recent years and realized that the self-destructive behavior had been masking the pain of the residential school experience.

> Most children in the bands were forced to attend the St. Joseph's Mission, a residential school operated by the Roman Catholic Oblate order, until it was closed 10 years ago. Two former officials of the school have been convicted of sexually abusing male students, and its former principal, Bishop Hugh O'Connor of Prince George, is scheduled to go to a preliminary hearing next month on charges of abusing female students. ...

> Bev Sellars, chief of the Soda Creek Indian band of the Cariboo region, said aside from incidents of sexual abuse, residential school children were brutally strapped, sometimes 'until they were black and blue' and permanently scarred. She said they were treated 'like dirt' and made to feel like 'part of a weak, defective race.' 'That to me is not training for success, it is training for self-destruction,' she said. 'And thousands did self-destruct. If they didn't commit suicide, they became addicted to anything that could numb or distract the pain, and the addictions unfortunately only became another thing to be ashamed of.'" (Wilson, 1991, *The Globe & Mail*, p. A4)

The destruction of identity that went on in residential schools was rationalized as being in the best interests of the children involved. Although few other examples reach the depth of brutality of the Canadian residential school experience, the *process* that these examples illustrate is extremely common. In far too many contexts, the message given to students and communities is that success in school and in the wider society requires that they abandon any identification or affiliation with the culture and experiences they brought to school. Students' prior experiences are seen as an impediment to academic growth rather than as the foundation upon which academic development can be built.

In short, the process of identity negotiation is interwoven into all educator-student interactions. This process is usually non-problematic when there is a cultural, linguistic and social class match between educator and student but often highly problematic when there are mismatches or discontinuities in culture, language or class. In these cases, educators must make special efforts to ensure that students' prior experiences and identities are affirmed rather than devalued.

In the past, the typical pattern has been that the more socially powerful group has devalued the identities of the less powerful group and rationalized this as being in the group's best interests. Under these conditions, subordinated group members often partially internalize the ways they are defined or positioned by the dominant group and come to see themselves as inferior. In *Pedagogy of the Oppressed,* Paulo Freire (1970/1981) calls this process *cultural invasion* which he describes as follows:

> In cultural invasion it is essential that those who are invaded come to see their reality with the outlook of the invaders rather than their own; for the more they mimic the invaders, the more stable the position of the latter becomes. For cultural invasion to succeed, it is essential that those invaded become convinced of their intrinsic inferiority. Since everything has its opposite, if those who are invaded consider themselves inferior, they must necessarily recognize the superiority of the invaders. (p. 151)

However, subordinated groups and individuals also actively resist cultural invasion and devaluation of identity. For example, indigenous peoples throughout the Americas (and elsewhere) have been resisting cultural invasion for more than 500 years and this struggle continues unabated (see the volume *Rethinking Columbus* published by Rethinking Schools [1991]). In the educational context, resistance can occasionally take the form of excelling academically, as illustrated in the case studies described by Zanger (1994). However, more frequently it results in withdrawal from academic effort and dropping out of school (see discussions in Darder [1991] and Walsh [1991]). [7]

The ways in which identities are negotiated in the classroom are strongly influenced by the assumptions in regard to culture and language in the wider society. Economically- and socially-powerful groups who have access to, and effectively control, the media can manufacture consent for social and educational policies that they see as serving their interests (Chomsky, 1987). For example, during the 1990s, groups such as *U.S. English* have escalated a national campaign to promote English-only programs as being in the best interests of bilingual children. Their goal is to change both the way educators interact with bilingual students and the structures that exist within schools (e.g. bilingual education). Arguments such as the following are intended to constrict the identity options for bilingual students in essentially similar ways to the constriction of identity that took place in residential schools for Native students:

- Bilingual students must be prevented from using their first language (L1) in school because "how else will they ever learn English?"

- Monolingual English programs are essential if students are to be given access to what *U.S. English* calls "the language of equal opportunity."

This type of discourse is discussed in more detail in subsequent chapters. For now the point is that the discourse articulated in the broader society in relation to bilingualism and cultural diversity can and does affect the ways in which educators define their roles with respect to teaching culturally diverse students. This, in turn, will affect the ways in which identities are negotiated in educator-student interactions. In other words, the pattern of inter-group power relations in the broader society is frequently replicated in the interpersonal power relations played out in the interactions between educators and culturally diverse students within the school.

The constriction of options for identity formation illustrated in an extreme way in the First Nations residential schools is clearly not inevitable. As illustrated in the Pajaro Valley example, there are many educators who define their role in a very different way in relation to culturally diverse students and communities. They aim explicitly to expand students' options for identity formation by affirming and building on students' prior experience and exploring with them how they can make powerful contributions within their societies. In other words, their pedagogy explicitly takes into account where students are coming from and where they are going. The teacher mediates between students' past and their future. The instructional focus is on empowerment rather than disempowerment.

Terri McCarty provides a contemporary example of the centrality of what she calls "the image of the child" in restructuring schools for empowerment. She describes the changes in pedagogy and assessment initiated by educators and researchers working together in the Navajo-English bilingual program at Rough Rock as fundamentally involving transformations in the images educators held of themselves and of their students:

> In classrooms, curriculum and pedagogy are the mirrors in which children see themselves reflected and through which they construct images of themselves as thinkers, learners, and users of language. The applied research at Rough Rock suggests the potentials children can exploit when the image they see and develop is one of self-affirmation. By engaging students in relevant, content-rich study that builds on their linguistic and experiential capital, whole language pedagogy opens up these potentials. (1993, p. 191) [8]

It is clear that the ways in which identities are negotiated in the school context between educators, students, and communities are intertwined with patterns of power relations in the wider society. In the next section, the nature of these power relations is explored further in order to define what constitutes *empowerment* in the school context.

Coercive and Collaborative Relations of Power

Coercive relations of power refer to the exercise of power by a dominant group (or individual or country) to the detriment of a subordinated group (or individual or country). The assumption is that there is a fixed quantity of power that operates according to a zero-sum logic; in other words, the more power one group has the less is left for other groups. Coercive relations of power are reflected in and shaped through the use of language or discourse [9] and usually involve a definitional process that legitimates the inferior or deviant status accorded to the subordinated group (or individual or country). In other words, the dominant group defines the subordinated group as inferior (or evil), thereby automatically defining itself as superior (or virtuous). The process of defining groups or individuals as inferior or deviant almost inevitably results in a pattern of interactions that confines them, either psychologically or physically.

For example, when teachers have low expectations of particular groups of students, they tend to provide fewer opportunities for academic development, thereby confining them intellectually.

The experience of First Nations students in residential schools, discussed above, illustrates the operation of coercive relations of power. In this case, the interactions between individual educators and students (henceforth termed *micro-interactions*) were merely reflecting the pattern of interactions between dominant and subordinated groups in the wider society (henceforth *macro-interactions*) where First Nations communities were widely disparaged. In both micro- and macro-interactions, the process of identity negotiation reflects the relations of power in the society.

Coercive relations of power generally operate to maintain the division of resources and status in the society, i.e. the societal power structure. They frequently invoke a particular form of discourse which William Ryan (1972) has called *blaming the victim*. The school failure of subordinated group students is attributed to alleged intrinsic characteristics of the group itself (e.g. bilingualism, parental apathy, genetic inferiority, etc.) or to programs that are seen as serving the interests of the group (e.g. bilingual education).

Collaborative relations of power, on the other hand, operate on the assumption that power is not a fixed pre-determined quantity but rather can be *generated* in interpersonal and intergroup relations. In other words, participants in the relationship are *empowered* through their collaboration such that each is more affirmed in her or his identity and has a greater sense of efficacy to create change in his or her life or social situation. Thus, power is created in the relationship and shared among participants. The power relationship is *additive* rather than *subtractive*. Power is *created with* others rather than being *imposed on* or *exercised over* others. [10]

Within this framework, *empowerment* can be defined as *the collaborative creation of power*. Students whose schooling experiences reflect collaborative relations of power develop the ability, confidence and motivation to succeed academically. They participate competently in instruction as a result of having developed a secure sense of identity and the knowledge that their voices will be heard and respected within the classroom. They feel a sense of ownership for the learning that goes on in the classroom and a sense that they belong in the classroom learning community.

In other words, empowerment derives from the process of negotiating identities in the classroom. Identities are not static or fixed but rather are constantly being shaped through experiences and interactions. There are multiple facets to our identities, some of which are difficult or impossible to change (e.g. gender, ethnicity) while other facets may be more malleable or subject to modification as a result of our experiences (e.g. core values, political affiliation, sense of self-worth in relation to intelligence, academic achievements, talents, attractiveness, etc.). For young children growing up, the sense of self-worth is usually cultivated through interactions with caregivers in the home. Ideally, interactions in the school further consolidate students' sense of self-worth but unfortunately, as we have seen, this has frequently not been the case for students whose communities are viewed as inferior or deviant in the wider society. [11]

Educators' interactions with students reflect the ways they have defined their own roles or identities as educators. These *role definitions* determine the way educators view students' possibilities and the messages they communicate to students in regard to the contributions they can make to their societies. Thus, our interactions with students are constantly sketching a triangular set of images:

• an image of our own identities as educators;

• an image of the identity options we highlight for our students; consider, for example, the contrasting messages conveyed to students in classrooms focused on critical inquiry compared to classrooms focused on passive internalization of information;

• an image of the society we hope our students will help form.

This can be illustrated in the fact that most large-scale studies of classroom interaction in the United States suggest that teacher-centered transmission of information and skills remains the predominant mode of instruction (e.g. Goodlad, 1984; Ramírez, 1992). Sirotnik (1983), in discussing the implications of Goodlad's study, points to the fact that the typical American classroom contains:

> a lot of teacher talk and a lot of student listening...almost invariably closed and factual questions...and predominantly total class instructional configurations around traditional activities — all in a virtually affectless environment. It is but a short inferential leap to suggest that we are implicitly teaching dependence upon authority, linear thinking, social apathy, passive involvement, and hands-off learning. (p. 29)

In other words, an image of the society that students will graduate into and the kind of contributions they can make to that society is embedded implicitly in the interactions between educators and students. These interactions reflect the way educators have defined their role with respect to the purposes of education in general and culturally diverse students and communities in particular. Are we preparing students to accept the societal status quo (and, in many cases, their own inferior status therein) or are we preparing them to participate actively and critically in the democratic process in pursuit of the ideals of social justice and equity that are enshrined in the American constitution?

This perspective clearly implies that in situations where coercive relations of power between dominant and subordinated groups predominate, the creation of interpersonal spaces where students' identities are validated will entail a direct challenge by educators (and students) to the societal power structure. For example, to acknowledge that culturally diverse students' religion, culture and language are valid forms of *self*-expression and to encourage their development is to challenge the prevailing attitudes in the wider society and the coercive structures that give rise to these attitudes.

A central component of the present framework is the argument that real change in the education of culturally diverse students requires a fundamental shift from coercive to collaborative relations of power. The history of humanity does not augur well for the imminence of such a paradigm shift, but environmental and social deterioration has reached a point where there may be little alternative if our species is to survive. The reality is that in the world of winners and losers, the "winner" ultimately joins the loser. Witness how industrialized societies are threatened by the destruction of the rainforests in the developing countries; or how poverty in the inner cities impacts on the wealthier sectors of society through increased crime, drugs, or costs associated with incarceration or welfare. Historical patterns of coercive relations of power are reaching a point of diminishing returns even for socially powerful groups. Simply put, educating students is a much better investment for our society than incarcerating them.

The challenge is to change the structure of power relations such that they become additive through collaboration rather than subtractive through coercion; in other words, the structure of macro- and micro-interactions needs to shift so that these interactions generate power for all participants rather than increase the disparities of power.

Figure 1.1 outlines the framework that has been sketched thus far. This framework also serves to organize the content of subsequent chapters.

The framework proposes that relations of power in the wider society (macro-interactions), ranging from coercive to collaborative in varying degrees, influence both the ways in which educators define their role and the types of structures that are established in the educational system. Role definitions refer to the mindset of expectations, assumptions and goals that educators bring to the task of educating culturally diverse students. Educational structures refer to the organization of schooling in a broad sense that includes policies, programs, curriculum, and assessment. This organization is established to achieve the goals of education as defined primarily by the dominant group in the society. For example, the historical patterns of educational segregation in the United States, Canada, South Africa and many other countries were designed to limit the opportunities that subordinated groups might have for educational and social advancement. By contrast, bilingual education in the United States was instituted to promote equality of educational opportunity at a time (late 1960s, early 1970s) when there was some degree of consensus in the society that this was a valid and important goal.

Educational structures, however, are not static; as with most other aspects of the way societies are organized and resources distributed, educational structures are contested by individuals and groups. The debates surrounding bilingual education illustrate just how volatile these issues can become.

Educational structures, together with educator role definitions, determine the micro-interactions between educators, students, and communities. These micro-interactions form an interpersonal or an interactional space within which the acquisition of knowledge and formation of identity are negotiated. Power is created and shared within this interpersonal space where minds and identities meet.[12] As such, the micro-interactions constitute the most immediate determinant of student academic success or failure.

These micro-interactions between educators, students and communities are never neutral; in varying degrees, they either reinforce coercive relations of power or promote collaborative relations of power. In the former case, they contribute to the disempowerment of culturally diverse students and communities; in the latter case, the micro-interactions constitute a process of empowerment that enables educators, students and communities to challenge the operation of coercive power structures.

Chapters 2 through 5 focus on aspects of bilingualism, language learning, and bilingual education. The second chapter discusses the history of the education of bilingual students in North America and outlines the way certain forms of discourse are currently being mobilized in the service of coercive relations of power. In order to throw some light on the research realities behind this debate, Chapter 3 focuses on the nature of proficiency in a language and

$\mathcal{F}igure\ 1.1$ **COERCIVE AND COLLABORATIVE RELATIONS OF POWER MANIFESTED IN MACRO- AND MICRO-INTERACTIONS**

COERCIVE AND COLLABORATIVE RELATIONS
OF POWER MANIFESTED IN MACRO- AND MICRO-INTERACTIONS
BETWEEN SUBORDINATED COMMUNITIES AND DOMINANT GROUP INSTITUTIONS

EDUCATOR ROLE DEFINITIONS ⟷ EDUCATIONAL STRUCTURES

MICRO-INTERACTIONS BETWEEN
EDUCATORS AND STUDENTS

forming an

INTERPERSONAL SPACE

within which
knowledge is generated
and
identities are negotiated

EITHER

REINFORCING COERCIVE RELATIONS OF POWER
OR
PROMOTING COLLABORATIVE RELATIONS OF POWER

discusses how misconceptions about language proficiency have fueled controversy about bilingual education. In Chapter 4, the kinds of classroom instructional environments that will accelerate academic language learning are examined. Chapter 5 reviews the research on bilingual education and the theoretical principles that underlie the consistent support for programs that strongly support the development of bilingual students' L1.

In Chapter 6, we focus on the specific changes necessary to transform the educational experience of culturally diverse students from the historical pattern of widespread academic failure to a pattern of academic success. This change process entails transformations in schools' orientation to students' language and culture, parental participation, pedagogy, and assessment such that the micro-interactions between educators, students, and communities generate collaborative empowerment.

Portraits of how this empowerment process has operated at the preschool, elementary, and secondary levels are presented in Chapter 7. In Chapter 8, we analyze in more detail the opposition to bilingual education by academic critics in order to illustrate the disregard for both empirical evidence and theoretical consistency that underlies their arguments.

In the final chapter, we return to the issue of how power is negotiated and distributed in both the domestic and international arenas. The goal is to show how the anti-bilingual education discourse mobilized by groups such as *U.S. English* forms part of a broader pattern of coercive relations of power. If educators understand that the purpose of this discourse is (a) to dismantle educational structures that promote student and community empowerment and (b) to limit possibilities for the collaborative creation of power, then they are in a better position to resist this process and more actively promote democratic participation and social justice both in their classrooms and in the wider society.

Endnotes to Chapter 1

1. With the recent escalation of anti-immigrant rhetoric in the United States, even the home is not a safe place to use a language viewed as alien by socially powerful groups. This is illustrated in the remarks of State District Judge Samuel Kiser to Marta Laureano, a bilingual Mexican-American involved in a child custody dispute in Amarillo, Texas. The judge told Laureano that she was abusing her five-year old daughter by speaking Spanish to her and ordered Laureano to speak only English at home. The father of the child, Timothy Garcia, who was seeking unsupervised visitation rights with his daughter, had complained that she was not proficient in English. As reported in Maclean's magazine (September 11, 1995, p. 13):

In court, Kiser told Laureano that she was relegating her daughter "to the position of housemaid." After a public outcry, Kiser backed down — a little. He apologized to housekeepers everywhere, "since we entrust our personal possessions and our families' welfare to these hardworking people." But otherwise, Kiser stood by his statements. Excerpts from his comments:

"If she starts first grade with the other children and cannot even speak the language that the teachers and others speak, and she's a full-blooded American citizen, you're abusing that child and you're relegating her to the position of housemaid. Now, get this straight: you start speaking English to that child, because if she doesn't do good [sic] in school, then I can remove her because it's not in her best interest to be ignorant.

"You are real big about talking about what's best for your daughter, but you won't even teach a five-year-old child how to speak English. And then you expect her to go off to school and educate herself and be able to learn how to make a living. Now that is bordering on abuse."

2. R.D. Laing (1969), the Scottish psychiatrist, has written insightfully about patterns of confirmation and disconfirmation in interpersonal relationships. The following quotations from his book *Self and Others* illustrate his perspective:

Even an account of one person cannot afford to forget that each person is always acting upon others and acted upon by others. The others are there also. No one acts or experiences in a vacuum. ...(pp. 81-82)

A woman cannot be a mother without a child. She needs a child to give her the identity of a mother. A man needs a wife for him to be a husband. ...All 'identities' require an other. ...(p. 82)

Every relationship implies a definition of self by other and other by self. ...Other people become a sort of identity kit, whereby one can piece together a picture of *oneself*. One recognizes *oneself* in that old smile of recognition from that old friend. ...It is difficult to establish a consistent identity for oneself — that is, to see oneself consistently in the same way — if definitions of oneself by others are inconsistent or mutually exclusive. ...To 'fit in with' them all or to repudiate them all may be impossible. Hence mystification, confusion, and conflict. (pp. 86-87)

This is the situation for many culturally diverse students; the messages about identity they receive from home and school are frequently contradictory. As expressed by Sudia Paloma McCaleb (1994), when a child feels that the culture of the home is not valued by that of the school, she:

is often forced to make difficult choices about whose teachings she is going to accept and whose she will reject. When the values and teachings of the home and school are quite different, serious intergenerational conflicts can result. ...While some students accept their bicultural identities, others want to deny their home culture completely. ...We are beginning to witness the tragedy that may result when students reject the home culture. As students pull themselves away from their roots and family ties, they need to find or become part of another group for support and care. Growing numbers of young people are succumbing to the attractions of gang involvement. (pp. 32-33)

Schools can go a long way towards preventing this process when educators affirm the home culture and involve parents as partners in the education of their children (see Chapter 6).

3. The term *First Nations* is the preferred self-descriptor of aboriginal communities in Canada, reflecting their status as the first nations of this continent. First Nations communities in Canada generally view the term *Indian* as reflecting the Eurocentric perspective of Columbus and his followers who thought they had discovered a new route to the Indies.

4. A similar picture emerges from an account of the project in the *Santa Cruz Sentinel*:

Another parent said she noticed her children are now starting to request that she bring more books home to read, and they are now requesting them in Spanish instead of English. The result, she said, is they are learning about their culture and language, and also realizing that there are as many good ideas in Spanish as there are in English.

Another parent said the reading and writing program has helped her to be more resolute in dealing with teachers and demanding that they teach her child Spanish, her native language.

The biggest benefit, however, may be that the children and their parents are being drawn closer by the constant expression and discussion of ideas and books they are working on together.

'Tell your children every day how much you love them, how much you value them and how much you appreciate them,' Ada said in closing. (Estrada, Santa Cruz Sentinel, Friday Oct. 31, 1986)

5. This project is not an isolated one. A variety of other recent projects that have transformed the relationships between schools and communities are described by Balderas (1995), Delgado-Gaitan (1994), McCaleb (1994), and Weinstein-Shr & Quintero (1995).

6. James Comer's (1980) work is a notable exception to this trend.

7. Zanger (1994) reports on the insights of a class of academically-successful Latino/Latina high school students into the social dynamics of their schooling experience. Students were asked to discuss the reasons for the high drop-out rate of other Spanish-speaking students at the school and to recommend ways to make the school better for students from Spanish-speaking backgrounds. The student body at the school was about 40% Latino/Latina, 40% African

American, and 20% White. A transitional bilingual program operated in the school and was staffed by Latino/Latina and White teachers but there were no Latino/Latina teachers in the monolingual program.

Three themes emerged from the data: marginalization, cultural respect, and student-teacher trust. Marginalization reflected students' feeling that they existed on the social and academic periphery of the school, were relegated to an inferior status in the school's social hierarchy, and were ignored and felt almost invisible.

Students' perception that their culture was not respected within the school was expressed by Elsa who said "You can't succeed in a place where no one respects you for what you are" (p. 179). Students resented the fact that their culture was not incorporated into the curriculum despite the fact that 40% of the student body was Latino/Latina.

Students' comments also reflected an erosion of trust and cooperation on both sides between teachers and students. Students felt that their teachers' ignorance of their backgrounds contributed to mutual alienation. Elsa, for example, complained that "teachers don't learn from us, they don't learn from anybody. They don't ask" (p. 186). Students expressed the "desire to establish more caring, supportive, even family-like relationships with teachers" (p. 186).

Zanger concludes that school restructuring must focus on transforming the mainstream so that neither students nor teachers feel left out. In Zanger's study, as in the research of Poplin and Weeres (1992), the quality of relationships established across cultural boundaries emerges as a central aspect of students' ability and willingness to become academically engaged. A similar perspective is elaborated by Walsh (1991) in her book *Pedagogy and the Struggle for Voice: Issues of Language, Power, and Schooling for Puerto Ricans*. The central purpose of her study "was to highlight how the past and present intersect in people's voices, infuse pedagogy, and sculpt the conditions and processes involved in coming to know" (p. 133).

8. According to McCarty, the instructional changes underway at Rough Rock appear to be bearing fruit with respect to students' academic achievement: "When individual and grade-cohort scores are analyzed for all K-6 students over the past two years, an overriding pattern emerges: Bilingual students who have the benefit of cumulative, uninterrupted initial literacy experiences in Navajo make the greatest gains on local and national measures of achievement" (1993, p. 191).

McCarty's case study of the restructuring process at Rough Rock parallels many other examples of dramatic educational improvement resulting from instruction that emphasizes affirmation of identity. Abi-Nader (1993), for example, documents how Spanish-speaking high school students' academic performance improved dramatically when cultural values associated with *familia* were incorporated into instruction. More than 65 percent of the graduates of this program went on to college, a striking contrast with the massive dropout rates of Latinos/Latinas in other school systems.

Hayes, Bahruth, and Kessler (1991) similarly document the impact on student success of incorporating a strong positive affective dimension into a program for migrant Mexican American students in an agricultural community in South Texas. As expressed in the title of their book (Literacy con Cariño), the focus was on literacy achieved through a nurturing process:

> Attention to caring about and valuing each student individually was the result of a conscious attempt to incorporate into the school culture the affection and caring the students experienced in their homes. Although many of the parents of these children were illiterate, their home lives often reflected rich oral traditions, deeply felt care and love, and a strong desire on the part of the parents for their children to succeed in school. (p. 2)

The case studies described by Igoa (1995) and Nieto (1996) again show the centrality of issues related to identity in students' orientation to effort and success at school. Finally, a large-scale study of Southeast Asian students carried out by Rumbaut and Ima (1987) reported greater academic success among students who were maintaining traditional values, ethnic pride, and close social and cultural ties with members of their ethnic group.

The clear message from these studies is that the more the school affirms rather than ignores or devalues students' personal and cultural identities, the more likely students are to succeed educationally.

This point has also been made forcefully by Donna Deyhle (1995) in an article entitled: "Navajo Youth and Anglo Racism: Cultural Integrity and Resistance." She analyzes the identity choices that Navajo students were forced to make as a result of a school district's refusal to implement a Navajo-English bilingual program. Administrators and teachers believed that Navajo students' language and culture were the source of their academic difficulties. In the words of one teacher "These kids we get are learning disabled with their reading. Because they speak Navajo, you know" (p. 418). Another teacher argued that "Bilingual education will become the greatest obstacle a Navajo student has to overcome and an impediment to the education of all other students" (p. 418). Deyhle locates these perspectives in the power relations operating in the wider society:

> To accept Navajo culture and language would be to confer equal status, which is unacceptable to the Anglo community. Navajo culture and students' lives are effectively silenced by the surrounding Anglo community. Navajo language and traditions are absent from the school curriculum. Teachers' ignorance of Navajo students' lives results in the dismissal of the credibility of Navajo life. (p. 419)

Deyhle documents how maintaining pride in their culture and language (cultural integrity) can contribute to students' academic success in this kind of context, although this path was "fraught with conflict, uncertainty, and pain" (p. 439).

9. I am using the term "discourse" to refer to the ways in which language is used to create what is generally accepted as "common sense," thereby orchestrating consent for initiatives that are in the interests of particular groups. Discourses are intimately linked to patterns of power relations in a society. Discourses constitute what can be thought and what counts as truth or knowledge. Internalized discourses constitute cognitive schemata, which might be thought of as computer programs in our heads, that allow for certain propositions to be pro-

cessed in a highly automatized way and accepted as valid while propositions that are inconsistent with the internalized discourse are automatically rejected. A major focus of schooling in virtually all societies is the transmission of internalized discourses that are consistent with, and reinforcing of, national, cultural or religious identities (see Foucault [1980] for a detailed discussion of discourse and its relation to power).

The relationship between discourse and power is elaborated by Corson (1993) who claims that language is mainly an instrument of power; it is "the vehicle for identifying, manipulating and changing power relations between people" (1993, p. 1). He goes on to argue that "rather than a privilege that is ascribed to the individual, power itself is a network of relations constantly in tension and ever-present in activity; rather than possessed and localized in individual hands, power is exercised through the production, accumulation and functioning of various discourses" (1993, p. 4-5). The ways in which discourse operates to "manufacture consent" (Chomsky, 1987) can be described in terms of Gramsci's notion of *hegemony* which, as summarized by Corson:

> describes the organization of consent through invisible cultural dominance, rather than through visible political power. …This non-coercive 'force' is said to penetrate consciousness itself, so that the dominated become accomplices in their own domination. So it is argued that power hegemonies are reinforced from both sides of the power relationship: in their language usages, the non-dominant adhere to the linguistic norms created by dominant groups, while not realizing that they are being 'voluntarily coerced.' (p. 6)

Within the discipline of psychology, Harré and Gillett (1994) have argued for the centrality of discourse in understanding all aspects of human behavior. They suggest that "the mind of any human being is constituted by the discourses that they are involved in, private and public" (p. 104). Private discourse is thought; public discourse is behavior. It is possible to learn much about private discourse (thought and consciousness) through its public manifestation. According to discursive psychology, each individual's structure of consciousness will appear in the way we converse. Our minds and identities are the confluence of the social relations in which we have participated. In Corson's (1995) terms, "each human individual stands at a unique intersection of discourses and relationships: a 'position' embedded in historical, political, cultural, social, and interpersonal contexts, that largely determines mind" (p. 3).

10. All of us intuitively understand the nature of collaborative relations of power. The notion refers to the kind of affirmation and power that is generated when two people love each other, or in the relations between parents and children, or when teachers connect at a personal level with their students rather than just transmitting content.

I came across a moving example of "collaborative relations of power" in reading a newspaper during a trip to Ireland in May 1995. A news report under the headline "1845 Famine Aid Gesture Is Recalled" read as follows:

An American Indian tribe which sent aid to Ireland during the Great Famine will be thanked personally by President Robinson [the Irish President] during a visit to the U.S. The generosity of the Choctaw nation will be marked by the President at the tribal headquarters in Durant, Oklahoma, next Monday. The Choctaw heard of the famine disaster in 1845 and sent aid to Ireland equivalent to [about $1.8] million today, despite their own meager resources. (Evening Herald, Tuesday, May 16, 1995, p. 6)

11. Peirce (1995) has also emphasized the ways in which relations of power affect interactions between language learners and target language speakers. She criticizes current second language acquisition theory for focusing on the individual in isolation from the social context and the power relations embedded in that context. She suggests that the notions of *social identity* and *investment* are key to understanding learners' interactions in the target language. Specifically, she argues that the concept of *motivation* is usually viewed as:

> a property of the language learner — a fixed personality trait. The notion of investment, on the other hand, attempts to capture the relationship of the language learner to the changing social world. It conceives of the language learner as having a complex social identity and multiple desires. The notion presupposes that when language learners speak, they are not only exchanging information with target language speakers but they are constantly organizing and reorganizing a sense of who they are and how they relate to the social world. Thus, an investment in the target language is also an investment in a learner's own social identity, an identity which is constantly changing across time and space. (1995, pp. 17-18)

12. I am using the term *interpersonal space* in a way that overlaps with Vygotsky's (1978) influential notion of the *zone of proximal development* (ZPD) which he defined as the distance between children's developmental level as determined by individual problem solving without adult guidance and the level of potential development as determined by children's problem solving under the influence of, or in collaboration with, more capable adults and peers. Expressed simply, the ZPD is the interpersonal space where minds meet and new understandings can arise through collaborative interaction and inquiry. Newman, Griffin, and Cole (1989) label this interpersonal space *the construction zone*. In the present volume, the dual processes of reciprocal negotiation of identity and collaborative generation of knowledge take place within this "construction zone" and are seen as being intimately related to each other. Teacher-student collaboration in the construction of knowledge will operate effectively only in contexts where students' identities are being affirmed. Essentially, this conception extends the ZPD beyond the cognitive sphere into the realms of affective development and power relationships. It also makes clear that the *construction zone* can also be a *constriction zone* where student identities and learning are constricted rather than extended.

Chapter 2
The Evolution of Xenophobia: Cultural Diversity as the Enemy Within

Many commentators have objected strenuously to the implementation of bilingual education programs because they appear to run counter to the American tradition of assimilating immigrant groups into the mainstream of society. To these commentators, the increased status that accrues to a language (e.g. Spanish) as a result of being recognized for instructional purposes in schools appears likely to hinder the efficient operation of the melting pot. Not only will individuals who speak that language be rewarded with jobs and other incentives, but children will also be encouraged to retain their language. To opponents of bilingual education, the apparent encouragement of ethnic distinctiveness is especially unpalatable at the present time in view of the rapid growth of the Spanish-speaking population. In California, for example, Latino/Latina students are projected to form 50% of the school population by the year 2030. Encouraging these students to retain their home language contributes, according to this view, to what Arthur Schlesinger Jr. (1991) called "The Disuniting of America."

A favorite theme of many commentators is that the melting pot worked well for previous generations of immigrants who "made it" without crutches, and Spanish-speaking students could also make it if they tried.

This attitude shows a profound ignorance of American educational history. The groups that have tended to experience persistent educational difficulty (African American, Latino/Latina, Native American, and Native Hawaiian students) were never given the opportunity to "melt" into the American mainstream. Unlike immigrant groups, these groups represent what John Ogbu

(1992) terms *involuntary minorities*. Their status has been that of internal colonies insofar as they have been subordinated and regarded as inherently inferior for generations by the Euro-American dominant group.

Ogbu's (1978, 1992) distinction between voluntary and involuntary minorities is important for understanding both the historical and current educational achievement of culturally diverse communities in the United States (and elsewhere).

Voluntary and Involuntary Minorities

Ogbu (1992) defines immigrant or voluntary minorities as people who have moved more or less voluntarily to another society usually because they seek better economic opportunities and/or greater political freedom. Ogbu suggests that:

> Voluntary minorities usually experience initial problems in school due to cultural and language differences as well as lack of understanding of how the education system works. But they do not experience lingering, disproportionate school failure. The Chinese and Punjabi Indians are representative U.S. examples. (p. 8)

By contrast, involuntary minorities are people who were originally brought into the United States (or any other society) against their will; for example, through slavery, conquest, colonization, or forced labor. According to Ogbu, "thereafter, these minorities were often relegated to menial positions and denied true assimilation into the mainstream society" (p. 8).

The division between voluntary and involuntary minorities is not always clear-cut. For example, Mexican Americans who immigrate to the U.S. may initially have many of the characteristics of voluntary minorities; however, they quickly encounter the barriers to full participation that Mexican Americans have historically experienced and their encounters with the dominant group become very similar to those of previous generations of Mexican Americans. [1]

Ogbu suggests that voluntary minorities are characterized by primary cultural differences from the dominant group whereas involuntary minorities are characterized by secondary cultural differences. Primary cultural differences are those that existed before two groups come into contact (e.g. differences in language, religion, child-rearing practices, etc.). Secondary cultural differences arise after two populations come into contact, particularly when the contact involves the domination of one group by another. Under these circumstances, the involuntary minority will often develop an ambivalent or oppositional collective identity in relation to the dominant group. Minority group members take on certain cultural behaviors that are opposed to dominant group norms in order to maintain their collective identity and sense of security and self-worth. According to Ogbu:

> Voluntary minorities seem to bring to the United States a sense of who they are from their homeland and seem to retain this different but non-oppositional social identity at least during the first generation. Involuntary minorities, in contrast, develop a new sense of social or collective identity that is in opposition to the social identity of the dominant group after they have become subordinated. They do so in response to their treatment by White Americans in economic, political, social, psychological, cultural, and language domains. Whites' treatment included deliberate exclusion from true assimilation or the reverse, namely, forced superficial assimilation. (p. 9)

Ogbu suggests that a major reason why academic difficulties among involuntary minorities tend to be persistent is that cultural and language boundaries become more rigid than is typically the case for voluntary minorities. As illustrated by Deyhle's (1995) case study of the education of Navajo students, this process is rooted in inter-group power relations:

> The presence of these cultural differences, by themselves, is a politically neutral phenomenon. Navajo youth, securely rooted in their culture, move back and forth between their community and the surrounding Anglo community. ...Cultural boundaries, however, are often turned into cultural borders or barriers during inter-group conflict. ...The Anglo community uses Navajo culture as a border, a reason to deny equality by claiming the privilege of one kind of knowledge over another. Navajo families are judged by what they don't have — money, middle-class Anglo values, higher education, and professional jobs — rather than by what they do have — extended families, permanent homes, strong Navajo values and religious beliefs. (1995, p. 438)

Thus, cultural boundaries frequently are entrenched by various forms of discrimination on the part of the dominant group. However, according to Ogbu, they are also maintained by the minority group as a means of insulating themselves culturally from the process of subordination. The cultural and language differences act as markers of the group's collective identity and help the group cope under conditions of subordination.

While the realities of minority group adaptation are likely to be considerably more complex in practice than revealed by Ogbu's typology, the distinctions he makes do throw light on the general patterns of academic achievement among culturally diverse students. His analysis points to the centrality of issues of identity in understanding school success and failure. Consistent with this perspective, Signitia Fordham's research with academically-successful African American adolescents highlights the conflict these students feel between loyalty to their peer group and doing well in school, which the peer group regards as selling out to White norms:

> ...within the school structure, Black adolescents consciously and unconsciously sense that they have to give up aspects of their identities and of their indigenous cultural system in order to achieve success as defined in dominant-group terms; their resulting social selves are embodied in the notion of racelessness. Hence, for many of them the cost of school success is too high; it implies that cultural integrity must be sacrificed in order to "make it." For many Black adolescents, that option is unacceptable. For the high achievers identified in this paper, achieving school success is not marked only by conflict and ambivalence...but with the need to camouflage efforts directed at behaviors that the group identifies as "acting White." (1990, p. 259)

In a similar vein, Ladson-Billings (1995) has reviewed research suggesting that academically successful African American students tended to be social isolates, with neither African American nor White friends. These students perceived accurately that teachers were likely to devalue their academic competence if they manifested cultural behaviors that were typical of African American youth. Ladson-Billings points out:

> The problem that African American students face is the constant devaluation of their culture both in school and in the larger society. Thus, the styles apparent in African American youth culture — e.g. dress, music, walk, language — are equated with poor academic performance. The student who identifies with "hip-hop" culture may be regarded as dangerous and/or a gang member for whom academic success is not expected. (1995, p. 485)

Ladson-Billings outlines a theory of "culturally relevant pedagogy" that encourages students to maintain their cultural integrity while succeeding academically. The theoretical assumptions underlying "culturally relevant pedagogy" are consistent with the assumptions of the present framework. Both approaches argue that the ways in which identities are negotiated in the micro-interactions between educators and students must challenge the coercive pattern of macro-interactions in the broader society (see Chapter 6).

In the next section, the historical patterns of inter-group contact and academic performance are examined in light of Ogbu's distinction between voluntary and involuntary minorities.

The Historical Context

Involuntary Minorities. In light of historical realities, the concerns about bilingual education being against American traditions and a potential catalyst for separatist tendencies are highly ironic. In fact, the education of Mexican Americans in the Southwest was openly dedicated until the late 1960's to *separating* Mexican-American students from the mainstream of American society by means of segregated schooling (conducted exclusively in English). In Texas, for example, the judgement of the court in the United States versus the State of Texas case (1981) documented the "pervasive, intentional discrimination throughout most of this century" against Mexican-American students (a charge that was not contested by the State of Texas in the trial) and noted that:

> ...the long history of prejudice and deprivation remains a significant obstacle to equal educational opportunity for these children. The deep sense of inferiority, cultural isolation, and acceptance of failure, instilled in a people by generations of subjugation, cannot be eradicated merely by integrating the schools and repealing the 'no Spanish' statutes. (1981, p. 14)

Noel Epstein (1977), although a critic of bilingual education policy, also noted "the widespread discrimination and humiliation that have often been severely inflicted against such students" (p. 55). He goes on to report that:

> As late as 1970, Charles E. Silberman reported, 'In a South Texas school, children are forced to kneel in the playground and beg forgiveness if they are caught talking to each other in Spanish; some teachers require students using the forbidden language to kneel before the entire class.' In the early 1970's, the U.S. Civil Rights

Commission reported comments from students who said that getting caught speaking Spanish meant that they were fined, forced to stand on a special black square or made to write 'I must not speak Spanish.' This may help explain why Hispanic Americans speak of the melting pot today in harsh terms which other Americans might not recognize. (p. 55)

This perspective on the melting pot is eloquently expressed in an essay by Isidro Lucas (1981) entitled "Bilingual Education and the Melting Pot: Getting Burned." He argues that:

> There is in America a profound, underground culture, that of the *unmeltable* populations. Blacks have proven unmeltable over the years. The only place allowed them near the melting pot was underneath it. Getting burned. Hispanics were also left out of the melting pot. Spanish has been historically preserved more among them than other languages in non-English-speaking populations. It was a shelter, a defense. (p. 21-22)

Segregated/inferior schooling was usually rationalized on the grounds that it was necessary in order to provide effective remedial instruction in English to students who were "language handicapped" (Schlossman, 1983). However, in the Southwest, Latino/Latina children were generally assigned to segregated schools purely on the basis of surname when in fact many knew more English than Spanish since English had been the dominant home language for generations (Sánchez, 1943). George Sánchez, in many articles, pointed to the racism that was rationalized by:

> ...thinly veiled [pedagogical] excuses which do not conform with either the science of education or the facts in the case. Judging from current practice, these pseudo-pedagogical reasons call for short school terms, ramshackle school buildings, poorly paid and untrained teachers, and all varieties of prejudicial discrimination. (1943, p. 16; quoted in Schlossman, 1983, p. 893)

The pattern of physical and/or psychological violence aimed at eradicating students' identity was clearly not a pattern confined to North America (see, for example, Skutnabb-Kangas, 1984). [2] It was, and unfortunately continues to be, more the rule than the exception in many countries around the world in spite of the re-discovery of principles of equity and justice in Western industrialized countries during the 1960s. This pattern is depicted in Table 2.1.

The historical pattern of inter-group relationships and school performance for voluntary or immigrant minorities shows many similarities with that described for involuntary minorities but also some important differences.

Voluntary Minorities. In the case of voluntary minorities, schooling was generally not segregated but the same overt goals (acculturation to the dominant culture) and methods (punishment for speaking the home language) were used. Contrary to popular belief, many first generation immigrant children experienced considerable difficulty in school. Cohen (1970) sums up the findings of a comprehensive review of the educational achievement of immigrant students in the early part of this century as follows:

> ...the evidence...suggests that in the first generation, at least, children from many immigrant groups did not have an easy time in school. Pupils from these groups were more likely to be retarded than their native white schoolmates, more likely to make low scores on IQ tests, and they seem to have been a good deal less likely to remain in high school" (1970, p. 24).

Many of these first generation immigrants may have become successful economically since much less education was required for economic and social advancement at the beginning of this century than is the case at the present time.

For the children of these immigrants, there was considerable variability across groups in academic performance; specifically:

> Children whose parents emigrated from England, Scotland, Wales, Germany, and Scandinavia seem to have generally performed about as well in school as native whites. ...The children of Jewish immigrants typically achieved at or above the average for native whites. It was central and southern European non-Jewish immigrants — and to a lesser extent, the Irish — who experienced really serious difficulty in school. (Cohen, p. 24)

Cohen suggests that the ethnic differences in school performance may arise from cultural/motivational factors and the degree of urbanization of the different groups. [3]

Figure 2.1   **BLAMING THE VICTIM IN THE EDUCATION OF BILINGUAL STUDENTS**

A. OVERT AIM

Teach English to bilingual children in order to create a harmonious society with equal opportunity for all.

COVERT AIM

Anglicize bilingual children because linguistic and cultural diversity are seen as a threat to social cohesion.

B. METHOD

Punish children for using L1 in schools and encourage them to reject their own culture and language in order to identify with majority English group.

JUSTIFICATION

1. L1 should be eradicated because it will interfere with the learning of English;
2. Identification with L1 culture will reduce child's ability to identify with English-speaking culture.

C. RESULTS

1. Shame in L1 language and culture.

2. Replacement of L1 by L2.

3. School failure among many children.

"SCIENTIFIC" EXPLANATIONS

1. Bilingualism causes confusion in thinking, emotional insecurity and school failure.
2. Bilingual children are "culturally deprived" (almost by definition since they are not Anglos).
3. Some culturally diverse groups are genetically inferior (common theory in 1920's recently revived by Lloyd Dunn [1987])

D. OUTCOMES

1. The educational disablement of bilingual children under these conditions only serves to reinforce the myth of bilingual group inferiority.
2. Even more intense efforts by the school to eradicate the "deficiencies" inherent in bilingual children (i.e. their language and culture).

It is clear from these data that a complex array of variables determines the academic achievement of culturally diverse students and that the argument that previous generations of immigrants made it "without the crutch of bilingual education" is seriously oversimplified. However, the data also show that the usual rationale for bilingual education similarly fails to account for the observed pattern. This rationale is that children cannot learn in a language they do not understand and therefore, if there is a home-school "linguistic mismatch," academic retardation will almost invariably result. The historical data show that Scandinavian and German children performed well despite a mismatch between the language of the home and the language of the school whereas Irish children instructed in their native language (English, for the most part) experienced difficulty.

In summary, the historical data reinforce the critical role that inter-group power relations and the negotiation of identity play in determining language learning and academic achievement among culturally diverse students. The major points are as follows:

• Subordinated groups that tend to experience the most severe academic disadvantage have never been given the opportunity to assimilate into the societal mainstream; on the contrary, they were subjected over generations to segregated and inferior schooling, they were punished for speaking their home language in school, and their pride in their cultural identity was systematically eradicated;

• The educational experiences of subordinated group students have reflected the pattern of interactions experienced by their communities in the wider society; both children and adults have been prevented from full participation and advancement in mainstream societal institutions (e.g. schools, the job market, etc.) through segregation and discrimination;

• Although early generations of immigrant children were punished for speaking their L1 and many groups did tend to experience academic difficulties, they were not discriminated against nor segregated educationally to the same extent as involuntary minorities; thus, an ambivalent and/or oppositional identity was not internalized by the group and later generations assimilated to the mainstream society and succeeded academically;

- Among both voluntary and involuntary minorities, school failure on the part of culturally diverse students was generally attributed to some inherent deficiency, either genetic or experiential (e.g. "cultural deprivation," bilingual confusion, etc.); this focus on inherent deficiencies of the bilingual child served to deflect attention away from the educational treatment that children were receiving.

Evolution of the Bilingual Education Debate

The debate about the merits or otherwise of bilingual education has preoccupied educators, politicians, the media and occasionally the general public in the United States for almost 30 years. Many commentators have warned that bilingual education is not only educationally ill-advised, it also threatens the social and political stability of the nation. Newspaper editorials across the country have detailed a catastrophic scenario of Latino/Latina activists demanding ever more intensive bilingual education as a ploy both to prevent bilingual children from learning English and to fuel separatist tendencies, resulting ultimately in the disintegration of the United States.

To outsiders, this paranoia about bilingual education might seem absurd, especially in view of the prevalence and high status of bilingual programs in many countries around the world. However, within the United States, these arguments are taken very seriously. The roots of this bilingual paranoia can be seen in the evolution of the policy debate during the past 30 years.

Phase I. 1967-1974. Initially, as Troike (1978) has observed, bilingual education was instituted in the late sixties on the basis of what appeared to be a self-evident rationale, namely that "the best medium for teaching a child is his or her mother tongue," but with relatively little hard evidence to back up this rationale. The reaction of many press commentators in the initial years of this experiment was one of "wait-and-see;" they didn't particularly like the idea but were willing to give it a chance to prove its potential for reducing educational inequities. Some were concerned, however, that bilingual education might have the opposite effect, namely of preventing Spanish-speaking students from entering the mainstream of English-speaking America, and also that it might give rise to the divisiveness that appeared to be associated with bilingualism in Canada. However, in general, this first phase of the modern bilingual education debate was marked by a tolerance for the educational potential of bilingual education and, although doubts were certainly raised, its rationale was not disputed in any sustained or systematic way.

An early expression of these views appeared in the *Christian Science Monitor* (Nov. 13, 1967). The editorial noted that several senators were drafting measures for bilingual education because they were concerned, "and very rightly so," about the educational lag among Spanish-speaking children. However, it went on to wonder:

> ...whether such an official recognition of Spanish might not actually worsen the situation rather than improve it. Might it not tend to fasten even more strongly upon children the disadvantage of being Spanish-speaking in an overwhelmingly English-speaking land?

Phase II. 1974-1986. The bilingual education debate became considerably more volatile after the *Lau v. Nichols* case in 1974. The judgement of the Supreme Court in this case acknowledged that the civil rights of non-English-speaking students were violated when the school took no steps to help them acquire the language of instruction:

> ...there is no equality of treatment merely by providing students with the same facilities, textbooks, teachers, and curriculum; for students who do not understand English are effectively foreclosed from any meaningful education. Basic English skills are at the very core of what these public schools teach. Imposition of a requirement that, before a child can effectively participate in the educational program, he must already have acquired those basic skills is to make a mockery of public education. We know that those who do not understand English are certain to find their classroom experiences wholly incomprehensible and in no way meaningful. (Crawford, 1992a, p. 253)

The Court did not mandate bilingual education but they did mandate that schools take effective measures to overcome the educational disadvantages resulting from a home-school language mismatch. The Office of Civil Rights, however, interpreted the Supreme Court's decision as effectively mandating transitional bilingual education unless a school district could prove that another approach would be equally or more effective. This interpretation of the Supreme Court decision by the Office of Civil Rights sparked outrage among media commentators and educators in school districts which, for the most part, were totally unprepared to offer any form of bilingual instruction.

The ensuing debate was (and continues to be) volatile. The concern with political divisiveness resulting from bilingual education was articulated clearly in a *New York Times* editorial entitled "Bilingual Danger" on November 22, 1976:

> The disconcerting strength gathered by separatism in Canada contains a relevant lesson for the United States and its approach to bilingual education. …it is no exaggeration to warn that the present encouragement given to making [Spanish-speaking] enclaves permanent, in the mistaken view that they are an expression of positive pluralism, points the road to cultural, economic and political divisiveness. The reason why such a warning appears appropriate is that political splinter groups within the Spanish-speaking community, and among educators, are misinterpreting the goals of bilingual education in New York as a means of creating a Spanish-speaking power base. …Without exaggerating the threat to America's nationhood now that English has prevailed, it nevertheless remains pertinent to warn against a misguided linguistic separatism that, while it may seem to promise its advocates limited political and ideological power, can only have the effect of condemning to permanent economic and social disadvantage those who cut themselves off from the majority culture. (quoted in *The Linguistic Reporter*, January 1977, pp. 1 & 7)

Although his reply was not printed in the *New York Times*, Joshua Fishman refuted the arguments of this editorial as follows:

> "The *New York Times* seems to fear that something divisive…might grow out of bilingual education in the USA. Having spent many years studying bilingual education throughout the world…I consider this to be highly unlikely, both because ethno-cultural divisiveness, where it obtains, is far too deeply imbedded in a pervasive socioeconomic matrix to be "caused" by any kind of education, as well as because bilingual education per se is unfailingly unifying rather than divisive. The hallmark of all bilingual education (including its compensatory USA variant) is that it includes a unifying supra-ethnic language of wider communication (in our case: English …). Indeed, if any educational pattern can be said to typify Quebec it is the absence (historically as well as currently) of bilingual education (education via two media of instruction), rather than its presence. All of which is not to say that there is no striving for "a Spanish-speaking power base in the

USA," or that such strivings may not be justified. ...What might counteract such strivings would be genuine opportunity for Hispanic participation in "political power" and a genuine end to the "economic and social disadvantage" of Hispanics in the USA, all of the foregoing having been promised in theory and so obviously denied in practice by the monolingual English establishment. If Hispanic (or rather minority) "divisiveness" increases in the USA, it will be because of the long tradition of English-dominated inequality, such as that long practiced in Quebec, rather than because of bilingual education which functions to link together populations that might otherwise be totally estranged." (*The Linguistic Reporter*, January 1977, p. 7)

As the debate evolved, the sociopolitical concerns of many commentators were backed up by psychoeducational arguments against bilingual education and in favor of all-English immersion programs. The argument in favor of bilingual education which was reflected in the Supreme Court's decision, namely, that "children can't learn in a language they don't understand," was no longer regarded as self-evident. As Noel Epstein (1977) pointed out, apparent counterevidence had appeared in the findings from French immersion programs in Canada which showed that English-background children who were taught initially through French in order to develop fluent bilingual skills did not suffer academically as a result of this home-school language switch (see Swain & Lapkin, 1982; Cummins & Swain, 1986). To many commentators in the United States, these results suggested that English immersion programs were a plausible educational alternative to bilingual programs. [4]

The intense opposition to bilingual programs during this period is well summed up in the following three quotations which vividly outline the concerns of many Americans about the increasing penetration of Spanish into mainstream institutions such as the educational system:

> Bilingual education is an idea that appeals to teachers of Spanish and other tongues, but also to those who never did think that another idea, the United States of America, was a particularly good one to begin with, and that the sooner it is restored to its component 'ethnic' parts the better off we shall all be. Such people have been welcomed with open arms into the upper reaches of the federal government in recent years, giving rise to the suspicion of a death wish. (Bethell, 1979, p. 30)

President Reagan also joined the fray in early March 1981, arguing that:

It is absolutely wrong and against American concepts to have a bilingual education program that is now openly, admittedly dedicated to preserving students' native language and never getting them adequate in English so they can go out into the job market and participate. (Democrat-Chronicle, Rochester, March 3, 1981, p. 2A)

The incompatibility that is implied in President Reagan's remark between preserving the native languages of bilingual students and the learning of English is a theme that occurs frequently in the opposition to bilingual programs. This assumed incompatibility is made explicit in the following excerpt from a *New York Times* editorial (October 10, 1981):

"The Department of Education is analyzing new evidence that expensive bilingual education programs don't work…Teaching non-English speaking children in their native language during much of their school day constructs a roadblock on their journey into English. A language is best learned through immersion in it, particularly by children…Neither society nor its children will be well served if bilingualism continues to be used to keep thousands of children from quickly learning the one language needed to succeed in America."

The general line of argument against bilingual education is clear: such programs are a threat to national unity and furthermore they are ineffective in teaching English to bilingual students since the primary language, rather than English, is used for a considerable amount of instruction in the early grades. The bilingual approach appears to imply a counter-intuitive "less equals more" rationale in which *less* English instruction is assumed to lead to *more* English achievement. It appears more logical to many opponents of bilingual education to argue that if children are deficient in English then they need instruction in English, not their native language. School failure is caused by *insufficient exposure* to English (at home) and it makes no sense to further dilute the amount of English to which bilingual students are exposed by instructing them through their L1 at school. Unless such students are immersed in English at school, they will not learn English and consequently will be prevented from participating in the mainstream of American society.

their L1 at school. Unless such students are immersed in English at school, they will not learn English and consequently will be prevented from participating in the mainstream of American society.

In summary, during this second phase the battle lines were drawn between two opposing but apparently equally plausible arguments: on the one hand, the *linguistic mismatch* hypothesis which argued that children can't learn in a language they don't understand; on the other, the *maximum exposure* hypothesis that if children are deficient in English, then surely they require maximum exposure to English in school. These psychoeducational hypotheses remain prominent in the third phase of this debate; however, in this phase the relatively narrow concern with bilingual education has joined forces with a broader set of concerns in relation to the more general infiltration of cultural diversity into American institutions.

Phase III. 1987-1996. During the 1980s and 1990s, the *U.S. English* organization coordinated much of the opposition to bilingual education, initiating and passing referenda in more than 20 states to make English the official language (see Cazden & Snow [1990], Crawford [1989, 1992a, 1992b] and Pruyn [1994] for detailed analysis of the U.S. English movement). Inspired by Senator S.I. Hayakawa's (1981) proposed constitutional amendment to make English the official language of the United States, *U.S. English* was formed in 1983 and within five years had grown to a 400,000 member organization with a $6 million annual budget (Crawford, 1992a). By 1995, the membership had mushroomed to more than 600,000.

The urgency of the *U.S. English* mandate was enhanced during the late 1980s by publications of a variety of neo-conservative academics (e.g. Dinesh D'Souza, 1991; E.D. Hirsch, 1987; Arthur Schlesinger, Jr., 1991) who warned about the dangers cultural diversity posed to the American way of life. These authors articulated a form of intellectualized xenophobia intended to alert the general public to the infiltration of the Other into the heart and soul of American institutions. Cultural diversity has become the enemy within, far more potent and insidious in its threat than any external enemy. Most influential was E.D. Hirsch's (1987) *Cultural Literacy: What Every American Needs to Know* which argued that the fabric of nationhood depended on a set of common knowledge, understandings and values shared by the populace. Multilingualism represented a threat to cultural literacy and, by extension, nationhood:

in fact, multilingualism enormously increases cultural fragmentation, civil antagonism, illiteracy, and economic-technological ineffectualness. (1987, p. 92)

Hirsch's "cultural literacy" represented a call to strengthen the national immune system so that it could successfully resist the debilitating influence of cultural diversity. Only when the national identity has been fortified and secured through "cultural literacy" should contact with the Other be contemplated, and even then educators should keep diversity at a distance, always vigilant against its potent destructive power.

It is in this context that we can understand statements such as the following from Arthur Schlesinger Jr. (1991) in his book *The Disuniting of America*:

> In recent years the combination of the ethnicity cult with a flood of immigration from Spanish-speaking countries has given bilingualism new impetus. …Alas, bilingualism has not worked out as planned: rather the contrary. Testimony is mixed, but indications are that bilingual education retards rather than expedites the movement of Hispanic children into the English-speaking world and that it promotes segregation rather than it does integration. Bilingualism shuts doors. It nourishes self-ghettoization, and ghettoization nourishes racial antagonism. …Using some language other than English dooms people to second-class citizenship in American society. …Monolingual education opens doors to the larger world. …institutionalized bilingualism remains another source of the fragmentation of America, another threat to the dream of 'one people.' (1991, pp. 108-109)

The claims that "bilingualism shuts doors" and "monolingual education opens doors to the wider world," are laughable if viewed in isolation, particularly in the context of current global interdependence and the frequently expressed needs of American business for multilingual "human resources." Schlesinger's comments become interpretable only in the context of a societal discourse that is profoundly disquieted by the fact that the sounds of the Other have now become audible and the hues of the American social landscape have darkened noticeably.

Speaker of the House, Newt Gingrich, has forcefully expressed views similar to those of Schlesinger in a recent *Los Angeles Times* article:

Today the counterculture left and its allies profess to smooth the path for immigrants by setting up bilingual education programs, making it possible for children to continue in their own language. In fact, they have actually made it more difficult. Bilingual education slows down and confuses people in their pursuit of new ways of thinking. It fosters the expectation of a duality that is simply not an accurate portrayal of America.

Immigrants need to make a sharp psychological break with the past, immersing themselves in the culture and economic system that is going to be their home. Every time students are told they can avoid learning their new language (which will be the language of their children and grandchildren), they are risking their future by clinging to the past. ...

Sadly, there are some ethnic leaders who prefer bilingualism because it keeps their voters and supporters isolated from the rest of America, ghettoized into groups more easily manipulated for political purposes often by self-appointed leaders. ...Bilingualism keeps people more actively tied to their old language and habits and maximizes the cost of the transition to becoming American. As a result, poor Americans and first-generation immigrant children have suffered pain and confusion.

Yet the personal problems caused by bilingualism are overshadowed by the ultimate challenge they pose to American society. America can absorb an amazing number of people from an astonishing range of backgrounds if our goal is assimilation. If people are encouraged to resist assimilation, the very fabric of American society will eventually break down. ...

The only viable alternative for the American underclass is American civilization. Without English as a common language, there is no such civilization. (L.A. Times, August 4, 1995)

As in the case of Schlesinger, empirical evidence is considered totally unnecessary to support claims that "bilingual education slows down and confuses people in their pursuit of new ways of thinking." If the Speaker's message is that his opinion is superior to scientific evidence, new ways of thinking might not be a bad idea.

Despite its disdain for empirical evidence, this discourse is broadcast through the media into every classroom in the nation. There is anger that schools have apparently reneged on their traditional duty to render the Other invisible and inaudible. [5] Under the guise of equity programs initiated in the 1960s, diversity infiltrated into the American classroom and became legitimated. In view of the demographic projections, there is extreme urgency to curtail the infiltration of diversity and particularly one of its most visible manifestations, bilingual education. [6]

This perceived urgency accounts for the escalation of the *U.S. English* rhetoric in recent years. Two examples of *U.S. English* advertisements in national media will illustrate the trend. The first example was one I encountered in the United Airlines in-flight magazine *Hemispheres* in April 1994. Entitled "Why a Hispanic Heads an Organization Called U.S. English" it features a photograph of Mauro E. Mujica, the Chairman/CEO of U.S. English with the following text underneath:

> "I am proud of my heritage. Yet when I emigrated to the United States from Chile in 1965 to study architecture at Columbia University, I knew that to succeed I would have to adopt the language of my new home. As in the past, it is critical today for new immigrants to learn English as quickly as possible. And that's so they can benefit from the many economic opportunities that this land has to offer. …U.S. ENGLISH is a national, non-partisan, non-profit organization committed to making sure every single immigrant has the chance to learn English. Our mission is the preservation of our common bond through our common language: English. …"

This pious mission statement might be more convincing if *U.S. English* were using even a fraction of its funds to sponsor English language classes for immigrants or to advocate for an expansion of English language and literacy classes for immigrant adults. There is currently enormous demand for English language and literacy classes among immigrants which far exceeds the availability of affordable classes.

The second advertisement appeared in some editions of *TIME Magazine* (March 20, 1995) and delivers the most direct frontal assault yet on bilingual education. The text of the full-page advertisement reads as follows:

Deprive a child of an education. Handicap a young life outside the classroom. Restrict social mobility. If it came at the hand of a parent it would be called child abuse.

At the hand of our schools and funded primarily by state and local government, it's called **bilingual education**. A massive bureaucratic program that's strayed from its mandate of mainstreaming non-English speaking students. Today more money is spent teaching immigrants in their native languages than teaching them in English.

To equate bilingual education with child abuse is so extreme that it betrays a sense of desperation. I believe that the roots of this desperation are to be found in the fact that bilingual education has withstood almost 20 years of intense attack and has consolidated its status as a viable and effective approach in a number of key states (e.g. California, New York). The research data (reviewed in Chapter 5) is getting increasingly harder to ignore. This research shows clearly that there is a direct positive relationship between the extent to which bilingual students develop their L1 literacy skills at school and how well they do in English academic skills. This pattern of findings is replicated in programs throughout the world.

In order to show that the escalating academic and media rhetoric in the third phase of the bilingual education debate reflects a discourse of disempowerment intended to reinforce coercive relations of power, it is necessary to examine carefully the empirical evidence related to the claims on either side. We take up this task in the next three chapters. The concluding section provides an overview of the specific issues considered in these three chapters.

Conclusion

Two general issues can be raised with respect to the psychoeducational arguments for and against bilingual education. First, what underlying assumptions are implied by these arguments and to what extent are these assumptions valid in light of the research evidence? Second, to the extent that the assumptions on either side of the debate are not valid, what sociopolitical functions do they serve? In other words, what policies and programs do they legitimate and to what extent do bilingual students benefit or suffer as a result of these policies and programs?

The arguments about the educational validity of bilingual education embody a variety of assumptions that *can* be tested against the available research evidence. For example, to what extent does research support the "linguistic mismatch" hypothesis that children exposed to a home-school language switch will suffer academic retardation? At the other pole of the debate, is it true that more exposure to English at school increases English academic achievement, or does less English instruction lead to more English achievement, as implied by the bilingual education rationale? Is bilingualism an educational disadvantage (as Arthur Schlesinger Jr. argues) or might it be a positive force in children's development under some conditions? Is there a positive or a negative relationship between children's L1 and L2 academic skills?

At a more basic level, many commentators on both sides of the issue suggest that lack of English proficiency is the major cause of children's academic disadvantage — is there any evidence for this assumption? It is also relevant to ask what exactly is meant by "English proficiency." Specifically, how are academic skills in English related to the acquisition of English conversational skills? Clarification of these issues is important in order to answer the central question regarding the most effective methods of promoting English and overall academic development.

Finally, the research evidence regarding the impact of broader social factors and patterns of classroom interaction can be examined. In reviewing some of these factors to this point, I have suggested that inter-group power relations have played a major role in determining culturally diverse students' academic progress. If so, why have these variables not been taken into account in the policy debate? What is the relationship between sociopolitical and psychoeducational factors in determining student outcomes?

These issues are discussed in the following chapters. The research on most of these issues is sufficiently clear to show that the major psychoeducational arguments against bilingual education are spurious. In fact, massive amounts of research evidence refute the argument that insufficient exposure to English is a major cause of bilingual students' academic failure and the related assumption that maximum exposure to English will result in academic success.

In view of the overwhelming evidence against the maximum exposure assumption, it is legitimate to ask what sociopolitical function such arguments serve. I argue that the sociopolitical function of such arguments is very similar to the sociopolitical function of previous arguments used to legitimate sink-or-swim (submersion) programs for minorities. The argument that bilingualism caused "language handicaps" legitimated eradicating bilingual children's L1 and making them ashamed of their cultural identity. In the same way, current arguments promoting maximum exposure to English serve to subvert bilingual programs such that relatively ineffective "quick-exit" programs are implemented rather than the considerably more effective programs aimed at promoting biliteracy. In both cases, a patently inferior form of education has been rationalized as being for children's own good and necessary to provide them with access to what *U.S. English* calls "the language of equal opportunity" (see Wong Fillmore, 1992, for a discussion of the attempts to sabotage the implementation of bilingual education).

Endnotes to Chapter 2

1. Any broad categorization, such as Ogbu's voluntary and involuntary minorities, is likely to obscure considerable variation within particular groups. There is enormous variation among different Latino/Latina groups in the U.S. as well as within groups such as Mexicanos (see, for example, Gibson, 1995; Suárez-Orozco, 1987, 1989; Trueba, 1988; Vásquez, Pease-Alvarez, & Shannon, 1994). In critiquing Ogbu's position, Erickson (1987) and Trueba (1988) point out that it does not explain the success of many involuntary minority students. The ethnographic research of Marcelo Suárez-Orozco among recently arrived students from war-torn Central American countries in the early 1980s also highlights this as an important issue. He focused not on why students dropped-out or experienced academic problems but on why they remained in school at all. He argues that "becoming a somebody" was an important motivation for students:

> Among many new arrivals in my sample feelings of desperation give way to a harsh sense of responsibility that they must now seize upon any opportunities. Achieving in school and working to ease parental hardships are intimately related to this psychosocial syndrome of propensity to guilt over one's selective survival. (1989, p. 107)

    Thus, Ogbu's distinction between voluntary and involuntary minorities should be seen as a broad categorization describing general patterns of power relations between dominant and subordinated groups but allowing for considerable intra-group variation within voluntary and involuntary minorities.

2. A particularly vicious example of punishment for speaking the home language comes from the Welsh context. The "Welsh not" came into existence after the 1870 Education Act in Britain as a means of eradicating the Welsh language. Any child heard speaking Welsh in school had a heavy wooden placard attached by rope placed over his or her shoulders. The placard reached to the child's shins and would bump them when the child walked. If that child heard another child speaking Welsh, he or she could transfer the "Welsh not" to the

other child. The child carrying this placard at the end of the day was beaten (Evans, 1978). Richard Llewellyn gives an account of this type of punishment in his autobiographical novel *How Green Was My Valley*:

> I heard crying in the infants' school as though a child had fallen and the voice came nearer and fell flat upon the air as a small girl came through the door and walked a couple of steps towards us. …About her neck a piece of new cord, and from the cord, a board that hung to her shins and cut her as she walked. Chalked on the board, in the fist of Mr. Elijah Jonas-Sessions, I must not speak Welsh in school. …And the board dragged her down, for she was small, and the cord rasped the flesh on her neck, and there were marks upon her shins where the edge of the board had cut. (Llewellyn, 1968, p. 267)

3. This same variability in academic performance among immigrant students is evident in contemporary data from a number of contexts. For example, Canadian data show many groups of first and second generation immigrant students from non-English-speaking backgrounds performing as well or better academically than English native speakers of the same social class (see Cummins, 1984, for a review). However, involuntary minority groups such as First Nations and francophone students outside Quebec show considerably lower levels of academic performance.

4. Many American commentators who cite the Canadian French immersion programs as counter-evidence to bilingual education and as a means of arguing for "English immersion" for bilingual students fail to realize that French immersion programs are, in fact, fully bilingual programs. These programs are taught by bilingual teachers, the goal is bilingualism and biliteracy, and children's L1 (English) is strongly promoted after the initial grades so that about half the instruction is through L1 in grades 4-6. It is absurd to use the success of these bilingual programs to argue for monolingual programs, taught by monolingual teachers, whose goal is to produce monolingualism.

5. This anger erupted in California in the fall of 1994 in the passing by a large majority of Proposition 187 which would (among other provisions) prohibit undocumented persons from enrolling in public schools and require school districts to verify the legal status of all students already enrolled or who seek to enroll in public schools. As pointed out by Heller and Leone (1995), these provisions are unconstitutional and, if implemented, would create and perpetuate a permanent illiterate underclass. Research has indicated that undocumented minor children are likely to remain in the U.S. and, at some point, legalize their immigration status.

6. The message of the demographic projections has been internalized by the socially-powerful establishment. Poor people currently tend not to vote in the United States. What if bilingual education were to be successful in promoting high levels of critical literacy among the rapidly increasing culturally diverse population and what if these people were to vote? Social control is at stake; hence the escalating campaign on a number of fronts (media, leg-

islative, political) to get rid of bilingual education and revert to traditional forms of assimilation and exclusion that allegedly served the nation well for more than 200 years (see Macedo, 1993, 1994).

Paranoia about the growing Spanish-speaking population was vividly illustrated in a memorandum written in the fall of 1988 by John Tanton, chairman of *U.S. English,* who warned about a Latino/Latina political takeover as a result of high immigration and birthrates:

> *Gobernar es popular* translates 'to govern is to populate.' In this society, where the majority rules, does this hold? Will the present majority peacefully hand over its political power to a group that is simply more fertile?… Can *homo contraceptivus* compete with *homo progenitiva* if borders aren't controlled?…Perhaps this is the first instance in which those with their pants up are going to get caught by those with their pants down. (quoted in Crawford, 1995, p. 68)

Chapter 3
The Two Faces of
Language Proficiency

Appropriate ways of conceptualizing the nature of language proficiency and its relationship to other constructs (e.g. "intelligence") have been debated by philosophers and psychologists since ancient times. However, the issue is not just an abstract theoretical question but one that is central to resolving a variety of controversial issues in the education of culturally diverse students. Educational policies are frequently based on assumptions about the nature of "language proficiency" and how long it takes to attain. For example, funding for English as a second language (ESL) and bilingual education classes in North America is based (at least in part) on assumptions about how long it takes bilingual students to acquire sufficient English proficiency to follow instruction in the regular classroom. Yet what exactly constitutes "English proficiency" is rarely analyzed by policy-makers or researchers.

Misconceptions about the Nature of Language Proficiency

Two major misconceptions regarding the nature of language proficiency remain common among educators in North America. These misconceptions have important *practical* implications for the way educators interact with culturally diverse students. Both involve a confusion between the surface or conversational aspects of children's language and deeper aspects of proficiency that are more closely related to conceptual and academic development.

The first misconception entails drawing inferences about children's ability to think logically on the basis of their familiarity with and command of standard English. Children who speak a non-standard variety of English (or their L1) are frequently thought to be handicapped educationally and less capable of logical thinking. This assumption derives from the fact that these children's language is viewed as inherently deficient as a tool for expressing logical relations. Since Labov's (1970) refutation of this position with respect to the language of African American inner-city children, it has had few advocates among applied linguists, although it is still a common misconception among some educators and academics who have little background in sociolinguistics.

A recent example of how persistent some of these linguistic prejudices are among academics who know little about language comes from Dunn's (1987) monograph on Spanish-speaking children. In expressing his concerns that bilingual education could result in "at least the partial disintegration of the United States of America" (pp. 66-67), Dunn argues that Latino/Latina children and adults "speak inferior Spanish" and that "Latin pupils on the U.S. mainland, as a group, are inadequate bilinguals. They simply don't understand either English or Spanish well enough to function adequately in school" (p. 49). He goes on to argue that this is due to the fact that these children "do not have the scholastic aptitude or linguistic ability to master two languages well, or to handle switching from one to the other, at school, as the language of instruction" (p. 71). He attributes the causes of this lower scholastic ability about equally to environmental factors and "to genes that influence scholastic aptitude" (p. 64). (See the special issue of the Hispanic Journal of Behavioral Science, vol. 10, 1988 for critical discussion of Dunn's views.)

The second misconception is in many respects the converse of the first. In this case, children's adequate control over the surface features of English (i.e. their ability to converse fluently in English) is taken as an indication that all aspects of their "English proficiency" have been mastered to the same extent as native speakers of the language. In other words, conversational skills are interpreted as a valid index of overall proficiency in the language.

This implicit assumption has had a major impact on the organization of bilingual education programs in the United States. The rationale for bilingual education, as it is understood by most policy makers and practitioners, can be stated as follows:

> *Lack of English proficiency is the major reason for bilingual students' academic failure. Bilingual education is intended to ensure that students do not fall behind in subject matter content while they are learning English, as they would likely do in an all-English pro-*

gram. However, when students have become proficient in English, then they can be exited to an all-English program, since limited English proficiency will no longer impede their academic progress.

Despite its intuitive appeal, there are serious problems with this rationale. First, it ignores the social and historical factors that influence bilingual students' academic performance. As suggested in Chapter 2, these social determinants are more fundamental than linguistic factors alone. Second, this rationale fails to specify what exactly is meant by proficiency in English and this vagueness has contributed directly to bilingual students' academic difficulties.

Some concrete examples will help illustrate how this process operates. These examples are taken from a study conducted in western Canada in which the teacher referral forms and psychological assessments of more than 400 bilingual students were analyzed (Cummins, 1984). Throughout the teachers' referral forms and psychological assessment reports there are references to the fact that children's English communicative skills appeared considerably better developed than their academic language skills. The following examples illustrate this point:

PS (094). Referred for reading and arithmetic difficulties in second grade, teacher commented that "since PS attended grade one in Italy, I think his main problem is language, although he understands and speaks English quite well."

GG (184). Although he had been in Canada for less than a year, in November of the grade one year, the teacher commented that "he speaks Italian fluently and English as well." However, she also referred him for psychological assessment because "he is having a great deal of difficulty with the grade one program" and she wondered if he had "specific learning disabilities or if he is just a very long way behind children in his age group."

DM (105). Arrived from Portugal at age 10 and was placed in a second grade class; three years later in fifth grade, her teacher commented that "her oral answering and comprehension is so much better than her written work that we feel a severe learning problem is involved, not just her non-English background."

These examples illustrate the influence of the environment in developing English conversational skills. In many instances immigrant students were considered to have sufficient English proficiency to take a verbal IQ test within about one year of arrival in Canada. Similarly, in the United States, bilingual students are often considered to have developed sufficient English proficiency to cope with the demands of an all-English classroom after a relatively short amount of time in a bilingual or ESL program.

There is little doubt that many English language learners can develop a relatively high degree of English conversational skills within about two years of exposure to English-speaking peers, television, and schooling. However, we cannot logically extrapolate from the considerable English proficiency that students may display in face-to-face communication to their overall proficiency in English. Consider the following example:

> *PR (289).* PR was referred in first grade by the school principal who noted that "PR is experiencing considerable difficulty with grade one work. An intellectual assessment would help her teacher to set realistic learning expectations for her and might provide some clues as to remedial assistance that might be offered."

No mention was made of the fact that the child was learning English as a second language; this only emerged when the child was referred by the second grade teacher in the following year. Thus, the psychologist does not consider this as a possible factor in accounting for the discrepancy between a verbal IQ of 64 and a performance IQ of 108. The assessment report read as follows:

> Although overall ability level appears to be within the low average range, note the significant difference between verbal and nonverbal scores. ...It would appear that PR's development has not progressed at a normal rate and consequently she is, and will continue to experience much difficulty in school. Teacher's expectations at this time should be set accordingly.

What is interesting in this example is that the child's English communicative skills are presumably sufficiently well developed that the psychologist (and possibly the teacher) is not alerted to the child's second language background. This leads the psychologist to infer from her low verbal IQ score that "her development has not progressed at a normal rate" and to advise the teacher to set low academic expectations for the child since she "will continue to experience much difficulty in school." There is ample evidence from many contexts of how the attribution of deficient cognitive skills to culturally diverse students can become self-fulfilling. Ortiz and Yates (1983), for example, report that more than three times as many Latino/Latina students were classified as "learning disabled" in Texas than would be expected based on their proportion in the school population. These classifications usually resulted in a one-way ticket into special education classes where students fell even further behind academically.

In many of the referral forms and psychological assessments analyzed in the Cummins (1984) study, the following line of reasoning was invoked:

> Because bilingual students are fluent in English, their poor academic performance and/or test scores cannot be attributed to lack of proficiency in English. Therefore, these students must either have deficient cognitive abilities or be poorly motivated.

The trend to exit students to all-English instruction as quickly as possible in many bilingual programs inevitably gives rise to a similar line of reasoning. It is commonly observed that students classified as "English proficient" after a relatively short stay in a bilingual program and then exited to an all-English program often fall progressively further behind grade norms in the development of English academic skills. Because these students appear to be fluent in English, their poor academic performance can no longer be explained by the fact that their English language abilities are still in the process of development. Policymakers and educators are also reluctant to blame the school for students' poor performance because the school has accommodated the students by providing a bilingual program (albeit usually one with minimal L1 instruction). Thus, the academic deficiency is typically attributed to factors within the child or his or her community, as in Dunn's (1987) argument outlined above.

In the case of both of the misconceptions outlined here, a close relationship is assumed between the two faces of language proficiency, the conversational and the academic. In order to address these misconceptions and clarify the relationship between language proficiency and bilingual students' academic progress, I have suggested that it is necessary to make a fundamental distinction between conversational and academic aspects of language proficiency

(Cummins, 1981, 1984). This distinction is similar to that proposed by a number of other investigators (e.g. Bruner, 1975; Donaldson, 1978; Olson, 1977; Skutnabb-Kangas & Toukomaa, 1976; Snow et al., 1991). In particular, it builds on the original distinction between surface fluency and academic proficiency made by Skutnabb-Kangas and Toukomaa who, in 1976, brought attention to the fact that Finnish immigrant children in Sweden often appeared to educators to be fluent in both Finnish and Swedish but still showed levels of verbal academic performance in both languages considerably below grade/age expectations.

All of these investigators have pointed to a distinction between *contextualized* and *decontextualized* language as fundamental to understanding the nature of children's language and literacy development. The terms used by different investigators have varied but the essential distinction refers to the extent to which the meaning being communicated is supported by contextual or interpersonal cues (such as gestures, facial expressions, and intonation present in face-to-face interaction) or dependent on linguistic cues that are largely independent of the immediate communicative context. To illustrate the nature of linguistic cues, a cohesive device such as *however* coming at the beginning of a sentence tells the proficient reader (or listener) to expect some qualification to the immediately preceding statement. Students who have not developed awareness of the role of such linguistic cues will have difficulty interpreting meaning in decontextualized settings where interpersonal or non-linguistic cues are lacking.

In the Australian context, Pauline Gibbons (1991) has given a particularly clear description of the difference between what she terms *playground language* and *classroom language*:

> This playground language includes the language which enables children to make friends, join in games and take part in a variety of day-to-day activities that develop and maintain social contacts. It usually occurs in face-to-face contact, and is thus highly dependent on the physical and visual context, and on gesture and body language. Fluency with this kind of language is an important part of language development; without it a child is isolated from the normal social life of the playground. ...

> But playground language is very different from the language that teachers use in the classroom, and from the language that we expect children to learn to use. The language of the playground is not the

language associated with learning in mathematics, or social studies, or science. The playground situation does not normally offer children the opportunity to use such language as: *if we increase the angle by 5 degrees, we could cut the circumference into equal parts*. Nor does it normally require the language associated with the higher order thinking skills, such as hypothesizing, evaluating, inferring, generalizing, predicting or classifying. Yet these are the language functions which are related to learning and the development of cognition; they occur in all areas of the curriculum, and without them a child's potential in academic areas cannot be realized. (p. 3)

In discussing the distinction between contextualized and decontextualized language, I originally used the terms *basic interpersonal communicative skills* (BICS) and *cognitive academic language proficiency* (CALP) and later (e.g. Cummins, 1981a, 1984) elaborated the distinction into a framework that distinguished the cognitive and contextual demands made by particular forms of communication.

Cognitive and Contextual Demands

The framework outlined in Figure 3.1 is designed to identify the extent to which students are able to cope successfully with the cognitive and linguistic demands made on them by the social and educational environment in which they are obliged to function. These demands are conceptualized within a framework made up of the intersection of two continua, one relating to the range of contextual support available for expressing or receiving meaning and the other relating to the amount of information that must be processed simultaneously or in close succession by the student in order to carry out the activity.

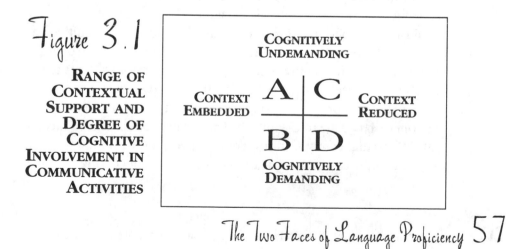

Figure 3.1

RANGE OF CONTEXTUAL SUPPORT AND DEGREE OF COGNITIVE INVOLVEMENT IN COMMUNICATIVE ACTIVITIES

COGNITIVELY UNDEMANDING

CONTEXT EMBEDDED — A | C — CONTEXT REDUCED

B | D

COGNITIVELY DEMANDING

The extremes of the context-embedded/context-reduced continuum are distinguished by the fact that in context-embedded communication the participants can actively negotiate meaning (e.g. by providing feedback that the message has not been understood) and the language is supported by a wide range of meaningful interpersonal and situational cues. Context-reduced communication, on the other hand, relies primarily (or, at the extreme of the continuum, exclusively) on linguistic cues to meaning, and thus successful interpretation of the message depends heavily on knowledge of the language itself. In general, context-embedded communication is more typical of the everyday world outside the classroom, whereas many of the linguistic demands of the classroom (e.g. manipulating text) reflect communicative activities that are close to the context-reduced end of the continuum.

The upper parts of the vertical continuum consist of communicative tasks and activities in which the linguistic tools have become largely automatized and thus require little active cognitive involvement for appropriate performance. At the lower end of the continuum are tasks and activities in which the linguistic tools have not become automatized and thus require active cognitive involvement. Persuading another individual that your point of view is correct, and writing an essay, are examples of quadrant B and D skills respectively. Casual conversation is a typical quadrant A activity while examples of quadrant C are copying notes from the blackboard or filling in worksheets.

The framework elaborates on the conversational/academic (or BICS/ CALP) distinction by highlighting important underlying dimensions of conversational and academic communication. Thus, conversational abilities (quadrant A) often develop relatively quickly among English language learners because these forms of communication are supported by interpersonal and contextual cues and make relatively few cognitive demands on the individual. Mastery of the academic functions of language (quadrant D), on the other hand, is a more formidable task because such uses require high levels of cognitive involvement and are only minimally supported by contextual or interpersonal cues. Under conditions of high cognitive demand, it is necessary for students to stretch their linguistic resources to the limit to function successfully.

As students progress through the grades, they are increasingly required to manipulate language in cognitively-demanding and context-reduced situations that differ significantly from everyday conversational interactions. In writing, for example, they must learn to continue to produce language without the prompting that comes from a conversational partner and they must plan large units of discourse, and organize them coherently, rather than planning only what will be said next.

Thus, the context-embedded/context-reduced distinction is not one between oral and written language. Within the framework, the dimensions of contextual embeddedness and cognitive demand are distinguished because some context-embedded activities are clearly just as cognitively-demanding as context-reduced activities. For example, an intense intellectual discussion with one or two other people is likely to require at least as much cognitive processing as writing an essay on the same topic. Similarly, writing an e-mail message to a close friend is, in many respects, more context-embedded than giving a lecture to a large group of people. [1]

The essential aspect of *academic* language proficiency is the ability to make complex meanings explicit in either oral or written modalities by means of *language itself* rather than by means of contextual or paralinguistic cues (e.g. gestures, intonation etc.). Experience of these uses of language in oral interactions prior to school clearly helps to prepare children to use and understand the increasingly decontextualized language demands of school. [2]

The distinctions incorporated into this framework have significant implications for instruction of English language learners. The progression of academic tasks should ideally go from quadrant A (context-embedded, cognitively undemanding), to quadrant B (context-embedded, cognitively demanding) and then to quadrant D (context-reduced, cognitively demanding). Cognitive challenge is essential for academic growth but the contextual support necessary for bilingual students to meet that challenge must also be present in the activities. If instruction stays at the level of quadrant A, there is no cognitive challenge; students are not pushed to go beyond what they already know and can accomplish. If instruction jumps prematurely to quadrant D, students are not given the contextual supports they need to meet the cognitive challenge. Quadrant C tasks (context-reduced, cognitively undemanding), as reflected in drills and mechanical exercises (e.g. out-of-context phonics instruction, filling in worksheets that reflect only memorization, etc.) usually fail to supply either cognitive challenge or "learner-friendly" language, and consequently are not very useful for promoting academic language acquisition.

Quadrant B activities provide both cognitive challenge and contextual support and are thus crucial for promoting academic growth. Cooperative learning is an example of a quadrant B activity insofar as the cooperation among students, together with teacher input, supplies the contextual support for students to engage in cognitively challenging projects or activities. As elaborated in the next chapter, quadrant B activities will also encompass an explicit focus on language awareness in order to assist students to develop strategies for picking up contextual clues embedded in both oral and written language itself.

Quadrant C tasks may be included prior to quadrant D tasks (or subsequent to quadrant D for consolidation of skills) if the teacher considers them necessary. However, teachers whose instructional philosophy emphasizes active language use and intellectually challenging content will tend to avoid quadrant C activities entirely.

Contextual support involves both internal and external dimensions. Internal factors are *attributes of the individual* that make a task more familiar or easier in some respect (e.g. prior experience, motivation, cultural relevance, interests, etc.). External factors refer to *aspects of the input* that facilitate or impede comprehension; for example, language input that is spoken clearly and contains a considerable amount of syntactic and semantic redundancy is easier to understand than input that lacks these features. As elaborated in the next chapter, teachers must focus on both internal and external contextual supports if bilingual students' academic progress is to be accelerated. For example, activating students' prior experience is crucial in making academic input in the target language comprehensible.

The central point is that language and content will be acquired most successfully when students are challenged cognitively but provided with the contextual and linguistic supports required for successful task completion. The process of providing these supports is usually referred to as *scaffolding* and is a central component in promoting academic success for English language learners. [3]

The next section considers how long it takes second language learners to master conversational and academic aspects of the target language.

How Long Does It Take English Language Learners to Master Different Aspects of Proficiency?

One application of the framework considered in Figure 3.1 is in the interpretation of data regarding the length of time required for bilingual students to develop proficiency in different aspects of English. Three large-scale studies have reported that, on the average, at least five years is required for immigrant students to attain grade norms on academic (context-reduced, cognitively demanding) aspects of English proficiency (Collier, 1987, 1989; Cummins, 1981b; Klesmer, 1994).

Collier's data are particularly interesting in that most students were from relatively affluent backgrounds attending a district (Fairfax County, Virginia) that was regarded as having an exemplary ESL program (and no bilingual education). She reports that children who arrived in the United States between ages 8 and 12, with several years of L1 schooling, required five to seven years to reach national norms in reading, social studies and science. Those who arrived before age 8 required seven to ten years to attain national norms, while those who arrived after age 12 often ran out of time before they could catch up academically in language-based areas of the curriculum. A considerably shorter period of time was usually required to catch up in math. [4]

Cummins (1981b) also reported that five to seven years were required for immigrant students from non-English-speaking backgrounds to catch up academically in English proficiency. Students who had been in Canada for three years were approximately one standard deviation (the equivalent of 15 IQ points) behind grade norms despite the fact that after three years most would have become relatively fluent in English conversational skills.

Klesmer's (1994) study involved a representative sample of almost 300 12-year-old English language learners (ELL) in a metropolitan Toronto school district. Detailed assessments of English proficiency and background data, as well as teacher ratings, were obtained. Klesmer reported that teachers considered most ELL students as average for their age in speaking, listening and reading after 24 to 35 months in Canada. In the area of writing, teachers considered ELL students to have almost reached the mean for Canadian-born students after 5 or 6 years. However, the test data showed significant gaps between the ELL students and a control group of English first language students (N=43) in all areas, except non-verbal ability, even after six years length of residence. The control group performed at the level of test norms whereas the ELL students were considerably below test norms on verbal academic measures after 6 years length of residence. Klesmer (1994) concludes that:

> there is strong evidence to suggest that the academic/linguistic development of ELL students follows a distinct pattern. It requires at least six years for ELL students to approach native English speakers' norms in a variety of areas; and it appears that, even after six years, full comparability may not be achieved. (p. 11) [5]

Other research suggests that a much shorter period of time (less than two years) is usually required for immigrant students to attain peer-appropriate levels of proficiency in conversational (context-embedded, cognitively undemanding) aspects of their second language (e.g. González, 1986; Snow and Hoefnagel-Höhle, 1978). These patterns are depicted in Figure 3.2.

There are two reasons why such major differences are found in the length of time required to attain peer-appropriate levels of conversational and academic skills. First, as outlined above, considerably less knowledge of language itself is usually required to function appropriately in interpersonal communica-

 **LENGTH OF TIME REQUIRED TO ACHIEVE AGE-APPROPRIATE LEVELS OF CONVERSATIONAL AND ACADEMIC LANGUAGE PROFICIENCY**

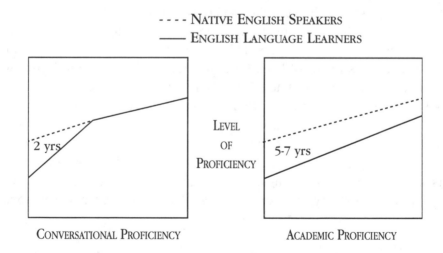

tive situations than is required in academic situations. The social expectations of the learner and sensitivity to contextual and interpersonal cues (e.g. eye contact, facial expression, intonation etc.) greatly facilitate communication of meaning. These cues are largely absent in most academic situations that depend on literacy skills and manipulation of language for successful task completion.

The second reason is that English L1 speakers are not standing still waiting for English language learners to catch up. A major goal of schooling for all children is to expand their ability to manipulate language in increasingly decontextualized situations. Every year English L1 students gain more sophisticated vocabulary and grammatical knowledge and increase their literacy skills. Thus, English language learners must catch up with a moving target. It is not surprising that this formidable task is seldom complete in one or two years.

By contrast, in the area of conversational skills, most native speakers have reached a plateau relatively early in schooling in the sense that a typical six year-old can express herself as adequately as an older child on most topics she is likely to want to speak about and she can understand most of what is likely to be addressed to her. While some increase in conversational sophistication can be expected with increasing age, the differences are not particularly salient in comparison to differences in literacy-related skills; compare, for example, the differences in literacy between a twelve and a six year-old student in comparison to differences in their conversational skills.

The preceding discussion of the nature of language proficiency and the length of time required to develop peer-appropriate levels of conversational and academic skills has immediate relevance for two practical issues. First, psychological assessment of bilingual students conducted in English is likely to underestimate their academic potential to a significant extent if any credence is placed in the test norms which are derived predominantly from native English-speaking students. As the numbers of culturally diverse students increase in school systems across North America, a radical restructuring of special education placement and assessment procedures will be required (Rueda, 1989).

Second, support for language and academic development will still be beneficial (and frequently necessary) even after students have attained conversational fluency in English. Exiting children prematurely from bilingual or ESL support programs may jeopardize their academic development, particularly if the mainstream classroom does not provide an environment that is supportive of language and content development. The kinds of instructional environment that are supportive of bilingual students' academic development are considered in the next chapter.

Conclusion

As discussed in Chapter 2, academic difficulties among bilingual students cannot be attributed solely to linguistic factors. However, misconceptions about language on the part of educators have clearly contributed to students' difficulties. [6] In fact, it is argued in Chapter 6 that the persistence of these misconceptions about language is a *symptom* of the underlying educational structure that disables culturally diverse students. For educators, a first step in becoming conscious of the ways in which this underlying structure operates to promote discriminatory assessment, placement and instruction of culturally diverse students is to examine critically the notion of "language proficiency" and how it affects performance on psychometric tests. Specifically, it is necessary to acknowledge that students' surface fluency in English cannot be taken as indicative of their overall proficiency in English. Similarly, the challenge for ESL and bilingual teachers is to develop *academic* skills in English, not just conversational skills. Academic skills in English usually require most of the elementary school years to develop to grade norms, and, as discussed in the following chapters, are more dependent on children's conceptual foundation in L1 than on their English conversational fluency.

It is also crucial for educators and policy-makers to face up to the implications of the fact that children are not failing in school only because of lack of English fluency. Lack of English fluency may be a secondary contributor to children's academic difficulty but the fundamental causal factors of both success and failure lie in what is communicated to children in their interactions with educators. This is clearly expressed by Isidro Lucas (1981) in describing a research study he carried out in the early 1970's with Puerto Rican students in Chicago designed to explore the reasons for student dropout. Although he prepared questionnaires in both Spanish and English, he never had to use the Spanish version. The reason was that:

> All my dropout respondents spoke good understandable English. They hadn't learned math, or social sciences, or natural sciences, unfortunately. But they had learned English…No dropout mentioned

lack of English as the reason for quitting. As it evolved through questionnaires and interviews, theirs was a more subtle story — of alienation, of not belonging, of being 'push-outs'…To my surprise, dropouts expressed more confidence in their ability to speak English than did the stay-ins (seniors in high school). For their part, stay-ins showed more confidence in their Spanish than did dropouts…I had to conclude that identity, expressed in one's confidence and acceptance of the native culture, was more a determinant of school stay-in power than the mere acquisition of the coding-decoding skills involved in a different language, English. (p. 19)

In short, understanding why and how bilingual students are failing academically requires that educators dig a little deeper than superficial linguistic mismatches between home and school or insufficient exposure to English. Underachievement is not caused primarily by lack of fluency in English. Underachievement is the result of particular kinds of interactions in school that lead culturally diverse students to mentally withdraw from academic effort.

One of the major reasons why students mentally withdraw from academic effort is that the instructional environment frequently does not facilitate or encourage active participation on their part. The message students get is that academic success is unlikely and thus academic effort is not worthwhile. Their identities disengage from the academic life of the school. What kinds of instructional environments are likely to reverse this pattern? This issue is discussed in the next chapter.

Endnotes to Chapter 3

1. In practice, the contextual and cognitive dimensions are not totally independent in that many context-reduced activities will tend to be more cognitively-demanding than context-embedded activities. This point is made by Frederickson and Cline (1990) in discussing the applicability of the framework for curriculum-based assessment of bilingual children:

   In observing and analysing classroom tasks, instructions and performances, we have often found it difficult to disentangle the "cognitive" from the "contextual". In some cases, movement along the contextual dimensions has actually been represented on the model as a diagonal shift, as it was found in practice that making tasks or instructions more context embedded also made them somewhat less cognitively demanding. Similarly, changes in cognitive demand may result in tasks actually being presented with greater context embeddedness. (p. 26)

Although there is clearly likely to be a correlation between degree of decontextualization and cognitive demand, I believe it is important to distinguish the two dimensions in order that the extent of this relationship can be investigated. In the one-dimensional distinctions proposed by other investigators (e.g. Donaldson's embedded/disembedded distinction), the degree of cognitive demand of particular tasks or activities is not represented and thus the instructional implications are more difficult to discern.

Robson (1995) summarizes some of the ways the framework has been used in the British context as follows:

> We found that the Cummins model was particularly relevant as a tool for formative assessment in that it could offer a framework for ongoing assessment, evaluation of tasks set and the planning of further teaching programmes and tasks for bilingual pupils. ... With reference to a bilingual pupil who may have learning difficulties, the Cummins model offers a framework for assessing progress over time, taking into account context, cognitive demand and language ability in relation to the tasks set. (pp. 41 & 43)

2. On the basis of her extensive ethnographic study among middle-class and lower-class families, Heath (1983) argues that the differences between social classes in learning to read derives from more than just differential access to literacy materials at home. What is more significant is the extent to which literacy activities are integrated with children's daily lives. The black and white *Maintown* (middle-class) children in her study experienced activities such as inventing narratives related to the stories that were read to them and comparing book characters with real people they knew. They learned to view language as an artifact separate from its use in face-to-face communicative contexts.

Heath (1986) enumerates some of the ways in which schools expect children to be able to use language before they begin formal schooling:

1. Use language to label and describe the objects, events and information that non-intimates present to them;

2. Use language to recount in a predictable order and format past events or information given to them by non-intimates;

3. Follow directions from oral and written sources without needing sustained personal reinforcement from adults or peers;

4. Use language to sustain and maintain the social interactions of the group;

5. Use language to obtain and clarify information from non-intimates;

6. Use language on appropriate occasions to account for one's unique experiences, to link these to generally known ideas or events, and to create new information or to integrate ideas in innovative ways.

Heath points out that those students who achieve academic success either bring to school all of these language uses, and the cultural norms that lie behind them, or they learn quickly to intuit the rules of these language uses for both speaking and writing. Bilingual children who have these functions of language available in their L1 can transfer them easily to English, given appropriate opportunities in English (see Chapter 5). Thus, both in-school and out-of-school occasions (in both L1 and L2) that require explanation of facts and assumptions not shared by others provide practice in the kind of context-reduced and impersonal language that is important for academic success. Heath suggests, for example, that a child who listens to a bank teller explain to her mother the rules for opening a savings account learns something about how to present information to someone who does not already share it, a use of language that will be invoked in much of the child's writing in school.

3. The general distinction that has been made between context-embedded and context-reduced language skills is consistent with the psychometric research of Ludo Verhoeven (1991a, 1991b, 1992, 1994) and Douglas Biber (1986). Verhoeven assessed context-embedded and context-reduced aspects of L1 and L2 proficiency among 72 Turkish-background kindergarten children living in The Netherlands. The context-embedded (or pragmatic in Verhoeven's terms) indices were derived from spontaneous speech whereas the context-reduced (or grammatical in Verhoeven's terms) indices were derived from test data assessing primarily vocabulary and sentence processing skills. Verhoeven found that context-embedded and context-reduced aspects of proficiency were clearly distinguishable (through factor analysis) in both languages. In addition, context-reduced proficiency in both languages was significantly related to non-verbal cognitive ability whereas this was not the case for context-embedded proficiency. Verhoeven concludes:

> The present study suggests that the proficiencies children have developed in L1 and L2 can not be conceived as monolithic traits. The present data show that in either language, context-based pragmatic skills can be distinguished from decontextualized grammatical skills. (1992, p. 134)

Verhoeven also found that both context-embedded and context-reduced proficiencies were significantly related across languages (Turkish-Dutch), a finding that is consistent with the results of Cummins et al. (1984) among Japanese-English bilingual students in Toronto, Canada and supportive of the *interdependence* hypothesis discussed in Chapter 5.

The conversational/academic distinction is also supported by Biber who used psychometric analysis of a large corpus of spoken and written textual material in order to uncover the basic dimensions underlying textual variation. Among the 16 text types included in Biber's analysis were broadcasts, spontaneous speeches, telephone conversation, face-to-face conversation, professional letters, academic prose and press reports. Forty-one linguistic features were counted in 545 text samples, totalling more than one million words.

Three major dimensions emerged from the factor analysis of this corpus. These were labelled by Biber as *Interactive vs. Edited Text, Abstract vs. Situated Content,* and *Reported vs. Immediate Style.* The first dimension is described as follows:

Thus, Factor 1 identifies a dimension which characterizes texts produced under conditions of high personal involvement and real-time constraints (marked by low explicitness in the expression of meaning, high subordination and interactive features) — as opposed to texts produced under conditions permitting considerable editing and high explicitness of lexical content, but little interaction or personal involvement. …This dimension combines both situational and cognitive parameters; in particular it combines interactional features with those reflecting production constraints (or the lack of them). (1986, p. 385)

The second factor has positive weights from linguistic features such as nominalizations, prepositions, and passives and, according to Biber, reflects a "detached formal style vs. a concrete colloquial one" (p. 396). Although this factor is correlated with the first factor, it can be empirically distinguished from it, as illustrated by professional letters, which, according to Biber's analysis, represent highly abstract texts that have a high level of personal involvement.

The third factor has positive weights from linguistic features such as past tense, perfect aspect and 3rd person pronouns which can all refer to a removed narrative context. According to Biber this dimension "distinguishes texts with a primary narrative emphasis, marked by considerable reference to a removed situation, from those with non-narrative emphases (descriptive, expository, or other) marked by little reference to a removed situation but a high occurrence of present tense forms" (p. 396).

Although Biber's three dimensions provide a more detailed analysis of the nature of language proficiency and use than the conversational/academic distinction (as would be expected in view of the very extensive range of spoken and written texts analyzed), it is clear that the distinctions highlighted in his dimensions are consistent with those distinguishing conversational and academic aspects of proficiency. For example, when factor scores were calculated for the different text types on each factor, telephone and face-to-face conversation were at opposite extremes from official documents and academic prose on Textual Dimensions 1 and 2 (Interactive vs. Edited Text, and Abstract vs. Situated Content).

4. Students who arrive after developing literacy in their L1 have a second advantage in that they are less likely to lose their L1 than students who arrive at younger ages (see e.g. Cummins et al., 1984). Bilingual students typically experience rapid loss of L1 in the first few years of learning English in preschool or in the early grades (Cummins, 1991; Wong Fillmore, 1991a). In short, students who arrive between ages 8 and 12 have the best prospects for developing proficient bilingual and biliterate abilities, a conclusion that agrees with the data of Skutnabb-Kangas and Toukomaa (1976).

5. Laosa (1995) has reported that grade 3 and 4 students who immigrated from Puerto Rico made gains in absolute terms with respect to English language academic proficiency during the two-year period but did not improve with respect to percentile placement in relation to test norms:

Taken together, the data suggest that there is in absolute terms not only an increase in the children's English-language proficiency during the first two years after migrating to the United States, but also that there is, though to a lesser extent, English language proficiency development occurring among children who stay in Puerto Rico. In either case, however, the rate of the children's development over time in the cognitive-academic components of English-language proficiency (i.e., reading and writing) is generally insufficient to permit them, as a group, to improve their standing in these important components of English-language proficiency relative to the level of similar-age students who are native speakers of English. (1995, pp. 53-54)

Students were performing below the 15th percentile relative to 3rd grade norms in the spring of their second year in the U.S.

6. Educators are not the only ones who sometimes have misconceptions about language. As I was preparing a paper to present at the American Association of Applied Linguistics (AAAL) conference in Long Beach, California, in March 1995, my eye was caught by a headline in the *Toronto Star* entitled "Charles Churlish on U.S. English." Since my presentation focused on the arguments of *U.S. English* in relation to bilingual education, I was intrigued at the prospect of royal assent for my position. Unfortunately, Prince Charles viewed "U.S. English" as virulent in quite another sense. The *Globe & Mail* (March 27, 1995) reprinted the following editorial written by Dale McFeatters of the U.S. Scripps Howard News Service:

Britain's Prince Charles complains that American English is having a "very corrupting" influence on "proper English," which, through the darndest coincidence, happens to be the brand of English he speaks.

Said the Prince, casually infuriating the Scots, Welsh and Irish as he did so, "We must act now to ensure that English — and that to my way of thinking means English English — maintains its position as the world language well into the next century."

His problem with Americans is that we tend to "invent all sorts of new nouns and verbs and make words that shouldn't be."

Our first reaction, as you can well imagine, was, "I say, old chap. Steady on." Think of the American words that have enriched the language: Gridlock. Carjack. Spin doctor. Deadbeat dad. Junk mail. Gangsta rap. Road kill. Cyberpunk. Grunge. Smog. Boombox.

Our second reaction was: Maybe the Prince has a point. (p.A11)

Bilingual and mother tongue teachers are no less subject to prejudice about language varieties than other members of the public. This was illustrated to me in a workshop I gave during the 1980s to a group of international language (mother tongue) teachers in Toronto, Canada. A participant raised the issue of how to deal with children's use of non-standard language in the classroom. Another teacher immediately raised his hand to share his way of helping children learn the standard form of the language (in this case Italian). He suggested that when children use a non-standard form in the classroom, the teacher should immediately stop the child and give her the "correct" term or expression. Another participant then asked what he would do if the child said that the non-standard form was what her parents used. The teacher responded that the child should be told that her parents were using the wrong word and she should go home and tell her parents what the "correct" word was.

It is clear that in this situation the teacher is communicating to the child that her parents not only have problems in English but, in addition, they don't even speak their home language properly. The effect is likely to be to reduce children's pride in their own cultural background and adversely affect their esteem for their parents. An alternative way of dealing with the same issue was suggested by a teacher of Italian at a different workshop. She suggested that when a non-standard word comes up in class the teacher can ask children what other words (in different dialects) they have for this object or idea. Her experience was that children soon realized the need for the standard form of the language in order to facilitate communication between communities whose native dialects are different. The appropriateness of the non-standard variety in its own context is also reinforced.

Chapter 4
Accelerating Academic Language Learning

The research reviewed in the previous chapter suggests that although there will be large variation among students, typically it takes between five and ten years for second language learners to catch up academically. For second language learners entering high school, the implications of these figures may appear daunting: students will run out of time to attain graduation requirements in English and academic content unless their progress can be accelerated. [1]

Several immediate implications follow when these time periods are considered together with recent demographic trends. McLaughlin (1995), for example, points out that more than one-fifth of American school-age children come from homes in which languages other than English are spoken; furthermore, the number of school children with limited proficiency in English grew two and a half times faster than regular school enrollment.

The growing numbers of students with limited English proficiency and the length of time required for these students to catch up academically means that increasing numbers of "mainstream" teachers will have bilingual students in their classrooms. This implies that *all* teachers should see themselves as teachers of academic language in addition to specific content areas. The time has long past when linguistic and other "exceptionalities" could be fully addressed by means of "satellite" programs that revolve around the mainstream (e.g. ESL, bilingual education, special education, etc).

By the same token, if academic language is central to all areas of the curriculum, then it should be taught by all teachers. If the task of teaching academic language is left only to the ESL or bilingual teacher, students' chances of catching up academically will be drastically diminished. Thus, an important part of leadership in culturally diverse schools is to ensure that an explicit policy is in place with respect to teaching language across the curriculum and that all teachers are prepared (in both senses of the term) to promote academic language development among bilingual students (see Corson, 1990, for a comprehensive treatment of school language policy development).

The instructional approach described in this chapter incorporates some central aspects of accelerating bilingual students' academic language development across the curriculum. The goal is to help students to attain grade expectations more rapidly than typically appears to be the case.

There are a considerable number of documented accounts of how bilingual students' academic progress improved dramatically as a result of particular kinds of classroom interventions and school restructuring efforts (e.g. Garcia, 1991; Hayes et al., 1990; Lucas, Henze, & Donato, 1990; McCarty, 1993; Rosier & Holm, 1980). These data suggest that students' academic progress can be accelerated quite significantly under optimal conditions. Here we sketch what some of those optimal conditions are with respect to classroom instruction.

In the context of the present chapter, the assumption is that students come from a variety of linguistic backgrounds with varying degrees of proficiency in English and differing levels of previous education. It is also assumed that they are in a mainstream classroom with minimal or no bilingual support. Thus, strategies associated with bilingual education and L1 support are not considered in detail here. Bilingual education is considered in the next chapter and both L1 support and other pedagogical strategies (e.g. parental involvement) are placed in a broader affective and sociopolitical context in Chapter 6 with respect to the concept of negotiation of identity.

If we consider Figure 3.1, the "target zone" or in Vygotsky's (1978) terms, *the zone of proximal development*, for pitching instruction for second language learners should be quadrant B — context-embedded and cognitively demanding. The rationale is that instruction must evoke intellectual effort on the part of students, i.e. be cognitively demanding, if it is to develop academic and intellectual abilities. If the instruction is cognitively undemanding, students will learn very little and quickly become bored in the process; if the instruction goes beyond what students can cope with cognitively, then they will also learn very little and become frustrated and mentally withdraw from academic effort. As indicated in Figure 3.1, the crucial dimension in helping students succeed in cognitively demanding tasks and activities is the contextual support that is activated in the learner (e.g. motivation, prior knowledge etc.) and embedded in the instruction.

Expressed differently, an English L1 student may succeed in a particular task (e.g. writing a science experiment report) with relatively little contextual support because English is her L1 and she has acquired the rules of this genre of writing from previous instruction; however, the same task may be much more cognitively challenging for a second language learner because of limitations in her current English language abilities and lack of previous instruction in how to write up science reports. The second student will require considerable contextual support if she is to succeed in the task.

Faced with this situation, some teachers who are unfamiliar with instructional strategies for second language learners have tended to "dumb down" the task (i.e. revert to quadrants A or C). This permits students to work within their level of English and academic competence but never pushes them to go beyond that level, which they must do if they are to catch up academically to English L1 students. [2]

The instructional approaches and techniques outlined below fall into the category of quadrant B. Among these are cooperative learning, drama and role-playing, total physical response, thematic teaching, use of visual representations such as graphs and semantic webs to make academic content and language comprehensible, language experience approaches, peer tutoring, dialogue journals, writers' workshop, etc. Most will be familiar to educators who have applied a whole language philosophy in their teaching since communication of meaning is a central theme.

The range of these techniques and strategies may appear overwhelming. How can any teacher become an "expert" in each of these areas?

Fortunately, good teaching does not require us to internalize an endless list of instructional techniques. Much more fundamental is the recognition that human relationships are central to effective instruction. This is true for all students, but particularly so in the case of second language learners who may be trying to find their way in the borderlands between cultures. They frequently don't have either the means or the desire to go back to their original culture but don't yet have the language skills or cultural understanding to participate fully in their new culture. For students to invest their sense of self, their identity, in acquiring their new language and participating actively in their new culture, they must experience positive and affirming interactions with members of that culture.

Teachers have the opportunity to nurture students' growing understanding of who they are and who they want to be. It is the teacher who guides students towards powerful ways of expressing themselves in their new language and communicates to them possibilities of who they can become and the roles they might play within their new society.

In other words, techniques and strategies will be effective only when teachers and students forge a relationship of respect and affirmation; when students feel that they are welcomed into the learning community of the classroom and supported in the immense challenges they face in catching up academically; and when students feel that their teachers believe in them and expect them to succeed in school and in life.

Respect and affirmation are the basis of any relationship and, in classroom interactions, respect and affirmation are central to motivating second language learners to engage actively and enthusiastically in academic effort. This perspective entails two implications for how teachers define their role: first, it implies that teachers must see their role as creating instructional contexts in which second language learners can become active partners in the learning process; second, it implies that teachers must view themselves as learners; in order to teach effectively they must learn from their students about students' culture, background, and experience.

How can this perspective be translated into practice? How can we implement effective instructional strategies in ways that will affirm bilingual students' developing sense of self? Effective instruction that will give students access to the power of language and accelerate their academic growth must include the following components:

- active communication of meaning;

- cognitive challenge;

- contextual support;

- building student self-esteem.

These components are infused into all phases of the four-part instructional framework outlined below. The framework is modified slightly from that developed by Chamot, Cummins, Kessler, O'Malley, & Wong Fillmore (1996). Aspects of this approach are elaborated in considerably more detail in a variety of useful sources including Chamot & O'Malley (1994), Faltis (1993), Kessler (1992), Leyba (1994), O'Malley & Pierce, 1996; Spangenberg-Urbschat & Pritchard (1994), and Wong Fillmore (1990).

The four phases, whose sequence can vary, are as follows:

• Activate prior knowledge/Build background knowledge;

• Present cognitively engaging input with appropriate contextual supports;

• Encourage active language use to connect input with students' prior experience and with thematically-related content;

• Assess student learning in order to provide feedback that will build language awareness and efficient learning strategies.

The central aspect of the framework is that these phases be included in the lesson plan but the sequence may vary. For example, presenting cognitively engaging input may precede activating prior knowledge for students whose knowledge of English is minimal and the assessment/feedback process will also likely operate throughout the lesson. [3]

Activate prior knowledge/Build background knowledge

There is general agreement among cognitive psychologists that we learn by integrating new input into our existing cognitive structures or schemata. Our prior experience provides the foundation for interpreting new information. No learner is a blank slate. In reading, for example, we construct meaning by bringing our prior knowledge of language and of the world to the text. As Fielding and Pearson (1994) point out, research conducted in the late 1970s and early 1980s consistently revealed a strong reciprocal relationship between prior knowledge and reading comprehension ability: "The more one already knows, the more one comprehends; and the more one comprehends, the more one learns new knowledge to enable comprehension of an even greater array of topics and texts" (1994, p. 62).

In second language learning, our prior knowledge plays a major role in helping to make the second language input comprehensible. Imagine, for example, that you have intermediate Spanish skills and you take advantage of an opportunity to take a course in child development in a Mexican university in order to improve your knowledge of the language. You already know a lot about child development from courses you have taken in English and from raising your own children. As you struggle to understand the lectures in Spanish, your prior knowledge of child development allows you to understand far more than if you had no knowledge of the content. Because you know much of the content already, you can make intelligent guesses or inferences about the meaning. By contrast, if you had enrolled in a course on South American literature, about which you knew very little, your intermediate Spanish would not have carried you nearly as far. And furthermore, because you understood far less of the input, you would have learned far less Spanish.

Thus, the primary rationale for activating students' prior knowledge, or if there is minimal prior knowledge on a particular topic or issue, building it with the students, is to make the learning process more efficient. Prior knowledge represents one central aspect of what students bring to the learning situation that makes input more context-embedded and comprehensible. It is important to *activate* students' prior knowledge because they may not explicitly realize what they know about a particular topic or issue; consequently, their prior knowledge may not facilitate learning unless it is brought to consciousness.

In a classroom with second language learners from diverse backgrounds, prior knowledge about a particular topic may vary widely. Thus, simple transmission of the information or skill will fail to connect with the prior knowledge and previous experience of many students, with the result that the input will be much less comprehensible for those students. Some students may have relevant information in their L1 but not realize that there is any connection with what they are learning in their L2. In other cases, there may be a considerable cultural gap between what is assumed by the text and what students know from their prior experience. This is particularly the case for older students whose previous schooling has been interrupted and who may have minimal L1 literacy skills.

Thus, a first step in making any input more context-embedded is to activate students' prior knowledge through brainstorming as a whole class, or in small groups or pairs. This is an appropriate situation for students to use their L1 in small groups or in pairs when their proficiency in English is limited. [4]

Finding out what students know about a particular topic allows the teacher to supply relevant concepts or vocabulary that some or all students may be lacking but which will be important for understanding the upcoming text or lesson. Building this context permits students to understand more complex language and to pursue more cognitively demanding activities. It frees up brain power.

Schifini (1994) suggests five strategies for tapping, focusing, and building on students' background knowledge:

1. **Use visuals to stimulate discussion.** Students work in small groups to make observations or speculate about visual stimuli that are in the text or supplied by the teacher. For example, in a science class, the teacher may show a picture of waves breaking on a beach and ask students to write down or discuss how ocean water moves. The most frequent responses from students are highlighted and used as an introduction to the text itself.

2. **Use manipulatives and multimedia presentations.** Schifini points out that "concrete objects such as historical artifacts, posters, replicas of newspaper coverage of major historical events, and laboratory experiences with everyday objects such as thermometers, rocks, leaves, batteries, and bulbs all build background through interaction" (p. 165).

3. **Sharing prior experiences with students from diverse backgrounds.** Schifini gives the example of students listening to the songs "We Shall Overcome" and "De Colores" and sharing their personal experiences or prior knowledge of discrimination and prejudice. Teachers can focus the discussion through questions such as "Why do you think people discriminate against other people?" "Have you ever felt discriminated against?" "How have we tried to decrease discrimination in this country?" etc. On the basis of this discussion, the teacher might then ask students to predict what they might read about in a text on the Civil Rights movement in the United States.

4. **Writing activities that focus students' prior knowledge.** Schifini suggests that quick-writes (e.g. one-minute brainstorming on paper), journal writing, and responding to written prompts (e.g. "People make war because _____") help students to become aware of their prior knowledge and extend their schemata.

5. **Linking prior knowledge to new concepts.** A technique proposed originally by Ogle (1986), K-W-L charts, is useful in relating prior knowledge to new information and concepts. A page is divided into three sections which students can fill out individually or in groups. "K" stands for "what I know;" Schifini points out that this activates prior knowledge and can help students

clarify misconceptions when discussed within groups. "W" stands for "what I want to find out" and helps students establish their own purposes for reading and can guide their interpretation of and extraction of information from text. "L" stands for "what I have learned and still need to learn" and encourages students to monitor their own learning and become actively involved in the assessment process. Anna Uhl Chamot (1996) has suggested that "H" can be added to the chart to signify "how I learned what I learned" in order to build students' awareness of learning strategies.

Although these strategies for activating prior knowledge constitute good instruction for all students, they are particularly important for second language learners because the activation and building of context permits them to function at a cognitively and linguistically higher level. These strategies also stimulate students to use the target language since extended discussion is usually required rather than single word answers to teacher questions.

Finally, activation of prior knowledge is a crucial way in which teachers can validate culturally diverse students' background experiences and affirm their cultural knowledge. A community of sharing is being created in the classroom; identity is being negotiated in ways that motivate students to express their growing sense of self and participate actively in the learning process. The sharing of cultural knowledge among teacher and students is multicultural education in action in a far more profound way than the more typical "heroes and holidays" approach.

In this regard, it is important to emphasize that curriculum materials and texts should be chosen carefully to ensure their relevance to students' cultural background and prior experience. If students' prior experience is excluded by virtue of the cultural loading of the text or material, it will be far more difficult for students to relate to it or for teachers to build background knowledge. Lisa Delpit has eloquently expressed this point:

> If we plan to survive as a species on this planet we must certainly create multicultural curricula that educate our children to the differing perspectives of our diverse population. In part, the problems we see exhibited in school by African American children and by children of other oppressed minorities can be traced to this lack of a curriculum in which they can find represented the intellectual achievements of people who look like themselves. Were that not the case,

these children would not talk about doing well in school as "acting White." Our children of color need to see the brilliance of their legacy, too. (1992, p. 245)

In summary, activating bilingual students' prior knowledge:

- makes the learning process more efficient;

- stimulates students to use the target language;

- permits teachers to get to know their students better as individuals with unique personal histories;

- creates a context in the classroom where students' cultural knowledge is expressed, shared and validated, thereby motivating students to invest themselves more fully in the learning process.

Present cognitively engaging input with appropriate contextual supports

Input in the second language can be presented either orally or through written text (as well as manually in the case of deaf and hard-of-hearing students). In presenting information orally to students, teachers can facilitate comprehension in a variety of ways:

- Facial expressions and gestures, acting out meanings, dramatization and role-playing, appropriate emphasis and change of pace in speech, etc. In other words, ham it up! If you are having a good time, your students probably are too.

- Visual support or graphic organizers such as maps, Venn diagrams, semantic webs, outlines of chronological or causal sequences, etc. Students can also be encouraged to develop these graphic organizers based on their prior knowledge and these can be elaborated to incorporate new information from the text or lesson (see Early, 1990; Faltis, 1993; Mohan, 1986).

Faltis (1993), following Wong Fillmore (1985), also points out that it is important for teachers to have consistent classroom routines and to provide clear *lesson markers* to signal to students where they are in the lesson at all times. This way students can focus on comprehension without having to figure out the structure of the lesson or what they are supposed to be doing.

In addition, teachers should *facilitate student participation* by asking questions that go beyond simple transmission of information, instead focusing on generating extended student responses and higher level thinking skills. Termed "instructional conversations" (Tharp & Gallimore, 1991; Goldenberg, 1991), this type of classroom discussion encourages students to construct "with the assistance of a skilled teacher — understandings of important ideas, concepts, and texts they would otherwise not understand on their own (Goldenberg, 1991, p. 8). Goldenberg's research suggests that such instructional conversations can promote more sophisticated understandings of significant concepts without sacrificing literal comprehension of a text. [5]

It is also important for teachers to model language that is comprehensible but goes beyond what learners themselves can produce (Krashen's i+1 and Gibbons' [1991] *comprehensible input plus*). Gibbons emphasizes that explicit attention to academic language is particularly important in schools with large numbers of bilingual students:

> In such a school it is very easy to fall into the habit of constantly simplifying our language because we expect not to be understood. But if we only ever use basic language such as *put in* or *take out* or *go faster,* some children will not have any opportunity to learn other ways of expressing these ideas, such as *insert* or *remove* or *accelerate.* And these are the words which are needed to refer to the general concepts related to the ideas, such as *removal, insertion* and *acceleration.* (p. 18) [6]

In the written mode, **reading** is crucial as a source of comprehensible input to accelerate students' academic growth. Reading is essential for students to get access to the language of text. This language is very different from the language of interpersonal conversation. The vocabulary usually consists of words that are much less frequent than those in everyday conversational language; grammatical constructions are more complex because meanings must be made more explicit; and textual language is not supported by the immediacy of context and interpersonal cues (e.g. gestures, intonation) that make conversational language easier to understand.

Academic success depends on students comprehending the language of text. **The language of text is found only in books** (except for a very small percentage of very boring people who talk like they write!). Thus, students' knowledge of academic language and their ability to use academic language coherently in their own writing is crucially dependent on the amount and variety of what they read (see Krashen 1993, for a comprehensive review of the research in this area).

Expressed differently, the most important instructional activities to accelerate second language learners' academic progress involve providing ample opportunities, encouragement, and incentives to read and write extensively in a variety of genres. For both first and second language learners, new vocabulary can be acquired incidentally through reading without any deliberate intention to learn or without explicit formal instruction (Harley, 1996; Krashen, 1993), although explicit strategy instruction (e.g. helping students identify the main idea of a text) can also play an important role (Chamot & O'Malley, 1994; Fielding & Pearson, 1994). [7]

Encourage Active Language Use to Connect Input with Students' Prior Experience and with Thematically-Related Content

As with language input, language use, or output, can take place in oral, written, and manual modalities. Active language use plays important roles in both cognitive and linguistic growth. [8]

At a cognitive level, writing about or discussion of complex issues with the teacher and peers encourages students to reflect critically and refine their ideas. As learners connect new information with what they already know, their cognitive power increases. They are enabled to understand more of the content and language that they hear or read. Cognitive and linguistic growth are seriously impeded when students are confined to passive roles within the classroom.

Linguistic growth is stimulated by active language use in at least three ways (Swain, 1995):

- Students must try to figure out sophisticated aspects of the target language in order to express what they want to communicate;

- It brings home to students and to their teachers what assistance they need with different aspects of language;

- It provides teachers with the opportunity to provide corrective feedback to build language awareness and help students figure out how the language works.

Gibbons (1991) emphasizes the importance of *reporting back* as a strategy for promoting academic language development. For example, after a concrete hands-on group experience, such as science experiment, students are asked to report back to the class orally about what they did and observed and then to write about it. As students progress from concrete hands-on experience to more abstract language use, they must include sufficient information within the language itself for the meaning to be understood by those who did not share in the original experience. She notes that:

> while hands-on experiences are a very valuable starting point for language development, they do not, on their own, offer children adequate opportunities to develop the more 'context-free' language associated with reading and writing. ...a reporting back situation is a bridge into the more formal demands of literacy. It allows children to try out in speech — in a realistic and authentic situation — the sort of language they meet in books and which they need to develop in their writing. Where children's own language background has not led to this extension of oral language, it becomes even more important for the classroom to provide such opportunities. (p. 31)

In addition to its cognitive and linguistic benefits, active language use in the classroom encourages students to express *themselves;* in other words, to explore their feelings, ideas, and experiences in a supportive context and thereby become more aware of their goals, values, and aspirations.

Among the instructional strategies for encouraging second language learners' active language use in oral and written modalities are the following:

Cooperative learning. As a result of considerable research since the early 1950s, cooperative learning is currently recognized as an extremely valuable instructional strategy for promoting participation and academic growth in culturally and linguistically diverse classrooms. Cooperative learning involves small groups of students working together to attain a common learning objective through activities based on interdependent cooperation (Abrami et al., 1995; DeVillar & Faltis, 1991; Holt, 1993; Kessler, 1992). Among the effective instructional practices for linguistically diverse students identified by Garcia (1991) was student collaboration on small group projects organized around learning centers. He reports that:

teachers in Latino language minority classrooms organized instruction in such a way that students were required to interact with each other utilizing collaborative learning techniques. It was during student–student interactions that most higher order cognitive and linguistic discourse was observed (Garcia, 1988). Students asked each other hard questions and challenged each other's answers more readily than they did in interactions with the teacher. Moreover, students were likely to seek assistance from other students and were successful in obtaining it. (1991, p. 4)

In organizing cooperative learning groups, it is usually advisable to form groups that are of mixed ability with respect to language proficiency and academic development and to assign a specific role to each student in the group (e.g. timekeeper, recorder, etc.). It is also important to be explicit to students about the social skills required for the group to work effectively (e.g. listening to each other, sharing materials and information, encouraging others, etc.).

Peer tutoring. Documentation of peer tutoring projects (e.g. Heath, 1993; Heath & Mangiola, 1991) demonstrate that both tutor and tutee benefit academically from this form of collaboration. Heath (1993) highlights the central role of cognitive apprenticeship which permits both students to shift roles or identities:

Their focus on another student's learning helps them decompose what is involved in learning language — oral and written, and to turn that reflection not only on the other as learner but also on themselves as learner and as model. ...Youngsters become something other than their usual student selves within the cross-age tutoring frame. They must play new roles as teachers, mentors, evaluators, and planners; they are accountable in new and different ways — to themselves, to their young charges, and to the adults with whom they must communicate about the achievements of their tutees. (1993, p. 188)

One form of cross-age tutoring that has enormous potential is the involvement of bilingual high school students as tutors for younger students from the same linguistic group. When bilingual support is not available in any other form, these tutors can play an enormously important role in helping younger students integrate into the life of the classroom and school. For example, a recently-arrived grade 5 student placed in a mainstream classroom could write stories or assignments in her L1 and, with the help of the tutor, translate these into English for sharing with the teacher and other students. She can thus show her intelligence and share her prior experience in ways that she could not do in English. In some school systems, the high school tutors receive either "work placement" academic credits or a stipend for this activity.

Drama. Heath suggests that drama is similarly powerful in enabling language learning through collaboration. She documents how inner city youth organizations have used dramas that young people write, cast, and direct to enable them to retain their first language or dialect while acquiring standard English and preparing for job entry. In the Canadian context, Regnier (1988) has also documented how inner city First Nations (Native) youth have written and performed dramas that reflect their lives and how this process has exerted a powerful impact on their sense of self and on their academic development.

Creative writing and publishing. The process approach to writing, advocated for more than 15 years by Donald Graves (1983) and his colleagues, has begun to bring about a major change in the way writing is taught in North American schools. This approach emphasizes writing as a communicative activity in which there is a real purpose (e.g. publication of a book within the classroom), a genuine audience (e.g. peers, teachers, parents), and support systems to assist children to work through the editing of successive drafts. This type of writing, in a variety of genres, can be highly effective in creating a sense of academic power, particularly among bilingual children who are developing literacy in two languages (see, for example, Brisk, 1985; Edelsky, 1986). There is probably no clearer illustration of what the term *empowerment* means than when a student's published story is placed in the class library and this student sees her friend borrowing the book from the class library to bring home and read with her parents. Daiute (1985) has expressed the potential of creative writing to promote a sense of academic efficacy among students:

> Children who learn early that writing is not simply an exercise gain a sense of power that gives them confidence to write — and write a lot. ...Beginning writers who are confident that they have something to say or that they can find out what they need to know can even overcome some limits of training or development. Writers who don't feel that what they say matters have an additional burden that no skills training can help them overcome. (pp. 5-6)

Once again it is clear how a student's sense of self is affected by the opportunities provided in the classroom for active language use and creative effort. [9]

Writing on a daily basis is especially important for second language learners because it requires them to engage with the most sophisticated aspects of academic language. It brings home to them and to their teachers what aspects of language they need assistance with and encourages them to become familiar with supports such as dictionaries, computer spell checkers, and word banks they may have kept on particular topics. Despite its cognitively challenging nature, if the appropriate supports are in place, writing can be highly satisfying and motivating for second language learners. Dialogue journals (where teachers respond in writing to students' journals) are an excellent way of encouraging second language learners' writing development in a genuinely communicative manner.

Theme-based learning. The movement towards an integrated thematic curriculum is very much consistent with attempts to accelerate second language learners' academic development. When the curriculum addresses similar themes (e.g. "habitats") in different content areas (e.g. language arts, science, math, social studies) students' understanding of the issues is deepened and their capacity for critical thinking extended. Thematically-organized curriculum builds students' background knowledge, thereby facilitating learning and active language use. Students can use the scientific knowledge they have on, for example, *habitats*, to inform their own creative writing on any number of issues (e.g. home, community, inter-group conflicts, etc.).

In the effective schools for culturally and linguistically diverse students investigated by Garcia (1991), instruction of basic skills and academic content was consistently organized around thematic units. He reports that in the majority of classrooms, students actually selected the themes in consultation with the teacher. The following example shows how this process worked in practice:

> In one third grade classroom, the teacher asked students early in the year, "What do you want to learn about?" Besides the usual responses from the students regarding their desire to learn to "read," "do math," "write," etc., one student indicated that he wanted "to learn about the chemicals that my father has that are making my little brother sick" — pesticides. The teacher, with the assistance of the students, determined what the students already knew about pesticides, made a list of questions to which the students hoped to find the answers, and developed a set of specific learning goals. Over the next five weeks, the classroom organized reading, writing, research, science, math, and social studies assignments that addressed these learning goals in

an integrated fashion. The teacher guided students through a variety of learning activities while making sure that students developed and utilized district-articulated grade-level skills in reading, writing, mathematics, and social studies. (1991, pp. 3-4)

Henderson and Landesman (1992) have also concluded that theme-based mathematics courses that use mixed-ability cooperative learning groups and hands-on activities enhance middle-school Mexican American students' math achievement. The authors suggest that thematic instructional techniques such as modeling and demonstration, connecting math concepts to real-life problems, and engaging students in discussion with other students are compatible with the learning styles of Mexican American children.

Assess Student Learning in Order to Provide Feedback that Will Build Language Awareness and Efficient Learning Strategies

We are concerned here not with formal test-based assessment but with assessment based on teacher observation and student classroom performance that will feed directly into the instructional process. Instruction and assessment are closely linked. Active language use by students is necessary if teachers are to have any data to use for assessment purposes. Thus, assessment involves monitoring of students' content learning and oral and written language use in order to provide appropriate guidance and feedback to students. This implies that students themselves should be active partners in the assessment process.

The performance and portfolio assessment strategies proposed by J. Michael O'Malley and Lorraine Valdez Pierce (1996) are useful in understanding the role of assessment in guiding instruction. Performance assessment refers to the process whereby students demonstrate specific skills and competencies in relation to a continuum of mastery as judged by a competent rater. Portfolio assessment involves gathering a record of student work over time to show the full scope of a student's academic progress. Student reflections and self-monitoring can also be included in the portfolio. O'Malley and Pierce suggest that portfolio assessment can be used for monitoring student progress, feedback to students, communication with other teachers and parents, monitoring the effectiveness of instruction, and as an aid to diagnosis and placement. The content of a portfolio will depend on the purpose for which it is to be used but might include a log of personal reading and responses to particular texts, a personal writing log, samples of students' published writing, and videotapes or audiotapes of students' reading or other language development activities.

A major goal of the assessment process is to help students monitor their own learning and thus become independent learners. This is why the "L" of the K-W-L charts is so important. Becoming conscious of what they have learned and what they still need to learn gives students a sense of control over their lives in the classroom.

The Cognitive Academic Language Learning Approach (CALLA) proposed by Anna Uhl Chamot and J. Michael O'Malley (1994) strongly emphasizes the importance of student self-evaluation and monitoring. They suggest that self-evaluation can take a number of forms such as discussion in cooperative groups, oral or written summaries or retelling of stories read, learning logs, dialogue journals with the teacher etc. As expressed by O'Malley (1996):

> The importance of self-assessment cannot be overstated. Self-assessment is the key to student empowerment because it gives students an opportunity to reflect on their own progress toward instructional objectives, to determine the learning strategies that are effective for them, and to develop plans for their future learning. With self-assessment, students are active participants in deciding what and how much to learn and in setting the criteria by which their learning is evaluated. (p. 3)

This self-assessment feeds directly into learning strategies that students can be taught to use that will assist them in overcoming difficulties they may be encountering. Learning strategies are purposeful behaviors or thoughts that the learner uses to acquire or retain new information or skills. They may be observable (e.g. note-taking, outlining, summarizing, asking clarification questions) or non-observable (activating prior knowledge, scanning key words, selective attention, predicting answers or information in forthcoming paragraphs, monitoring comprehension, making inferences, visualizing). Teachers should model strategies for students and encourage them to participate in peer discussions about their most useful strategies (Chamot, 1996).

In summary, feedback to students based on assessment should ideally include discussion or suggestions to students regarding strategies that they can use to achieve their learning goals or overcome difficulties. The goal is to develop students' awareness of their own cognitive processes in order to improve the efficiency of their academic learning. For second language learners who are trying to catch up academically to the moving target of English L1 speakers, it is clearly crucial to maximize the efficiency of their learning.

Feedback to students is equally important with respect to their developing English language skills. Wong Fillmore (1989, 1991) has strongly emphasized the importance of corrective feedback to avoid fossilization of second language skills. Particularly in situations where input in L2 comes as much from other L2 learners as from native speakers of L2, teachers must model appropriate forms of the target language and provide corrective feedback to students in ways that do not impede communication. The goal is to develop students' understanding of how language works, i.e. their *language awareness*.

The most powerful way of providing this feedback is in the context of students' writing. As students write drafts for publication or sharing, teachers can focus initially on helping them clarify their ideas and express them powerfully; then students' attention can be drawn to formal features of the language (e.g. grammar, word choice, spelling etc.) that are important for effective communication in the public sphere. In writing, students are in a position to assimilate this feedback without it impeding their communication; in fact, this type of feedback is clearly necessary to enhance the power of their communication. In conversation, by contrast, immediate feedback will usually interfere with communication and should therefore be delayed. For example, if the teacher notices that many students are having difficulty with a particular construction, it is perfectly appropriate to teach a mini grammar lesson on that aspect of language and immediately provide students with opportunities to apply the concept or structure in their authentic oral or written communication. However, grammar or other aspects of language (e.g. vocabulary, spelling, phonics, etc.) taught in isolation from students' oral and written communication will tend to stay isolated from their communication. In other words, taught out of context, grammar teaching will be largely ineffective except for performance on formal tests of grammar.

Many of the vitriolic controversies that have plagued language and literacy teaching during the past 30 years (e.g. debates on the role of grammar teaching for first and second language learners, phonics v. whole language instruction, etc.) can be avoided by acknowledging that development of language awareness is a valid and important goal for all learners. Language awareness should include knowledge of at least the following dimensions of language form and function:

- The structure of language systems (e.g. how sounds are formed, regional and class-based accents, grammar, vocabulary, cognates, etc.);

- Ways of accomplishing different functions and purposes of language (e.g. explaining, classifying, questioning, analyzing, etc.);

- Conventions of different musical and literary forms (e.g. rap, poetry, haiku, fiction, country music ballads, etc.);

- Appropriateness of expression in different contexts (cultural conventions of politeness, street language versus school language, the language of everyday speech versus the language of books, language register as a badge of identity in groups as diverse as sports teams, families, political parties, gangs, etc.);

- Ways of organizing oral or written discourse to create powerful or persuasive messages (e.g. oratorical speeches, political rhetoric, influential written documents, advertisements, letters to public officials, etc.);

- Diversity of language use in both monolingual and multilingual contexts (code-switching in bilingual communities, language maintenance and loss in families, political implications of the spread of English worldwide, etc.).

All of these dimensions of language can be related to ELL students' own experience and be integrated with role-plays, dramas, project research, etc. When placed under the umbrella of language awareness, the teaching of phonics or grammar ceases to be a contentious issue. The development of students' awareness of sound-symbol relationships and grammatical conventions is a legitimate and important aspect of instruction. However, to be truly effective, teaching about phonics and grammar must become part of a broader project of promoting language awareness, where students can see the relevance of language forms as well as the sociolinguistic and sociopolitical dimensions of language for all aspects of their own lives. Language and its use should be a frequent focus for student projects (both individual and group) at virtually all grade levels. It will certainly help students to become interested in language if teachers are able to communicate their own fascination with language and how it is used. [10]

Another argument for focusing on language awareness in the classroom is that second language learners become resources for other students in the class since their knowledge of additional languages is recognized and validated. They become language resources who can share their knowledge and experience of language and language learning with their peers who are limited (at this point in time) to only one language.

One final suggestion regarding assessment and language awareness concerns demystifying the language and conventions of standardized tests. There is hardly a student in the United States who has not taken a standardized test at some point in his or her school career. These tests have frequently been used to place culturally diverse students in "low-ability" tracks and they tend to exert a pernicious effect on teachers' academic expectations for these students despite the cultural and linguistic biases of virtually all such tests (see Cummins, 1984). One way to involve students actively in demystifying the construction and social functions of standardized tests is to provide opportunities for them, working in groups, to construct their own tests on topics with which they are familiar or on which they have carried out research. For example, the teacher might explain how multiple-choice items are constructed (e.g. the role of distractors) and groups might construct a set of items on topics with which they are familiar (such as baseball, popular music, television programs, popular slang etc.) and administer their items to the other groups. Alternatively, each group might research aspects of a particular topic (e.g. the American Civil War, the European arrival in North America, endangered species, etc.) and construct items based on their research.

Within this conception, standardized tests are viewed as one genre of language whose conventions students should be familiar with if their academic worth is to be recognized. Students are developing language awareness in the context of a highly challenging (but engaging) cognitive activity. I believe that this approach would develop "test-taking skills" (and a lot more) far more effectively than drill and practice approaches.

Conclusion

This chapter has presented no formulas on how how to accelerate bilingual students' academic progress. The diversity of student backgrounds, language proficiencies, and educational provision and policies would make any such attempt futile.

What the chapter has attempted to do is present both a philosophy of instruction and a variety of strategies that educators across North America have found useful in promoting bilingual students' language and literacy development in situations where students are integrated into mainstream classes taught exclusively or primarily through English.

In this regard, the importance of extensive reading and writing in the development of academic language proficiency cannot be over-emphasized. Reading texts which students can relate to their personal histories or their understanding of the world generates the motivation to keep on reading. Writing narratives and analyses that express their growing sense of self, their identity, allows students to map out where they have come from and where they are going.

Perhaps the most important thing that teachers can do to promote students' mastery of academic English is to organize the classroom as a learning community where everyone's voice can be heard. When students feel strong respect and affirmation from their teachers and peers, it generates a powerful sense of belonging to the classroom learning community and motivation to participate fully in the society beyond.

The following two chapters elaborate on these themes in the context of bilingual education and educational restructuring. These chapters highlight crucial aspects of the instructional environment that have not been considered in depth in this chapter; for example, the role of L1 instruction in promoting L2 literacy development and the importance of establishing strong partnerships to encourage culturally diverse parents to participate actively in their children's education.

Endnotes to Chapter 4

1. The difficulties for second language learners at the high school level are illustrated in a study conducted by David Watt and Hetty Roessingh (1994) who followed several cohorts of second language learners in one Calgary high school over a three year period. Instruction was exclusively through English. They report that almost 75% of the ELL student population in this school failed to complete graduation requirements. For students who had minimal English skills on entry to high school, the drop out rate was 95.5%; for those whose English skills on entry were advanced, the rate was 50%. These figures are influenced by the fact that Alberta has a ceiling of age 19 for enrollment in high school, but they nonetheless suggest massive wastage of educational and economic potential.

2. The argument that instruction should be pitched primarily at the context-embedded, cognitively demanding level (quadrant B) is clearly compatible with Krashen's (1981) notion of *comprehensible input* and with Vygotsky's (1978) *zone of proximal development* (ZPD) (see Chapter 1, note 12). Krashen's Input hypothesis postulates that learners acquire L2 competence by understanding messages that contain structures that are a bit beyond their current level. He terms this i+1 and suggests that "we can understand language that contains structures we do not 'know' by utilizing context, extra-linguistic information, and our knowledge of the world" (1994, p. 54). Gibbons (1991) terms this *comprehensible input plus!* which she describes as "the learner needing to hear models of language which are *comprehensible but also beyond what the learners are able to produce themselves*" (p. 17).

Faltis (1993) suggests that the notion of comprehensible input is similar to that of the ZPD in that development depends on the extent to which language input is made comprehensible to the learner by an adult; however, the concepts differ in the role assigned to learner output or language use. Krashen minimizes the impact of output on language acquisition. By contrast, according to Faltis, "the goal of working in the zone is to adjust speech around the learner's interactional level of competence, where output is indispensable for learning" (p. 118).

In the present framework, for instructional purposes, I believe that it is largely futile to try and separate the theoretical effects of input and output; they are two sides of the same coin and, at a practical level, both are important for second language acquisition (e.g. see Swain, 1986, 1995). Thus, while recognizing the central importance of comprehensible input, I prefer to talk in terms of *communicative interaction* which avoids the connotation of the term *comprehensible input* that language learning is largely a passive process of receiving input (although Krashen himself has always emphasized the active constructive nature of the process of comprehension). I believe that providing ample opportunities and incentives for active language use, in both oral and written modalities, is crucial to accelerate second language learners' academic progress.

Krashen's Input Hypothesis is clearly valid when interpreted as proposing that comprehensible input (i+1) is a major causal variable in L2 acquisition. However, a stronger form of the hypothesis, namely that comprehensible input is *the* causal variable in L2 acquisition, seems problematic insofar as it inevitably underemphasizes the role of active student language use in promoting academic mastery of the language. Despite these misgivings in relation to a strong version of the Input Hypothesis, I believe that there is a theoretical sense in which this strong form of the hypothesis may be tenable. Krashen's argument that only input can change cognitive structures (i.e. cause language acquisition), whereas output merely reflects current internalized language structures, echoes the distinction between *accommodation* and *assimilation* made by the eminent Swiss developmental psychologist Jean Piaget. Piaget emphasized that cognitive structures change only through *accommodation* to new input that creates a cognitive conflict or disequilibrium with current cognitive structures; in other words, new input shows that the internal model of the world in the child's head does not correspond to external reality, causing modifications to the internal model. *Assimilation*, by contrast, simply plays out current cognitive structures, assimilating external reality to internal reality until conflicting input requires a change or accommodation.

Krashen's views on input and output appear analogous to Piaget's concepts of accommodation and assimilation and may be valid in an abstract theoretical sense in that new input is certainly required to change cognitive or linguistic structures whereas output appears to have a more indirect role. However, for instructional purposes, I believe that it is crucial to emphasize active language use by students because this not only generates more focused input from teachers and other communication partners but also deepens students' intellectual comprehension of issues by allowing them to relate new input to their personal experience and analyze it critically in collaboration with peers.

Active language use is also crucial in the process of negotiating identity. It is through "output" (oral and written) that we present ourselves to others and (hopefully) develop a sense of belonging within our social groups. As argued in Chapter 1, this is a critical aspect both of second language acquisition and of academic development (see also Peirce, 1995).

3. Obviously, there are many valid ways of thinking about the sequence of instruction in the lesson. One clear scheme proposed by Connie Williams and others in California involves three phases: *INTO—THROUGH—BEYOND*. As elaborated by Francisca Sánchez (1992), *INTO* involves a focus on use of students' prior knowledge to connect it to the text/topic; *THROUGH* involves (a) a focus on providing comprehensible messages to students and presentation of key content; (b) a focus on engaging students in meaningful communication as a result of personal interaction with the text/topic; (c) a focus on divergent exploration of themes and concepts introduced in the text/lesson; *BEYOND* involves a focus on extending ideas presented in the lesson and a focus on the process of learning (see also Crawford, 1994, for discussion of communicative and thematic approaches to second language acquisition, and Handscombe, 1994, for a very clear synthesis of prioritics in educating second language children).

4. Handscombe and Becker (1994) provide a telling example of the powerful messages conveyed to bilingual students when they are encouraged to use their L1 and share their prior knowledge with the teacher and other students. Taraneh was a student of Iranian background in a culturally diverse grade 3/4 class in the Metropolitan Toronto area taught by Nancy Becker. She had been in Canada for 10 months but had been educated prior to this through Urdu in Pakistan.

> While Tareneh's previous schooling had been in Urdu, her parents had taught her to read and write in Farsi/Persian and Nancy encouraged her to bring a book to school in what Tareneh always referred to as "my language" so that she could hear Tareneh read it. Tareneh was delighted to do this and chose to bring a book about a stuffed Panda. The book had appealing drawings to help the monolingual English users with the meaning, while Tareneh rattled her way fluently through the text. The girls in the class were particularly impressed with her skill at deciphering the impossible-looking squiggles on the pages. Their demonstrated interest did much to bolster Tareneh's self-esteem. The very next week, when Nancy asked if she would like to bring another book in Farsi, she arrived with one in English,

making it clear that she knew what she needed to learn at this moment and would take all the help she could get, especially now that everyone knew how literate she really was. (1994, pp. 25-26)

It is particularly important to communicate strong reinforcing and welcoming messages to refugee children who may have survived considerable trauma prior to arriving in North America (see Criddle & Mam [1987] and Kaprielian-Churchill & Churchill [1994] for moving accounts of refugees' struggle for survival in their homeland and the challenges they face trying to reestablish their lives and identities in a new society).

5. Further evidence for the efficacy of *instructional conversations* is provided in the work of Ratleff (1993), Patthey-Chavez, Clare, & Gallimore (1995), and Swedo (1987). For example, Swedo's research with handicapped English language learners reported that:

Academic activities associated with the most intensive and prolonged levels of task engagement drew heavily upon, and encouraged expression of students' experiences, language background and interests. They also fostered feelings of success and pride in accomplishment, gave children a sense of control over their own learning, and included peer collaboration or peer approval. Furthermore, they were holistic in nature in that they did not involve learning or drilling of isolated, decontextualized segments of information. (p. 3)

6. The natural tendency of teachers to simplify instruction and reduce cognitive challenges is illustrated in an ethnographic study carried out by Ron Mackay (1986) in an Eastern Arctic community where a large proportion of the Inuit students were in the process of learning English. Mackay contrasted the ways in which two teachers (one grade 6 and the other grade 7) presented subject matter content to their students. The grade 6 teacher-student interaction tended to involve a wide range of classroom tasks and activities which frequently had a developmental sequence to them. Mackay describes this progression in terms of the degree of contextual support for the instructional message and the cognitive demands placed on the learner in order to successfully carry out the instructional activity or task (as depicted in Figure 3.1). The progression in the grade 6 class was from cognitively undemanding and highly contextualized activities (quadrant A) to cognitively undemanding decontextualized activities (quadrant C) to cognitively demanding contextualized activities (quadrant B) and finally to cognitively demanding decontextualized activities (quadrant D).

By contrast, the grade 7 subject matter teacher often tended to start out with, or move rapidly to tasks that required not only an understanding of the subject matter covered in class but also an almost native-like mastery of the use of English. If, as was usually the case, students experienced difficulty in this type of cognitively demanding decontextualized task, the teacher would typically reduce the activity to a much simpler one (e.g. completing worksheets). Instruction tended to remain at this level (quadrant C) and not progress to cognitively demanding activities or contextualized tasks addressing language development. Thus, the grade 6 teacher built up or scaffolded the language demands for the students more effectively than the grade 7 teacher. The instructional sequence in the grade 7 class tended to go from cognitively demanding decontextualized (quadrant D) to cognitively undemanding decontextualized (quadrant C).

7. Corson (1993, 1995) has pointed out that the academic language of texts in English depends heavily on Graeco-Latin words whereas everyday conversation relies more on an Anglo-Saxon-based lexicon: "Most of the specialist and high status terminology of English is Graeco-Latin in origin, and most of its more everyday terminology is Anglo-Saxon in origin" (1993, p. 13). Examples of Graeco-Latin words are: intelligence, attention, preserve, introduce, abolish, consequences, civilization, etc. Corson suggests that this division constitutes a barrier to academic achievement for those students who may have limited exposure to the Graeco-Latin lexicon outside of school; for example, students who have very limited access to books in their homes. Harley (1995) and Corson (1995) cite the research of Nagy, Garcia, Durgunoglu and Hancin (1993) and Hancin-Bhatt and Nagy (1994) to suggest that competency in a Romance language may give students an advantage in interpreting the Graeco-Latin vocabulary typical of English text when they continue to develop literacy in their L1 (e.g. Spanish). For example, knowledge of the Spanish word *enfermo* potentially gives students access to the English cognate *infirm*, a more literary and less frequent semantic relative of *sick*.

8. In the case of deaf and hard-of-hearing students, there are compelling reasons for emphasizing the use of American Sign Language (ASL) as a major medium of classroom communication in the context of bilingual/bicultural programs. Among these are the following:

- The central role that linguistic interaction plays in developing in children a conceptual foundation for future academic growth. If much of deaf students' mental energy in the classroom is taken up with the laborious task of acquiring oral English (as has been the case in North America for most of this century), then there is little time or mental energy left over for using language as a tool for learning and intellectual exploration. As a result of their artificial character, the various forms of sign English do not exploit the communicative possibilities of the manual medium to the same degree as ASL (Johnson, Liddell, & Erting, 1989; Mason, 1994).

- The importance of reinforcing students' sense of pride in their cultural identity as a prerequisite for confident engagement with academic tasks; when the culture and language of the Deaf community are not validated in the classroom, students will tend to internalize the message that their culture and language are inferior. The only identity option available to them within this kind of coercive educational structure is to become a deficient or "handicapped" member of the mainstream community. When ASL is not used as a medium of instruction, the message of inferiority is communicated to students in all the classroom interactions they experience. In the past, it was not uncommon for deaf school children to have their hands tied behind their backs as punishment for being caught signing. The current anger and militancy of many within the Deaf community can be understood in the context of this history of discrimination and coercion that deaf individuals experienced in schools and other institutions.

- The equalization of power relations between Deaf and Hearing communities that would result from using ASL as a medium of instruction and requiring that all professionals involved in teaching or assessing deaf students be competent in ASL.

9. Process writing appeared innovative in the North American context when introduced by Graves and his colleagues. However, similar techniques for promoting writing development based on experiential learning together with the use of the printing press for publication and dissemination of students' writing to a wide audience of corresponding schools were articulated by Célestin Freinet in France as early as the 1920s. By the time of Freinet's death in 1966, 10,000 schools around the world were engaged in sister class exchanges that operated in essentially similar ways to the contemporary computer-mediated school exchanges made possible by modern technology, and particularly the Internet. The pedagogical foundations for this type of global learning network are discussed by Cummins and Sayers in their book *Brave New Schools: Challenging Cultural Illiteracy through Global Learning Networks* (New York: St. Martin's Press, 1995).

10. Two useful resources for fascinating information about language are John Edwards' book *Multilingualism* and David Crystal's (1987) *Cambridge Encyclopedia of Language*. Among the facts included in Crystal's volume are the following:

- There are about 5,000 languages co-existing in fewer than 200 countries around the world. This explains why most countries in the world are multilingual.

- One of the most multilingual people ever to have lived was Cardinal Giuseppe Mezzofanti who lived between 1774 and 1849 and was the librarian at the Vatican. The eminent Cardinal could speak 50 languages, understand 70 and translate 114!

- Chinese has the most mother tongue speakers (1,000 million), English comes next with 350 million, and then Spanish with 250 million. Although fewer in mother tongue speakers, English is estimated to exceed Chinese in terms of total number of speakers [1400 million] (Edwards, 1994).

Discussion of facts such as these can stimulate a variety of language awareness activities in the classroom. For example, students could research how many languages are spoken and understood by students in the class (these could then be graphed by languages); which student in the class speaks the most languages (give student a certificate or some form of recognition); what are the major countries in which Chinese, English, and Spanish are spoken (identify on a world map and connect with voyages of discovery/colonization etc.). In other words, the facts are not inert but rather act as catalysts for further student investigation.

There is a growing literature on *critical language awareness* that provides direction for integrating the study of language and discourse into the classroom (e.g. Clark, Fairclough, Ivanič, & Martin-Jones, 1990, 1991; Corson, 1993).

Chapter 5
Bilingual Education: What Does the Research Say?

As we have seen, both opponents and advocates of bilingual education in the United States justify their positions in terms of what is in the best interests of children. Advocates argue that bilingual education can help make instruction comprehensible for English language learners and facilitate parental participation in their children's education. Opponents, by contrast, have suggested that bilingual education reduces children's exposure to English, thereby limiting their academic opportunities. These claims are frequently clothed in vivid rhetoric: for example, the claim by *U.S. English* that bilingual education constitutes child abuse or Schlesinger's (1991) suggestion that "bilingualism shuts doors" whereas "monolingual education opens doors to the larger world."

In this chapter, these opposing claims are examined in relation to the research evidence. An extensive body of research on bilingualism and bilingual education exists within the United States. When this research is combined with the research carried out worldwide for more than 70 years on these issues, the evidence is truly monumental. As far back as 1963, entire volumes were being filled with reviews of the research on bilingualism (e.g. Vildomec, 1963).

Thus, I have always been puzzled by the frequent lament from policy-makers that "research on bilingual education is sparse" or that "the research evidence is conflicting and therefore no conclusions regarding the efficacy of bilingual education can be drawn." What has been missing from the policy debate is any attempt to think theoretically about the research evidence. By *theoretical thinking* I mean articulating predictions based on the opposing claims and evaluating these predictions in relation to the research evidence. For example, what predictions can be derived from the opposing *linguistic mismatch* and *maximum exposure* hypotheses and how do these predictions stack up against the research evidence?

In order to evaluate what the research evidence on bilingual education is saying, it is necessary first to examine the relationship between theory, research, and policy decisions. I suggest that when the role of theory is understood, there is overwhelming consistency in the research on bilingualism and bilingual education. Following this, a definition of bilingual education is offered and the different types of bilingual programs that have been implemented in various parts of the world are described. The third section makes explicit the theoretical positions underlying the claims of opponents and advocates of bilingual education in the United States and then predictions derived from these theoretical positions are examined, first in relation to recent large-scale studies carried out in the United States, and then in relation to the international research on bilingual education.

Theory, Research, and Policy

A major reason why many policy-makers and educators in the United States regard the research basis for bilingual education as inadequate is that they have failed to realize that data or "facts" from bilingual programs (or any other programs) become interpretable for policy purposes only within the context of a coherent theory. It is the *theory* rather than the individual research findings that permits the generation of predictions about program outcomes under different conditions. Research findings themselves cannot be *directly* applied across contexts. For example, the fact that kindergarten and grade 1 Punjabi-background students in a Punjabi-English bilingual program in Bradford, England, learned English just as successfully as a control group in a traditional English-only program (Rees, 1981), tells us very little about what might happen in the case of Latino/Latina students in the United States.

Yet when this pattern is repeated across a wide range of situations, it suggests that some stable underlying principle is at work. This principle can then be formally stated as a theoretical proposition or hypothesis from which predictions can be derived and tested. For example, the *linguistic mismatch* hypothesis would predict that in every situation where there is a switch between home language and school language, students will encounter academic difficulties. The *maximum exposure* hypothesis would predict that any form of bilingual education that reduces the amount of instructional time through the medium of English will result in academic difficulties in English. These predictions can be tested against the research evidence.

Similarly, if we observe that across a wide variety of social, political, and linguistic contexts, instruction through a minority language for part or all of the school day does not result in any long-term academic loss in the majority language, it suggests that some theoretical principle is operating that can account for the consistency of findings despite wide variation in contexts. This is, in fact, what the research data clearly show and the underlying principle has been termed *the linguistic interdependence principle* (Cummins, 1981, 1984). I suggest in this chapter that it provides a reliable, albeit partial, basis for policy decisions regarding the education of bilingual students.

In short, although research findings cannot be applied directly across contexts, the accumulation of research findings does have relevance for policy. This relevance is achieved by means of integrating the findings within a coherent theory from which predictions regarding program outcomes under different conditions can be generated. In contrast to research findings, theories are almost by definition applicable across contexts. The validity of any theoretical principle is assessed precisely by how well it can account for the research findings in a variety of contexts. If a theory cannot account for a particular set of research findings, then it is an inadequate or incomplete theory. Thus, if there is counter-evidence to predictions derived from the linguistic mismatch or maximum exposure hypotheses, then they must be rejected as inadequate theoretical principles to explain the research data.

Types of Bilingual Education Programs

The term *bilingual education* usually refers to the use of two (or more) languages of instruction at some point in the student's school career. In other words, it is generally defined in terms of the *means* through which particular educational goals are achieved. When used in this sense, proficiency in two languages is not necessarily a goal of bilingual education. For example, the most common form of bilingual education in the United States, transitional bilingual education, aims only to promote students' proficiency in English. When it is assumed that students have attained sufficient proficiency in the school language to follow instruction in that language, home language instruction is discontinued.

However, the term *bilingual education* is sometimes defined in relation to *goals*, to refer to educational programs that are designed to promote bilingual skills among students. When used in this broader sense, bilingual education may entail instruction primarily or exclusively through only one language, as for example, when instruction is delivered through a minority language in order to provide students with the maximum opportunity to learn that language. Second language immersion programs of this type are implemented widely in certain countries.

For example, French immersion programs have operated across Canada for about 30 years and currently involve approximately 300,000 students. There are three broad types of French immersion program: *early*, starting usually in Kindergarten with 100% French until English is introduced in grades 2, 3 or 4; usually about half the time is spent through each language by grade 5 or 6; *middle* starting in grades 4 or 5 with between 50% and 100% French initially; and *late*, starting in grade 7 or 8 with 50% to 100% French initially. The early immersion program is the most common variant and countless evaluations have shown that students make good progress in acquiring French fluency and literacy at no cost to their English (L1) academic skills despite considerably less instructional time through English (Lambert & Tucker, 1972; Swain & Lapkin, 1982).

Two-way bilingual immersion programs (sometimes termed two-way bilingual education or developmental programs) implemented in the United States are modelled after the early French immersion programs but involve students from English home backgrounds together with students from another language background (e.g. Spanish, Chinese, etc.). Initial instruction is given predominantly through the medium of the minority language. After the initial grades, these programs maintain close to 50% of instruction in the minority language throughout elementary school.

Typologies of bilingual education programs have generated a myriad of different types depending on the combination of program goals, status of the student group (e.g. dominant/subordinated, majority/minority etc.), proportion of instructional time through each language, and sociolinguistic and sociopolitical situation in the immediate community and wider society (see Skutnabb-Kangas, 1984, for a review). [1] For our purposes, it is sufficient to distinguish four broad types based on the population groups the program is intended to serve. Three of these program types are intended primarily for minority or subordinated group students while the fourth is intended for majority or dominant group students.

Type I programs involve the use of indigenous or Native languages as mediums of instruction; examples are the various Native language bilingual programs in the U.S. (e.g. McCarty, 1994), Inuktitut bilingual programs in Northern Quebec and the Eastern Canadian Arctic (Patrick, 1994; Stairs, 1990), and Maori bilingual or immersion programs in New Zealand (Benton, 1988; Smith, 1992). The indigenous group has usually been conquered or colonized at some time in the past and the bilingual programs are often aimed at revival or revitalization of languages that have become endangered.

Type II programs involve the use of a *national minority language* which sometimes has official language status in the society. Examples are the use of Gaelic in Ireland and Scotland and Welsh in Wales as well as Basque and Catalan in Spain. The right to L1 instruction for official language minorities (both French and English) in Canada constitutes another example. Many other examples exist across the world, from China and Singapore in Asia to a variety of programs in Africa and other continents (see Skutnabb-Kangas & Phillipson, 1994, for discussion of linguistic human rights related to bilingual education around the globe). The minority language or languages involved usually have long-term status in the society and often some degree of official recognition. Maintenance or revitalization of these languages is usually the primary goal of such programs. Some programs could be classified as either Type I or Type II; for example, the Basques are usually regarded as the indigenous population of the northern parts of the Iberian peninsula and thus programs aimed at revitalization of Basque could also be classified as Type I.

Type III programs involve *international minority languages* that are the languages of relatively recent immigrants to a host country. Many of the bilingual programs in countries such as the United States, Australia, or Sweden fall into this category. Most of these are transitional programs designed to facilitate students' academic progress. In some situations, Type II and Type III programs merge into one another, as in the case of some Spanish-English bilingual programs in the United States that may serve both long-term Spanish-speaking groups as well as more recent immigrant groups.

Type IV programs are intended for dominant or majority group students and are intended to develop bilingual and biliteracy skills among such students. French immersion programs in Canada and two-way bilingual programs in the United States are examples of Type IV. Two-way bilingual programs also fall into the category of Type II or Type III since they also serve linguistic minority students. The European Schools model (Beardsmore, 1993; Skutnabb-Kangas, 1995) which involves instruction through four languages at various points in the students' school career also qualifies as Type IV as do Swedish immersion programs for Finnish students in Finland (Buss & Laurén, 1995).

Contrary to the impression one might get from the current U.S. debate on the issue, bilingual programs are not a recent innovation. In fact, bilingual education was common in Greek and Roman times (Lewis, 1976) as well as in the United States prior to the first world war (Kloss, 1977; Schlossman, 1982). Currently some form of bilingual education is implemented in the vast majority of countries around the world (Fishman, 1976). [2] In the next section, theoretical positions underlying the opposing claims related to bilingual education in the United States are outlined.

Theory Underlying Opposition to Bilingual Education

Three major psychoeducational claims have been articulated to argue against bilingual education: (a) the claim that "time on task"(or "maximum exposure") is the major variable underlying language learning and hence immersion in English is the most effective means to ensure the learning of English; (b) the claim that under these conditions of immersion, language minority students will quickly (within 1-2 years) pick up sufficient English to survive academically without further special support; (c) the claim that English immersion should start as early as possible in the student's school career since younger children are better language learners than older children. Examples of each of these claims are presented below:

Rosalie Pedalino Porter (1990) clearly articulates the "time-on-task" principle in stating:

> My personal experience and professional investigations together impel me to conclude that the two overriding conditions that promote the best learning of a second language are (1) starting at an early age, say at five, and (2) having as much exposure and carefully planned instruction in the language as possible. Effective time on task — the amount of time spent learning — is, as educators know, the single greatest predictor of educational achievement; this is at least as true, if not more so, for low-socioeconomic-level, limited-English students. Children learn what they are taught, and if they are taught mainly in Spanish for several years, their Spanish-language skills will be far better than their English-language ones. (1990, pp. 63-64)

Gary Imhoff (1990) in outlining the *U.S. English* position on bilingual education suggests that while native language instruction might be acceptable "for the first few months" (p. 51), the educational rationale for bilingual education beyond this initial adjustment period is seriously deficient. Especially problematic is the rejection by bilingual education advocates of the "time on task" principle:

> Bilingual-education advocates also tend to dismiss the idea that practice makes perfect, expressed in educational terms as "time on task," and hold instead that non-English-speaking students will learn English better if less time is spent teaching it. (1990, p. 51)

Nathan Glazer (Glazer & Cummins, 1985) has articulated his position in regard to teaching methodology and length of time required to develop English proficiency in responding to questions posed by the editors of the journal *Equity and Choice*:

> ...all our experience shows that the most extended and steady exposure to the spoken language is the best way of learning any language. ...How long? It depends. But one year of intensive immersion seems to be enough to permit most children to transfer to English-language classes. (1985, p. 48)

These claims are in direct contrast to those made by academic advocates of bilingual education, as outlined below.

Theory Proposed by Bilingual Education Advocates

It is important first to highlight the fact that most bilingual education theorists have distanced themselves from the usual rationale for bilingual programs, namely the *linguistic mismatch* hypothesis, outlined earlier. While the claim that children cannot learn through a language they do not understand has been persuasive to many policy-makers and educators (and, in fact, underlies the quick-exit transitional focus of most U.S. bilingual education), it is seriously flawed. It fails to account either for the success of English background children in Canadian French immersion or in U.S. two-way bilingual programs or the fact that, under certain conditions, English language learners can succeed academically in English-only programs (see Cummins, 1984).

Academic advocates of bilingual education have consistently rejected compensatory (or transitional) bilingual programs; instead, they have argued for enrichment (or two-way) bilingual programs that promote biliteracy for all children, regardless of language background (e.g. Collier, 1989; Fishman, 1976; Lambert, 1975; Swain, 1979). They suggest that reinforcing children's conceptual base in their L1 throughout elementary school (and beyond) will provide a foundation for long-term growth in English academic skills. Based on the time periods required to catch up academically with English L1 peers, researchers have also cautioned that we should not expect bilingual children to approach grade norms in English academic skills before the later grades of elementary school.

The two theoretical principles proposed in support of bilingual education have been termed the *additive bilingualism enrichment principle* and the *interdependence or common underlying proficiency principle*. Each will be considered in turn.

The Additive Bilingualism Enrichment Principle

In the past many bilingual students have experienced difficulties in school and have performed more poorly than monolingual children on verbal I.Q. tests and on measures of literacy development. These findings led researchers in the period between 1920 and 1960 to speculate that bilingualism caused language handicaps and cognitive confusion among children. Some research studies also reported that bilingual children suffered emotional conflicts more frequently than did monolingual children. Thus, in the early part of this century bilingualism acquired a doubtful reputation among educators, and many schools redoubled their efforts to eradicate children's L1 on the grounds that this language was the source of children's academic difficulties.

However, virtually all of the early research involved bilingual students in both Europe (e.g. Wales) and North America who were in the process of replacing their L1 with the dominant language, usually with strong encouragement from the school. As documented in previous chapters, many students were physically punished for speaking their L1 in school. It appears more reasonable to attribute the academic difficulties of bilingual students to the treatment they received in schools rather than to their bilingualism.

Consistent with this interpretation are the results of more recent studies which suggest that bilingualism can positively affect both intellectual and linguistic progress. A large number of studies have reported that bilingual children exhibit a greater sensitivity to linguistic meanings and may be more flexible in their thinking than are monolingual children (Bialystok, 1991; Cummins and Swain, 1986; Diaz, 1986; Göncz & Kodžopeljić, 1991; Hakuta and Diaz, 1985;

Mohanty, 1994; Ricciardelli, 1989, 1992). Most of these studies have investigated aspects of children's metalinguistic development; in other words, children's explicit knowledge about the structure and functions of language itself.

A variety of explanations have been suggested to account for the observed superiority of bilingual children on certain types of cognitive and linguistic measures: for example, the fact that bilinguals have two words for the same idea or object and two ways of expressing the same thought may lead them to "objectify" or become more aware of their linguistic operations, as suggested by Vygotsky (1962) (see Cummins, 1984 ; Diaz & Klinger, 1991; and Lambert & Tucker, 1972, for reviews). [3]

In general, it is not surprising that bilingual children should be more adept at certain aspects of linguistic processing. In gaining control over two language systems, the bilingual child has had to decipher much more language input than the monolingual child who has been exposed to only one language system. Thus, the bilingual child has had considerably more practice in analyzing meanings than the monolingual child.

The evidence is not conclusive as to whether this linguistic advantage transfers to more general cognitive skills;

McLaughlin's review of the literature, for example, concludes that:

> It seems clear that the child who has mastered two languages has a linguistic advantage over the monolingual child. Bilingual children become aware that there are two ways of saying the same thing. But does this sensitivity to the lexical and formal aspects of language generalize to cognitive functioning?

> There is no conclusive answer to this question — mainly because it has proven so difficult to apply the necessary controls in research (1984, p. 44).

An important characteristic of the bilingual children in the more recent studies (conducted since the early 1960's) is that, for the most part, they were developing what has been termed an *additive* form of bilingualism (Lambert, 1975); in other words, they were adding a second language to their repertory of skills at no cost to the development of their first language. Consequently, these children were in the process of attaining a relatively high level of both fluency and literacy in their two languages. [4] The children in these studies tended to come either from dominant language groups whose L1 was strongly reinforced in the society (e.g. English-speakers in French immersion programs) or from minority groups whose L1 was reinforced by bilingual programs in the school. Bilingual children who lack this educational support for literacy development in L1 frequently develop a *subtractive* form of bilingualism in which L1 skills are replaced by L2 (Wong Fillmore, 1991b). [5]

This pattern of findings suggests that the level of proficiency attained by bilingual students in their two languages may be an important influence on their academic and intellectual development (Cummins, 1981a). Specifically, there may be a threshold level of proficiency in both languages which students must attain in order to avoid any negative academic consequences and a second, higher, threshold necessary to reap the linguistic and intellectual benefits of bilingualism and biliteracy.

Diaz (1985; Diaz & Klinger, 1991) has questioned the threshold hypothesis on the grounds that the effects of bilingualism on cognitive abilities in his data were stronger for children of relatively low L2 proficiency (non-balanced bilinguals). This suggests that the positive effects are related to the initial struggles and experiences of the beginning second-language learner. This interpretation does not appear to be incompatible with the threshold hypothesis since the major point of this hypothesis is that for positive effects to manifest themselves, children must be in an additive situation where both languages are developing. If beginning L2 learners do not continue to develop both their languages, any initial positive effects are likely to be counteracted by the negative consequences of subtractive bilingualism. Thus, positive effects will not be sustained unless high levels of bilingual proficiency are attained (see Figure 5.1).

The findings of a series of Australian studies (Ricciardelli, 1989, 1992) are consistent with the threshold hypothesis and illustrate the types of advantage that bilingual information processing might confer on the developing child. Ricciardelli conducted two studies to investigate the influence of bilingualism on children's cognitive abilities and creativity. The first involved 57 Italian-English bilingual and 55 English monolingual children who were aged 5 or 6 at the time of the study. This study found that children who were proficient in both Italian and English performed significantly better than children who were proficient in English only (the high English monolingual group) and those bilinguals who were proficient in English but less proficient in Italian, on several measures reflecting creative thinking (the Torrance Fluency and Imagination measures), metalinguistic awareness (Word Order Correction), and verbal and non-verbal abilities.

Figure 5.1 — EFFECTS OF BILINGUALISM

The second study was conducted in Rome with 35 Italian-English bilingual and 35 Italian monolingual 5 and 6 year-old children. Again, those children who were proficiently bilingual in Italian and English performed significantly better than the other groups on the Torrance Fluency and Imagination measures as well as on Word Order Correction and Word Reading. Ricciardelli concludes that these data are consistent with the threshold hypothesis:

> On the whole, the results from this experiment provide additional support for the Threshold Theory, and they are broadly consistent with those found in [the previous study], in that, an overall bilingual superiority on the cognitive measures was found only for those children who had obtained a high degree of bilingualism (1989, p. 151).

Another series of seven studies, carried out between 1978 and 1987 in a totally different socio-cultural context (Orissa, India), shows an entirely consistent pattern of results (Mohanty, 1994). Mohanty studied large numbers of monolingual and bilingual Kond tribal children who had varying degrees of contact with the dominant language of Orissa, namely Oriya. The monolingual children came from areas where the original Kui language of the Konds had given way to Oriya monolingualism as a result of contact with speakers of the dominant language. In other areas, a relatively stable form of Kui-Oriya bilingualism exists where Kui is used predominantly in children's homes but contact with Oriya through peers and others in the neighborhood results in most children having a considerable degree of bilingualism by the time they start school, which is conducted through the medium of Oriya. Despite the differences in language use, the Konds are relatively homogenous with respect to Kond identity, socio-economic, and cultural characteristics. The context thus provides a unique opportunity to study the impact of bilingualism in relative isolation from the social, political and economic factors which frequently confound comparisons between monolingual and bilingual groups.

Mohanty's studies show a clear positive relationship between bilingualism and cognitive performance including measures of metalinguistic ability. He suggests that bilinguals' awareness of language and their cognitive strategies are enhanced as a result of the challenging communicative environment in which their bilingual abilities have developed. He interprets the findings as supporting both the threshold and interdependence hypotheses.

In summary, the following conclusion emerges from the research on the academic, linguistic and intellectual effects of bilingualism:

The development of additive bilingual and biliteracy skills entails no negative consequences for children's academic, linguistic, or intellectual development. On the contrary, although not conclusive, the evidence points clearly in the direction of metalinguistic, academic, and intellectual benefits for bilingual children who continue to develop both their languages.

In light of the considerable international research evidence suggesting cognitive and linguistic advantages resulting from additive forms of bilingualism, one wonders what research Arthur Schlesinger Jr. consulted to arrive at his conclusion that "bilingualism shuts doors?"

The Linguistic Interdependence Principle

The argument proposed by bilingual education opponents that deficiencies in English should be remediated by intensive instruction in English appears at first sight much more intuitively appealing than the alternative argument that instruction in Ll will be more effective than instruction in English in promoting English skills. This latter argument appears to invoke a "less equals more" type of logic that is unlikely to convince skeptics.

However, when empirical evidence rather than "common sense" is made the criterion for evaluating the merits of these two positions, it becomes very clear that the maximum exposure or time-on-task claim is seriously flawed. The issues revolve around two alternative conceptions of bilingual proficiency, termed the Separate Underlying Proficiency (SUP) and Common Underlying Proficiency (CUP) models.

The SUP and CUP Models of Bilingual Proficiency. The argument that if bilingual children are deficient in English, then they need instruction in English, not in their Ll, implies: (a) that proficiency in Ll is separate from proficiency in English, and (b) that there is a direct relationship between exposure to a language (in home or school) and achievement in that language. The SUP model is illustrated in Figure 5.2.

The second implication of the SUP model follows from the first: if Ll and L2 proficiency are separate, then content and skills learned through Ll cannot transfer to L2 and vice versa. In terms of the balloon metaphor illustrated in Figure 5.2, blowing into the Ll balloon will succeed in inflating L1 but not L2. When bilingual education is approached with these "common-sense" assumptions about bilingual proficiency, it is not at all surprising that it appears illogical to argue that L2 proficiency can be more effectively developed through L1 instruction.

However, despite its intuitive appeal, the empirical evidence clearly refutes the SUP model by showing significant transfer of conceptual knowledge and skills across languages. In order to account for the evidence (reviewed below), we must posit a common underlying proficiency (CUP) model in which the literacy-related aspects of a bilingual's proficiency in Ll and L2 are seen as common or interdependent across languages. Two ways of illustrating the CUP model (the linguistic interdependence principle) are shown in Figures 5.3 and 5.4.

Figure 5.3 expresses the point that experience with either language can promote development of the proficiency underlying both languages, given adequate motivation and exposure to both either in school or in the wider environment. In Figure 5.4 bilingual proficiency is represented by means of a "dual iceberg" in which common cross-lingual proficiencies underlie the obviously different surface manifestations of each language. In general, the surface features of Ll and L2 are those conversational features that have become relatively automatized or less cognitively demanding whereas the underlying proficiency is that involved in cognitively demanding tasks. [6]

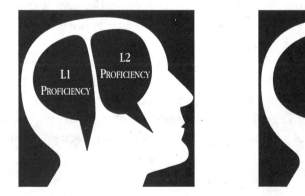

Figure 5.2

THE SEPARATE UNDERLYING PROFICIENCY (SUP) MODEL OF BILINGUAL PROFICIENCY

Figure 5.3

THE COMMON UNDERLYING PROFICIENCY (CUP) MODEL OF BILINGUAL PROFICIENCY

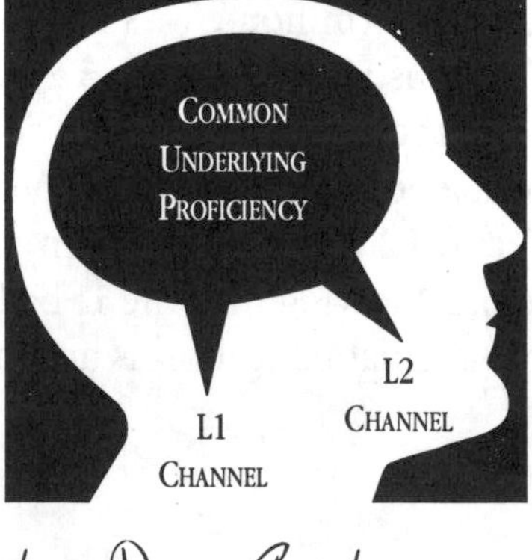

The linguistic interdependence principle can be formally stated as follows:

To the extent that instruction in Lx is effective in promoting proficiency in Lx, transfer of this proficiency to Ly will occur provided there is adequate exposure to Ly (either in school or environment) and adequate motivation to learn Ly.

In concrete terms, what this principle means is that in, for example, a Spanish-English bilingual program, Spanish instruction that develops Spanish reading and writing skills (for either Spanish L1 or L2 speakers) is not just developing *Spanish* skills, it is also developing a deeper conceptual and linguistic proficiency that is strongly related to the development of literacy in the majority language (English). In other words, although the surface aspects (c.g. pronunciation, fluency, etc.) of different languages are clearly separate, there is an underlying cognitive/academic proficiency that is common across languages. This "common underlying proficiency" makes possible the transfer of cognitive/academic or literacy-related skills from one language to another. Transfer is more likely to occur from the minority to the majority language because of the generally greater exposure to literacy in the majority language outside of school and the strong social pressure to learn it. However, as Verhoeven's (1991a, 1991b, 1992, 1994) studies (reviewed below) demonstrate, under some conditions two-way transfer across languages can occur.

In short, the development of academic skills in English depends not just on exposure to English (as "time-on-task" advocates argue) but equally on the

Figure 5.4

THE "DUAL ICEBERG" REPRESENTATION OF BILINGUAL PROFICIENCY

knowledge and concepts that children have inside their heads that help them make sense of English. Thus, instruction that builds up Latino/Latina children's reading and writing in Spanish is creating a conceptual foundation upon which academic skills in English can be built; a child who knows how to write sentences and paragraphs in Spanish doesn't have to learn what sentences and paragraphs are all over again in English.

Clearly, the notions of *time-on-task/maximum exposure* and *interdependence/common underlying proficiency* make diametrically opposite predictions in relation to the effects of bilingual education. If the time-on-task notion were valid we would expect that all students in bilingual programs would suffer academically in English when less instructional time was spent through English. By contrast, the interdependence notion would predict that transfer of underlying conceptual knowledge across languages would offset any impact of less instructional time through English.

Maximum Exposure v. Linguistic Interdependence: The Research Evidence

The results of virtually all evaluations of bilingual programs for both majority and minority students are consistent with predictions derived from the interdependence principle. The interdependence principle is also capable of accounting for data on immigrant students' L2 acquisition (e.g. Cummins, 1981b; Skutnabb-Kangas and Toukomaa, 1976) as well as from studies of bilingual language use in the home (e.g. Dolson, 1985). Correlational studies also consistently reveal a moderate degree of cognitive/academic interdependence across languages. [7]

The most clear-cut evidence with respect to the validity or otherwise of time-on-task versus interdependence notions comes from the Ramírez report, so-named after its principal investigator, J. David Ramírez. We examine the findings of this report and further analyses of its data (Beykont, 1994) in the next section and then sample from some of the international evaluations of bilingual education which show entirely consistent patterns of outcomes.

The Ramírez Report. The Ramírez report was released on February 11th, 1991, by the U.S. Department of Education. The study involved 2352 Latino/Latina elementary schoolchildren in nine school districts, 51 schools and 554 classrooms. It compared the academic progress of children in three program types: (a) English immersion, involving almost exclusive use of English throughout elementary school, (b) early-exit bilingual in which Spanish was used for about one-third of the time in kindergarten and first grade with a rapid phase-out thereafter, and (c) late-exit bilingual that used primarily Spanish instruction in kindergarten, with English used for about one-third of the time in grades 1 and 2, half the time in grade 3, and about sixty per cent of the time thereafter. One of the three late-exit programs in the study (site G) was an exception to this pattern in that students were abruptly transitioned into primarily English instruction at the end of grade 2 and English was used almost exclusively in grades five and six. In other words, this "late-exit" program is similar in its implementation to early-exit. Students were followed through to the point where each program model assumes they would be ready for mainstreaming into the regular program; in the case of the early-exit and immersion students this was grade 3 while late-exit students were followed to the end of grade 6.

It was possible to compare directly the progress of children in the English immersion and early-exit bilingual programs but only indirect comparisons were possible between these programs and the late-exit program because these latter programs were offered in different districts and schools from the former. The comparison of immersion and early-exit programs showed that by the end of grade 3 students were performing at comparable levels in English language and reading skills as well as in mathematics. Slightly more of the early-exit bilingual students were reclassified as fully English proficient by the end of grade 3 than was the case for immersion program students (72% vs 67%). Students in each of these program types progressed academically at about the same rate as students in the general population but the gap between their performance and that of the general population remained large. In other words, they tended not to fall further behind academically between first and third grade but neither did they bridge the gap in any significant way.

While these results do not demonstrate the superiority of early-exit bilingual over English immersion, they clearly do refute the argument that there is a direct relation between the amount of time spent through English instruction and academic development in English. If the "time-on-task" notion were valid, the early-exit bilingual students should have performed at a considerably lower level than the English immersion students, which they did not.

The "time-on-task" notion suffers even further indignity from the late-exit bilingual program results. In contrast to students in the immersion and early-exit programs, the late-exit students in the two sites that continued to strongly emphasize primary language instruction throughout elementary school (at close to 40% of instructional time) were catching up academically to students in the general population. This is despite the fact that these students received considerably less instruction in English than students in early-exit and immersion programs and proportionately more of their families came from the lowest income levels than was the case for students in the other two programs. It was also found that parental involvement (e.g. help with homework) was greater in the late-exit sites, presumably because teachers were fluent in Spanish and students were bringing work home in Spanish.

Differences were observed among the three late-exit sites with respect to mathematics, English language (i.e. skills such as punctuation, capitalization etc.) and English reading; specifically, according to the report:

> As in mathematics and English language, it seems that those students in site E, who received the strongest opportunity to develop their primary language skills, realized a growth in their English reading skills that was greater than that of the norming population used in this study. If sustained, in time these students would be expected to catch up and approximate the average achievement level of this norming population (Ramírez, 1992, pp. 37-38).

By contrast, students in site G who were abruptly transitioned into almost all-English instruction in the early grades (in a similar fashion to early-exit students) seemed to lose ground in relation to the general population between grades 3 and 6 in mathematics, English language and reading.

The report concludes that:

> Students who were provided with a substantial and consistent primary language development program learned mathematics, English language, and English reading skills as fast or faster than the norming population used in this study. As their growth in these academic skills is atypical of disadvantaged youth, it provides support for the efficacy of primary language development in facilitating the acquisition of English language skills (1992, pp. 38-39).

An additional conclusion highlighted by Ramírez (1992) was that learning English language skills by ELL students requires six or more years of special instructional support, a finding clearly consistent with the results of studies reviewed in Chapter 3 (e.g. Collier, 1987; Cummins, 1981b).

These findings are entirely consistent with the results of other bilingual programs and show clearly that, as predicted by the interdependence principle, there is no direct relationship between the instructional time spent through the medium of a majority language and academic achievement in that language On the contrary, there appears to be an inverse relation between exposure to English instruction and English achievement for Latino/Latina students in this study. [8]

Beykont's Analysis of Ramírez Site E Data. Beykont (1994) has carried out further analyses of the Ramírez data from Site E which involved Puerto Rican students in New York City. The sample of two cohorts for whom data were available from grades 3 through 6 consisted of 139 students (74 girls and 65 boys), the majority of whom were born in the United States. The progression of Spanish and English reading scores from grades 3 through 6 was related to a variety of predictor variables (preschool attendance, parental attitudes towards bilingual education, classroom organization [grouping patterns]). Beykont used sophisticated methodology for measuring change over time that relied on repeated measures of growth (Rogosa & Willett, 1985).

Among the findings of her study are the following:

• Students made significant progress between grades 3 and 6 in both English and Spanish reading. Spanish reading scores remained higher than English reading throughout this period but students approached grade norms rapidly in both languages.

• Academic progress in English reading was faster for those students whose initial (grade 3) Spanish reading scores were high and slower for those with low initial Spanish reading scores. A strong relationship was also observed between English and Spanish reading at the grade 3 level.

• Students whose parents held favorable attitudes towards bilingual education made faster progress in both English and Spanish reading between grades 3 and 6 than those whose parents held unfavorable or ambivalent attitudes.

• Students tended to show higher English and Spanish academic performance in classrooms that relied on smaller groups rather than on larger or whole class grouping.

Beykont concludes that:

In fact, children's consistently rapid progress in both English and Spanish reading through the sixth grade is remarkable, considering that the academic performance of native speakers typically levels off starting in the fourth grade, when children are expected to move beyond "learning to read" and start "reading to learn" difficult content matter. ...Of those Puerto Rican children who stayed in the program, about 50% of cohort 1 read at or above the sixth grade level in both English *and* Spanish; an additional 21.4% read at or above grade level in Spanish only and the rest read one or two years below grade level in English and Spanish. In cohort 2, which was followed for three years [to the end of grade 5], about 37% read at or above fifth-grade level in English *and* Spanish; an additional 31% read at or above fifth-grade level in Spanish only by the end of the study. ...These results clearly indicate that early assessment of English skills conceals the long-term benefits of extensive Spanish instruction for biliteracy development (p. 140). [9]

International Evaluations of Bilingual Education

As mentioned above, the international literature on bilingual education is voluminous (for example, see reviews by Baker, 1988, 1993; Corson, 1993; Cummins, 1984, 1993; Reid & Reich, 1992; Spolsky & Cooper, 1978). We provide just three examples here to illustrate the database that does exist. The first is an enormous study carried out in South Africa more than 50 years ago while the other two are more recent studies carried out in The Netherlands and Basque Country respectively.

Malherbe's Afrikaans-English bilingual education study. In 1938, E.G. Malherbe conducted a survey of almost 19,000 South African students from Afrikaans and English backgrounds in different types of school program. The results were published in 1946 in his book *The Bilingual School*. The aim of the study was to compare the effects of bilingual versus monolingual instruction for children from each language background. More than half (51%) of the sample received English-only instruction, 28% Afrikaans-only instruction and 21% were in bilingual schools receiving instruction in both languages. Almost one-third (32%) of the students spoke only English at home, 25% only Afrikaans, and 43% were from homes that were bilingual in varying degrees.

Students in the bilingual schools generally received their instruction in the early grades through their L1 and thereafter through both languages. Both cognitive ability and home language were controlled in comparisons of the effects of monolingual and bilingual schooling.

Among the findings reported by Malherbe (1946, 1969, 1978) were the following:

- Students gained considerable L2 skills when L2 was used as a medium of instruction rather than taught only as a school subject.

- Students instructed bilingually did at least as well in both languages as students instructed monolingually. In other words, there was considerable transfer of academic skills across languages and no evidence of a "time-on-task" effect.

- Bilingual instruction was equally appropriate for students with lower cognitive ability as for those whose cognitive abilities were higher. Malherbe expresses this finding as follows: "Not only the bright children but also the children with below normal intelligence do better school work all round in the bilingual school than in the unilingual school. What is most significant is that the greatest gain for the bilingual school was registered in the second language by the lower intelligence groups" (1969, p. 48).

In short, this massive and well-controlled study clearly refutes the time-on-task/maximum exposure notion which would have predicted that students in bilingual schools would perform considerably worse than those in monolingual schools as a result of less time through each language. Rather, the findings are entirely consistent with the notion of a common underlying proficiency which allows for transfer of academic skills across languages.

Verhoeven's Turkish-Dutch bilingual program evaluation. Verhoeven (1991a, 1991b, 1994) reported the results of two experimental programs in transitional L1 literacy instruction with Turkish-background students in The Netherlands. He summarizes the results as follows:

> With respect to linguistic measures, it was found that a strong emphasis on instruction in L1 does lead to better literacy results in L1 with no retardation of literacy results in L2. On the contrary, there was a tendency for L2 literacy results in the transitional classes to be better than in the regular submersion classes. Moreover, it was found that the transitional approach tended to develop a more positive orientation toward literacy in both L1 and L2. ...Finally, there was positive evidence for...[the] interdependence hypothesis. From the study on biliteracy development it was found that literacy skills being developed in one language strongly predict corresponding skills in another language acquired later in time (1991a, p. 72).

Verhoeven (1994) reports stronger cross-lingual relationships for literacy and pragmatic language skills than for lexical knowledge. Phonology (as measured by phoneme discrimination tests) was also significantly related across languages which Verhoeven interprets as reflecting the influence of metalinguistic factors on phonological performance in both languages. [10]

Evaluations of Basque-Spanish bilingual programs. A series of evaluations of Basque-Spanish bilingual programs in the Basque Country of Spain (Gabina et al., 1986; Sierra and Olaziregi, 1989; 1991) similarly showed a minimal relationship between instructional time spent through the medium of a majority language (in this case, Spanish) and academic achievement in that language. The three studies were similar in design in that each compared the Basque and Spanish achievement of elementary school students in three program types: (a) Spanish language instruction with Basque taught as a second language (Model A); (b) Spanish and Basque both used for instruction about 50% of the time (Model B); and (c) Basque as the language of instruction with Spanish taught as a subject (Model D). Students in Model D came from both Basque- and Spanish-speaking homes whereas a large majority of students in the other two programs came from Spanish-speaking homes. In all three studies, stratified random samples were chosen that were representative of the population of the Basque Country.

A similar pattern of results emerged in the three studies and at both grade levels studied (Grades 2 and 5). Extremely large differences were evident between Models D and A in command of both oral and written Basque, with Model B in an intermediate position. With respect to Spanish, however, the program differences at both grade levels were small. For example, in the second study involving Grade 5 students (Sierra and Olaziregi, 1989) there was only a six-point difference in overall Spanish scores between Models A and D (79.81, standard deviation 7.99, versus 73.77, standard deviation 9.31) compared to a 56 point difference in Basque scores (23.17 versus 79.04).

The goals of the Basque bilingual (Model B) and minority language immersion (Model D) programs are different than those of most bilingual programs in the United States insofar as promotion of additive bilingualism is the major objective in the Basque Country whereas academic achievement in the majority language is the primary goal of U.S. bilingual programs. Nevertheless, the findings are remarkably consistent in showing that instruction through the medium of a minority language for a substantial part of the school day entails minimal or no academic disadvantage with respect to achievement in the majority language (see also Artigal, 1991). [11]

In summary, the research evidence shows consistent support for the principle of linguistic interdependence in studies investigating L1-L2 relationships and in evaluations of bilingual education from around the world. The consistency and strength of research support indicates that highly reliable policy predictions can be made on the basis of this principle.

If the research data are so clear-cut in relation to the linguistic interdependence principle, why is there such controversy about the effectiveness of bilingual education in the United States?

There are two interrelated reasons why bilingual education continues to be highly controversial. First, as discussed in previous chapters, bilingual education was instituted in the late 1960s as an explicit challenge to the historical legacy of coercive relations of power; it was intended to create more equitable opportunities for bilingual students to achieve academic success. As such, it is not surprising that it would generate a backlash from those who wished to maintain the societal status quo and the inequities associated with the status quo. Furthermore, in the late 1980s the attempt to undermine bilingual education became associated with a broader struggle against all forms of cultural diversity, particularly multicultural education. The consideration of alternative perspectives on history (e.g. reinterpreting the 1492 Columbus "discovery" of America or examining Native perspectives on "how the West was won") was seen as weakening the fabric of nationhood, and bilingual education stuck out as a particularly visible and audible manifestation of this "disuniting" of America. Thus, regardless of what the research said, it was necessary to discredit bilingual education in order to halt the unravelling of nationhood.

The second reason why controversy has swirled around bilingual education is that the results of many so-called bilingual programs are mixed. The majority of bilingual programs instituted in the United States are quick-exit programs that make minimal or no attempt to promote literacy in students' L1. This weak variety of bilingual education is a consequence of the political pressure to remove students from bilingual programs as quickly as possible. Other programs may involve little more than a classroom assistant who works with the bilingual students (in either L1 or L2) while the classroom teacher instructs those who are fluent in English. Under these conditions, it is hardly surprising that students fall behind since they seldom interact with the teacher nor get access to mainstream curriculum content. In general, many programs have been set up to fail and, as Lily Wong Fillmore (1992) has argued, there have been concerted attempts to subvert bilingual education in a large number of school districts. She suggests that "a close examination of bilingual education where it has performed poorly will often show the extent to which it has been sabotaged from within by the people who were supposed to make it work" (p. 370). Only a minority of programs have attempted to promote strong literacy skills in students' L1 which the data reviewed in this chapter suggest is the approach most likely to promote development of English academic skills.

Despite the mixed quality of many bilingual programs, overall trends, even before the release of the Ramírez report, show the program to be more successful than English-only programs. Willig's (1985) meta-analysis of the research suggested that:

> When statistical controls for methodological inadequacies were employed, participation in bilingual education programs consistently produced small to moderate differences favoring bilingual education for tests of reading, language skills, mathematics, and total achievement when the tests were in English, and for reading, language, mathematics, writing, social studies, listening comprehension, and attitudes toward school or self when tests were in other languages (Willig, 1985, p. 269).

Krashen and Biber (1988) similarly reviewed the results of several bilingual programs in California in which bilingual students approached grade norms during the elementary school years and surpassed the academic performance of similar students in English-only programs. Collier's (1992) synthesis of research studies concluded that "the greater the amount of L1 instructional support for language-minority students, combined with balanced L2 support, the higher they are able to succeed academically in L2 in each succeeding academic year, in comparison to matched groups being schooled monolingually in L2" (p. 205).

More recently, Wayne Thomas and Virginia Collier (1995) have reported the findings of an on-going study involving 42,000 bilingual students in five school districts in various regions of the United States. Student background and educational program variables have been related to student outcomes over a six- to ten-year period. They summarized their preliminary, tentative findings as follows:

For students who are schooled in the U.S. from kindergarten on, the elementary school program with the most success in language minority students' long-term academic achievement, as measured by standardized tests across all the subject areas, is two-way developmental bilingual education. As a group, students in this program maintain grade-level skills in their first language throughout their schooling and reach the 50th percentile or NCE [normal curve equivalent] in their second language after 4-5 years of schooling in both languages. They also generally sustain the gains they make when they reach secondary level. Program characteristics are: (1) Integrated schooling, with English speakers and language minority students learning each others' languages; (2) Perception among staff, students, and parents that it is a "gifted and talented" program, leading to high expectations for student performance; (3) Equal status of the two languages...creating self-confidence among language minority students; (4) Healthy parent involvement among both language minority and English-speaking parents, for closer home-school cooperation; (5) Continuous support for staff development emphasizing: whole language, natural language acquisition through all content areas, cooperative learning, interactive and discovery learning, cognitive complexity for all proficiency levels. Students in well-taught bilingual classes that continue through at least sixth grade, with substantial cognitive and academic development of first language, are also able to reach the 50th percentile or NCE and maintain their academic performance at secondary level. ...ESL pullout in the early grades, taught traditionally, is the least successful program model for students' long-term academic success (1995, pp. 1-2). [12]

In summary, both large-scale and small-scale studies consistently show that strong promotion of bilingual students' L1 throughout elementary school contributes significantly to their academic success. However, bilingual education, by itself, is no panacea. Bilingual programs that are remedial in orientation or that fail to promote literacy skills in L1 will experience much less positive outcomes. Even programs that incorporate strong L1 promotion must also include active encouragement of parental participation and cognitively challenging instruction if optimum results are to be obtained.

Conclusion

This review of psychoeducational data regarding bilingual academic development shows that a theoretical and research basis for at least some policy decisions regarding bilingual students' education does exist. In other words, policy-makers can predict with considerable reliability the probable effects of educational programs for bilingual students implemented in very different sociopolitical contexts.

First, they can be confident that if the program is effective in continuing to develop students' academic skills in both languages, no cognitive confusion or handicap will result; in fact, students may benefit cognitively from access to two linguistic systems.

Second, they can be confident that spending instructional time through the minority language will not result in lower levels of academic performance in the majority language, provided of course, the instructional program is effective in developing academic skills in the minority language. This is because at deeper levels of conceptual and academic functioning, there is considerable overlap or interdependence across languages. Conceptual knowledge developed in one language helps to make input in the other language comprehensible.

These two psychoeducational principles open up significant possibilities for the planning of bilingual programs by showing that, when programs are well-implemented, students will not suffer academically either as a result of bilingualism *per se* nor as a result of spending less instructional time through English. If academic development of bilingual students is the goal, then students must be encouraged to acquire a conceptual foundation in their L1 to facilitate the acquisition of English academic skills.

This does not mean, however, that exposure to literacy in English should be delayed unduly. The interdependence principle posits that transfer of academic skills and knowledge will occur across languages under appropriate conditions of student motivation and exposure to both languages. It does *not* argue that initial instruction in the early grades should be totally through the minority language. Such an approach may be effective under certain conditions, as the outcomes of many two-way bilingual programs and second language immersion programs suggest. However, in other situations where bilingual students may have varying levels of proficiency in their L1 and English on entry to the program, it may be more effective to promote literacy in both L1 and English simultaneously or in close succession. The goal here would be to work for transfer across languages from an early stage by encouraging grades 1 and 2 students to read literature in both languages and write in both languages (e.g. produce and publish bilingual books). This type of approach has been implemented very successfully since 1971 in the Oyster Elementary School two-way bilingual program in Washington, DC. Children are reported to be reading in both languages by the middle of first grade and by grade 3 are reading two years above national norms (Crawford, 1995). In the context of French immersion programs in Canada, I have argued that L1 (English) reading and writing instruction should be introduced in grade 1 rather than delaying it for several years as happens frequently now (Cummins, 1995a, 1995b). The goal would be to work for more effective transfer across languages by ensuring that all children are literate in both languages by the end of grade 1.

In short, the data reviewed in this chapter clearly imply (a) that bilingualism and biliteracy should be promoted as central educational goals for all students and (b) that bilingual instruction should place a strong emphasis on developing literacy in the minority language. However, there is no one prescribed model for achieving these goals and flexibility of approach is necessary to take account of the varying entry characteristics of students, the availability of resources (e.g. bilingual teachers, minority language curriculum materials) and the political and economic climate within which the program is being instituted. [13]

While the psychoeducational principles discussed in this and the previous chapter clarify many of the disputed issues related to bilingual education, they do not, by themselves, constitute a fully adequate basis for planning educational interventions for bilingual students who come from groups that have been characterized by persistent school failure. The psychoeducational principles do not address the fundamental causes of bilingual students' educational difficulties, which, as noted in Chapter 2, are sociopolitical and sociohistorical in nature. Also, they do not fully explain the fact that, under some circumstances, bilingual programs have been dramatically successful in *reversing* children's academic difficulties. Thus, a framework for intervention is required that takes account of the interactions between sociopolitical and psychoeducational factors and that allows us to specify the essential components of effective education for culturally diverse students. Promotion of an additive form of bilingualism and biliteracy is one significant component but there are others that are equally significant and that must be in place for bilingual programs or any other programs to attain their goals. The components of an effective program are discussed in the next two chapters.

Endnotes to Chapter 5

1. Among the typologies of bilingual education that have been proposed, the most elaborate is Mackey's (1970) which distinguishes 90 different potential varieties depending on the intersection of home language(s), curricular organization of languages, and language(s) of the neighborhood and country.

   Perhaps the most useful typology for understanding the intersections between educational and sociopolitical factors in bilingual/multilingual education for both minority and majority students is that developed by Skutnabb-Kangas (1984). According to this typology, the *language of instruction* can be primarily the majority language, the minority language or both; the *program* can be designed for the majority group, the minority group or both together (a "two-way" or integrated program); *societal goals* of bilingual education can include direct assimilation of minority students, segregation (possibly with a view to repatriation) of minority students, equality for minority students, or enrichment and/or instrumental benefits (e.g. jobs) for both minority and majority students; finally, the *linguistic aims* include monolingualism (or strong dominance) in the majority language, monolingualism (or strong dominance) in the minority language, and bilingualism. Transitional bilingual programs in the United States illustrate the linguistic aim of monolingualism in the majority language while some European programs (e.g. in Bavaria) that have provided primarily L1 instruction for children of guest-workers illustrate the linguistic aim of monolingualism in the minority language.

   Churchill (1986) has also provided a useful typology of policy responses to diversity and minority language rights in OECD countries. He distinguishes six stages of response to the learning needs of minority groups:

   • *Stage 1: Learning Deficit.* The minority group's "problem" is defined in terms of lacking the majority language. The policy response is to provide additional teaching of the majority language.

   • *Stage 2: Socially-Linked Learning Deficit.* The minority group's "problem" is defined in terms of low socio-economic status together with language deficits. Additional assistance beyond just language programs is provided to assist achievement and assimilation (e.g. social workers, etc).

   • *Stage 3: Learning Deficit from Social/Cultural Differences.* The minority group's "problem" is defined in terms of low self-esteem and various multicultural interventions, usually of a fairly superficial order, are implemented as a remedy.

   • *Stage 4: Learning Deficit from Mother Tongue Deprivation.* The premature loss of the home language is seen as inhibiting cognitive and academic growth. Some form of minority language teaching is provided in the school to support continued development of the home language, usually only during the early years of schooling.

   • *Stage 5: Private Use Language Maintenance.* The minority group's language is seen as threatened with extinction if not supported. Some form of bilingual education is provided to support language maintenance, particularly in the early years of schooling.

- *Stage 6: Language Equality.* The majority and minority languages are seen as having equal rights in the society and special supports are provided for the non-dominant language(s). Policy responses can include recognition of the minority language as an official language together with various educational and other institutional supports for language equality and two-way language learning.

  Churchill's stages can also be seen as forms of collective role definitions similar to the notion of role definition elaborated in Chapters 1 and 6 of this volume.

2. A variety of bilingual program evaluations conducted in Canada during the past 20 years involving languages other than English and French are reviewed in Cummins and Danesi (1990). The results of all of these studies are consistent with the notion of linguistic interdependence. Two Australian studies of note document a Lebanese-English bilingual program (Gibbons, White, & Gibbons, 1994) and an Aboriginal language program (Gale et al., 1981). A small part of the vast experience with bilingual education in India is documented by Mohanty (1994) while a considerable number of international bilingual education programs are described in Spolsky and Cooper (1978).

3. Diaz and Klinger (1991) have outlined an explanatory model to account for the empirical data. Their first proposition states that exposure to two languages at an early age in a systematic additive fashion results in an objective awareness of grammatical rules and language functions. The second proposition holds that this greater awareness of the cognitive functions of language leads to increased and more efficient use of language as a tool for thought. Finally, they suggest that bilinguals' increased reliance on private speech and verbal mediation will promote the development of cognitive executive functions. Along the same lines, Bialystok (1991) and Bialystok and Hakuta (1994) have interpreted the research data as indicating that bilingual children have enhanced awareness of the analysis and control components of linguistic processing. They argue that processing systems developed to serve two linguistic systems are necessarily different from the same processing systems that operate in the service of only one.

   Malakoff and Hakuta (1991) have further explored the relation between bilingualism and metalinguistic awareness in two studies that investigated bilingual students' translation from one language to another. They report that translation skill is widely found in bilingual children in late elementary school. This ability appears to be related both to language proficiency in the two languages and to a separate metalinguistic ability that is unrelated to proficiency in the two languages. They also suggest that translation offers an excellent pedagogical tool to enhance students' metalinguistic awareness and their pride in bilingualism.

4. Landry and Allard (1991) have suggested that the additive/subtractive distinction should be viewed not as a linguistic dichotomy but as extremes on a continuum that encompasses the cognitive, affective, and behavioral aspects of language experience. Landry and his colleagues have conducted a series of large-scale studies of minority francophone students in various parts of Canada. He summarizes the conclusions of these studies as follows:

Recent research studies…have demonstrated that the attainment of additive bilingualism among minority francophones is strongly related to the proportion of schooling through French [students' L1]. Students who experienced more French-medium schooling developed higher levels of both conversational and academic proficiency in French, they desired to integrate more with the francophone community, they identified more as francophone, and they utilized the French language to a greater extent. Furthermore, students' English proficiency was not in any way diminished through participation in a strong French-medium bilingual program, a result that illustrates the additive nature of their bilingualism. …Among anglophone students who are members of a community with extremely high ethnolinguistic vitality, spending a large proportion of instructional time through French [their L2] had a positive impact on both their French proficiency and attitudes towards the francophone community without any negative impact on their mother tongue. (1993, p. 893) [translation by Jim Cummins]

The findings of Landry's studies are consistent with other large-scale Canadian evaluations of bilingual programs for minority francophone students outside Quebec (e.g. Hébert et al., 1976) and provide strong support for the interdependence of bilingual academic skills across languages. In other words, they demonstrate that minority students who are educated for up to 80% of the time through their L1 (as in the case of most Canadian bilingual programs for minority francophone students) develop literacy skills in English (the majority language) that are equivalent to similar students who have been instructed entirely through English.

In light of these data, Landry and Allard (1991) propose a *counterbalance model of bilingual experience* which states that "additive bilingualism for a minority group's members is only possible when the frequency of opportunities for linguistic contact in L1 can compensate for the dominance of L2" (p. 205). In most cases, this will require that the school and family context be almost completely unilingual in L1. While L1 schooling is an essential contributor to additive bilingualism, by itself it is inadequate to compensate fully for low levels of linguistic vitality at the sociological level or for low levels of linguistic contact in the family or social milieu. Despite French-medium schooling, most francophone students in their studies were dominant in English.

5. For bilingual students without the benefit of L1 literacy promotion in school, language shift can be extremely rapid. This pattern is illustrated in a small-scale longitudinal study of Portuguese-speaking children in Toronto, Canada (Cummins, 1991). The developing bilingual skills of 20 children were monitored from Junior Kindergarten [JK] (a two hour program for 4 year-olds) through Senior Kindergarten and grade 1. Language use in the home was tape-recorded, interviews with the children were conducted in both languages, and English reading measures were administered at the end of grade 1. It was found that even at the JK level, language shift was already well underway. Although parents used Portuguese predominantly with their children, a significant minority of children were already using

more English with their parents, especially with mothers. In addition, English had already become the dominant language among siblings. Only seven of the 4-year old children (out of 20) showed a marked preference for Portuguese, three showed roughly equal use of each language, while the remainder (10) used English as their predominant language. By the time the children completed grade 1, only 2 (out of 14) were rated as more conversationally proficient in Portuguese than in English and only three were rated as equally proficient in each language.

There were indications that the development of conceptual knowledge in both languages was closely related and that loss of Portuguese was associated with lower academic achievement in English. For example, the various preschool indices of language development in Portuguese and English were positively related across languages and about equally related to English reading performance at the grade 1 level. This pattern suggests a general developmental process encompassing conceptual growth and oral skills in both languages. There was also a large difference of about one standard deviation in English reading skills in favor of children who were maintaining Portuguese language skills (N=6, ratings of 3-5 on Portuguese oral proficiency) as compared to those who were losing the language (N=8, ratings of 1-2 on Portuguese oral proficiency).

Wong Fillmore (1991b) has also documented the loss of language skills in early childhood in an interview study involving more than 1,000 families. More than 60% of the families judged monolingual English daycare or preschool provision to have exerted a negative impact on family communication as a result of loss of L1 skills on the part of children. By contrast, preschool programs that utilized children's L1 exclusively were associated with significantly less language loss. Wong Fillmore argues on the basis of both the quantitative and qualitative data of this study that communication between children and parents in the home frequently breaks down as children progress through the grades as a result of the fact that they no longer share a common language.

6. The metaphor of language proficiency as an iceberg was first proposed by Roger Shuy (1978) to distinguish between surface and deeper levels of language proficiency. Basic grammar, vocabulary, and phonology are "visible" above the surface but the less obvious semantic and functional proficiencies below the surface are much more significant for academic progress. The idea of representing bilingual proficiency (and the interdependence hypothesis) as a dual-iceberg came to me in discussion with Roger Shuy and John Oller at a workshop organized by Margarita Calderón on a very hot February 1979 day in Riverside, California.

7. Many studies conducted since the mid-eighties support the interdependence principle (see Cummins, 1989, for a comprehensive review). Kemp (1984), for example, reported that level of Hebrew (L1) cognitive/academic abilities strongly predicted English (L2) academic skills among 196 seventh grade Israeli students.

In a three-year longitudinal study conducted in Newark, New Jersey, Ramírez (1985) followed 75 Latino/Latina elementary school students enrolled in bilingual programs. He reported that Spanish and English academic language scores were so strongly related that they represented the same underlying dimension over the three years of data collection.

Hakuta and Diaz (1985) with a similar sample of Latino/Latina students found an increasing correlation between English and Spanish academic skills over time. Between kindergarten and third grade the correlation between English and Spanish went from 0 to .68 (representing close to 50% of shared variance). The low cross-lingual relationship at the kindergarten level is likely due to the varied length of residence of the students and their parents in the United States which would result in varying levels of English proficiency at the start of school.

A case study of five schools attempting to implement the theoretical framework for the education of language minority students developed by the California State Department of Education (1981) showed consistently higher correlations between English and Spanish reading skills (range r= .60-.74) than between English reading and oral language skills (range r= .36-.59) (California State Department of Education, 1985). It was also found that the relation between L1 and L2 reading became stronger as English oral communicative skills grew stronger (r=.71, N=190 for students in the highest category of English oral skills). See Crawford (1995) for a detailed account of the Case Studies project and its highly positive outcomes for bilingual students' achievement in schools such as the Eastman Avenue school in Los Angeles.

Geva and Ryan (1987) have reported evidence with Hebrew-English bilinguals in Toronto that L1 cognitive/academic skills are significantly related to L2 cognitive/academic skills. They show that not only underlying non-verbal intellectual factors are involved in this process but also memory storage capacity and analytic processes required in performing academic tasks. In other words, they have made explicit some of the cognitive processes that are involved in mediating the transfer from L1 to L2.

European research also supports the interdependence hypothesis. McLaughlin (1986), for example, reviewed research carried out by German linguist Jochen Rehbein (1984) which found that:

> the ability of Turkish children to deal with complex texts in German was affected by their ability to understand these texts in their first language. Rehbein's investigations suggest that there is a strong developmental inter-relationship between the bilingual child's two languages and that conceptual information and discourse strategies acquired in the first language transfer to the second (1986, p. 34-35).

McLaughlin goes on to compare the principle of linguistic interdependence to the notion of "set" (proposed by psychologists in the Georgian Republic of the former Soviet Union). "Set" is a general competence that underlies both languages of a bilingual. McLaughlin describes "set" as:

> some unconscious 'feel' for language that permits its practical use in communicative settings. It is this competence in the first language that provides the basis for second-language learning (1986, p. 44).

Thus, in the former Soviet Union, the teaching of Russian to linguistic minority groups was based on strong promotion of children's first language in the early years of schooling with additive bilingualism as the goal (McLaughlin, 1986).

A study of Italian-English bilinguals in Australia and Italy (Ricciardelli, 1989, 1992) reported significant relationships between Italian and English proficiency among both the Australian and Italian samples. In the Italian data, for example, she reported:

> ...there is a large degree of overlap between the standard cognitive measures which were given in the two languages. ...These [findings] suggest that bilinguals' linguistic abilities are interdependent and are not separate, and therefore any instruction which bilingual children receive in either language is capable of promoting academic skills in both languages (1989, p. 137).

Medina and Escamilla (1992) compared the outcomes of a transitional bilingual program for 125 Vietnamese-speaking students with a maintenance program for 298 Latino/Latina students between kindergarten and grade 2. The data indicated that students in maintenance programs retained oral command of their L1 significantly better than those in transitional programs while performance in English was equivalent for the two programs. These data again suggest that the amount of time through the majority language is largely unrelated to achievement in that language.

Finally, Cummins, Harley, Swain and Allen (1990) reported highly significant correlations for written grammatical, discourse and sociolinguistic skills in Portuguese (L1) and English (L2) among Portuguese grade 7 students in Toronto. Cross-language correlations for oral skills were generally not significant. Significant cross-linguistic relationships for reading and writing skills were also observed among Japanese-background students in the Cummins et al. study as well as in an earlier study (Cummins, Swain, Nakajima, Handscombe, Green & Tran, 1984). This latter study also found a strong cross-lingual relationship for a variable labelled "interactional style" which reflected fluency and ease in interpersonal situations. It was suggested that personality constituted the underlying attribute that accounted for the similar interactional styles in each language just as cognition accounted for the cross-lingual interdependence of context-reduced language abilities.

8. Wayne Thomas (1992) has conducted supplementary analyses of the Ramírez data which lead him to view the report's conclusions as very conservatively worded. He suggests that:

> In fact, late-exit success across sites seems directly proportional to the degree of use of primary language instruction. Based on this author's supplementary analyses, it appears that both structured-immersion and early-exit students can be expected gradually to fall behind the norm group by amounts that fall slightly short of statistical significance over a three-year period. (p. 235)

Thomas goes on to point out that standardized test items "tend to sample more cognitively complex skills with more sophisticated usage of English with each passing grade, especially at secondary levels" (p. 238). He suggests that this may explain how second language learners "may appear to make quick progress in the early elementary years, even relative to the national norm group, but may quickly fall behind their native-speaking counterparts in the post-elementary school period as their initial acquisition of mostly low-level English skills becomes inadequate to cope with the increasing cognitive demands of the tests, as well as the requirements of more advanced courses that lead to higher education" (p. 238). Thus, initial gains made by students in English-only programs may be illusory:

> Because the structured-immersion students have sacrificed cognitive development and content in their early emphasis on learning English, their long-term ability to deal with increasingly complex material may be hampered, especially as they enter their years of post-elementary school instruction. ...The Ramírez study found that late-exit students, with both L1 and L2 support, were catching up to the norm group even as their academic work became cognitively more complex in the upper elementary grades. (p. 239)

In contrast to Thomas's assessment that the Ramírez report findings are expressed in an overly cautious manner, a review of the study by an expert panel of the National Research Council (NRC) considered many of the group comparisons to be inadequately controlled when strict experimental criteria were invoked. The review questioned whether comparability had been achieved between programs in different school districts and even in different schools within the same district. Thus, direct comparisons of growth curves across programs were rejected by the NRC panel. This, however, does not in any way invalidate the general patterns of growth that were observed within programs and the fact that the late-exit students were approaching grade expectations in English academic skills by the end of elementary school despite considerably less English-medium instruction than alternative programs. Crawford (1995) notes one additional finding highlighted by the NRC panel:

> The NRC did, however, accept as "compelling" one finding of the Ramírez report: when comparisons were made between kindergarten and 1st grade classrooms in the same school, early-exit bilingual students scored significantly higher in English reading than the immersion students. More generally, the panel found no evidence that native-language instruction impedes the acquisition of English. To the contrary, it noted the "convergence" of evidence in the Ramírez report and other research that "suggests, under certain conditions, the importance of primary-language instruction in second-language achievement in language arts and mathematics." (1995, p. 152)

9. It is worth noting that attrition and socio-economic status were controlled in these analyses. Students who left the study by the end of third grade had somewhat higher (marginally significant) levels of English achievement and those who left by the end of the fifth grade had somewhat higher levels of Spanish achievement. Thus, the impressive progress revealed by the analyses is not caused by weaker students leaving the program. If anything, the opposite is the case.

10. Verhoeven (1994) suggests that his data only partially support the interdependence hypothesis. Strong support is evident for interdependence on tasks that require metalinguistic skills or that assess literacy development. However, he suggests that the much more limited degree of transfer on lexical and morphosyntactic tasks is inconsistent with the theory, as is the transfer that was evident in pragmatic aspects of language proficiency. The pragmatic index was derived from the number of different content words and the mean length of utterance in children's spontaneous speech.

The small relationship across languages for oral syntactic functioning is not surprising to me. Consistent findings were reported by Harley, Allen, Cummins, and Swain (1990) in studies involving French immersion and Portuguese-speaking students in Toronto. Syntactic functioning in conversational contexts represents very specific linguistic knowledge that appears largely independent of the common underlying proficiency which is more conceptual and cognitive in nature. By contrast, the limited cross-lingual relationship Verhoeven observed for lexical knowledge is more surprising and at variance with the results of a number of other studies reviewed above (see Note 7).

The strong cross-lingual relationship Verhoeven observed for pragmatic language proficiency is not in any way at variance with the interdependence hypothesis. In fact, as noted above (Note 7), a similar finding was reported by Cummins et al. (1984) who hypothesized that personality traits could account for the similar pragmatic or interactional style behavior in both languages. It is true that my major interest has been in accounting for cross-lingual relationships as they affect academic achievement and thus I have not emphasized cross-lingual relationships involving conversational or pragmatic aspects of proficiency. At more advanced stages of L2 development many aspects of conversational/pragmatic skills will reach plateaus and not show significant cross-lingual relationships because there will be very little variance (e.g. phonology and fluency in everyday conversation). One could certainly devise tests that would show variance even at advanced levels of L2 but these would likely be tapping metalinguistic abilities as much as, or more than, basic conversational skills. Because of this plateau effect after a few years of L2 conversational development (at least among school-age children), cross-lingual relationships in conversational skills did not seem to me particularly relevant to pursue. However, a finding of L1-L2 interdependence in conversational/pragmatic skills in the early stages of acquiring L2 is not in any sense at variance with the interdependence hypothesis (see Cummins, 1981a).

Verhoeven also suggests that the interdependence hypothesis largely neglects the role of social factors in explaining differential literacy success. This is simply inaccurate. I have always posited the interdependence of L1 and L2 as an intervening factor strongly influenced by broader societal factors (Cummins, 1981a, 1986, 1989) and the present volume continues the elaboration of these relationships between social (macro-interactional) and cognitive/linguistic factors.

11. Some cautions with respect to the interdependence principle are in order. First, while considerable evidence has accumulated for transfer of literacy skills from one language to another, instruction oriented to promoting this form of transfer may not always be appropriate in bilingual education contexts. This, at least, is the persuasive argument made by Harris (1990) in his analysis of Aboriginal schooling in Australia. He suggests that the gap in

world views between Aboriginal and western cultures is so great that bilingual education programs should clearly separate western and Aboriginal cultural domains, with English used exclusively for the former and Aboriginal languages for the latter. Using the Aboriginal language as a means of teaching the concepts of western schooling risks undermining the Aboriginal culture and contributing to language and cultural shift. This analysis has implications for indigenous groups around the world who are concerned that bilingualism is but a step towards monolingualism in the majority societal language.

A second caution concerns the application of the interdependence principle to ASL-English bilingual bicultural programs for deaf students. While I believe there is persuasive evidence that the conceptual foundation established in ASL will facilitate the acquisition of English literacy (see Cummins and Danesi [1990]), others (Mayer & Wells, in press) have raised doubts about the possibility of *linguistic* transfer in view of the major difference in modality and structure between ASL and English. This theoretical issue has important practical implications; specifically, it relates to the issue of whether students can move from the conceptual base of ASL directly to the acquisition of written English or whether the teaching of some form of sign English is necessary as an intervening step, as argued by Mayer and Wells. Hopefully, empirical evidence will throw light on this issue as bilingual-bicultural programs for deaf students continue to expand (see Israelite, Ewoldt, & Hoffmeister [1992], Johnson, Liddell & Erting [1989], and Mason [1994] for analyses of issues related to ASL-English bilingual bicultural education).

12. The Thomas/Collier study was summarized prior to publication in a November 1995 article in TIME magazine:

> Though some states end bilingual education after three years, the study found that children who had received six years of bilingual education in well-designed programs performed better than 70% of all 11th graders, including native speakers, on standardized English tests. One of the report's authors, professor Virginia Collier, says children placed in an English-language environment before they are fluent "are just left out of the discussion in their mainstream classes. It shows up in the long term, when the academic going gets tough."
>
> The George Mason study also found that the highest achievers are products of the avant-garde experiment in so-called two-way schools, where half the curriculum is taught in English, half in a foreign language. An example is the Oyster Bilingual Elementary School in the District of Columbia, whose students are 58% Hispanic, 26% white, 12% black, and 4% Asian. After six years of Spanish-English curriculum, the school's sixth-graders score at ninth-grade level in reading and 10th-grade level in math. (Hornblower, 1995, p. 45)

13. Related to the misconception that the teaching of English literacy skills should be delayed for several years is an inappropriate linking of the threshold and interdependence hypotheses. For example, it is not uncommon to see these hypotheses interpreted as implying that

"English reading should be delayed until students have attained a threshold level of proficiency in their L1." I can understand how it may be tempting to connect the two hypotheses in this way but I have never advocated this type of linkage. The threshold and interdependence hypotheses developed independently and were proposed to account for two very different sets of data: the threshold hypothesis attempted to account for the effects of bilingualism on children's cognitive development, while the interdependence hypothesis focused on the relationship between L1 and L2 academic proficiencies, accounting for data in the areas of bilingual education, immigrant language learning, age and L2 learning, and correlational and experimental studies of L1/L2 relationships. The fact that L1 academic proficiency is a strong predictor of L2 proficiency suggests that, optimally, schools should strongly promote L1 literacy but it does not specify when L1 or L2 literacy should be introduced nor in what instructional proportions. There are many viable options for bilingual programs in this regard.

Chapter 6
The Deep Structure of Educational Reform

S ince the mid-1960s, educators in the United States have implemented a series of educational reforms aimed at reversing the pattern of school failure among culturally diverse students. These have included Head Start programs at the preschool level, myriad forms of bilingual education programs, the hiring of additional teaching assistants and remedial personnel, and the institution of safeguards against discriminatory assessment procedures.

These reforms have probably had some impact but the achievement gap between students from dominant and subordinated groups remains extremely large. For example, the National Center for Educational Statistics (1994) reports that although the dropout rate among 16- to 24-year-olds has fallen over the past 20 years, it remains relatively high for Hispanics "at 28 percent, compared to 8 percent for whites and 14 percent for blacks" (p. 36). The gap in reading scores also remains large. White 17-year-olds scored 292.8 in 1980 and 297.4 in 1992, compared to 243.1 and 260.6 for blacks and 261.4 and 271.2 for Hispanics (1994, p. 41).

Why has the rhetoric of "equality of educational opportunity" failed to translate into equity of educational outcomes? There are obvious reasons related to the rapid increase in poverty in American inner cities and rural areas and the huge disparities in educational spending between affluent and impoverished districts. For example, in many states high-expenditure districts spend almost three times as much per pupil as low-expenditure districts (Taylor & Piché, 1991). These disparities in the distribution of resources reflect the power structure of the society. Despite the rhetoric of equity, coercive relations of power are still evident in the distribution of resources and differential access to quality education among social groups. As Andrew Hacker (1995) concludes in his book *Two Nations: Black and White, Separate, Hostile, Unequal,* "legal slavery may be in the past, but segregation and subordination have been allowed to persist" (p. 229).

Since schools reflect the societies that support them, it is hardly surprising that issues related to equity are hotly contested in schools. Inter-group power relations in the broader society are reflected in the organization of schooling (curriculum, language of instruction, assessment practices, tracking, degree of parental participation, etc.) and in the mindset that educators bring to the teaching of culturally diverse students. These educational structures and the role definitions that educators adopt directly affect the interactions that culturally diverse students experience in schools.

I argue in this chapter that one of the major reasons why previous reform efforts have had only limited success is that the relationships between teachers and students and between schools and communities have remained largely unchanged. Interventions have often effected only superficial change, leaving the deep structure of relationships between educators and culturally diverse students largely untouched. Many individual educators have attempted to challenge inequities in schools, but in a large number of school contexts, this kind of advocacy for culturally diverse students has not been encouraged. The result has been that the power relations operating in both school and wider society have usually been accepted unconsciously rather than challenged. These power relations are still very much in evidence in schools, as Jonathon Kozol's (1991) book *Savage Inequalities* makes painfully clear. [1]

A central assumption of the present analysis is that implementation of genuine educational reform aimed at reversing centuries of discrimination requires *personal redefinitions* of the ways in which *individual educators* interact with the students and communities they serve. In other words, legislative and policy reforms aimed at changing educational structures may be necessary conditions for effective change, but they are not sufficient. Implementation of change is dependent on the extent to which educators, both collectively and individually, redefine their roles with respect to culturally diverse students and communities. This is the deep structure of educational reform. I suggest that reversal of the pattern of school failure requires that educator-student interactions be oriented towards *empowerment*, defined as the collaborative creation of power. Creating contexts of empowerment in the classroom entails a direct challenge to the coercive relations of power operating in the wider society that are at the root of culturally diverse students' school failure.

The empowerment framework described in this chapter (Figure 6.1) elaborates on the framework sketched in Chapter 1. The framework proposes that the causes of underachievement are rooted in the continuation of historical patterns of coercive relations of power between dominant and subordinated groups. These relations of power are reflected in the culture of the school. The culture of the school refers to the structural organization of the school and to the collective role definitions that educators adopt in relation to culturally diverse students and communities. Educational structures and educator role definitions together determine the interactions that students experience in the school system. Culturally diverse students will succeed educationally to the extent that the patterns of interaction in school challenge and reverse those that prevail in the society at large.

The ways in which identities are negotiated between educators and students in these micro-interactions can be analyzed in relation to four overlapping dimensions of schooling: (a) incorporation of bilingual students' language and culture; (b) community participation; (c) orientation to pedagogy; and (d) assessment practices. The extent to which culturally diverse students and communities either accept or resist the culture of the school and the societal power structure will also directly affect the ways in which identities are negotiated in the school context.

Central to the framework is the claim that the process of identity negotiation and the challenge to coercive relations of power are at least as important for students' academic development as any particular program or instructional technique. Instructional techniques become effective only to the extent that they contribute to the collaborative creation of power.

Macro-Interactions and the Culture of the School

When patterns of school success and failure among culturally diverse students are examined within an international perspective, it becomes evident that power and status relations between dominant and subordinated groups exert a major influence. As noted in Chapter 2, several theorists (e.g. Blauner, 1969; Ogbu, 1978, 1992) have pointed to the fact that subordinated groups that fail academically have generally been discriminated against over many generations. They react to this discrimination along a continuum ranging from internalization of a sense of ambivalence or insecurity about their identities to rejection

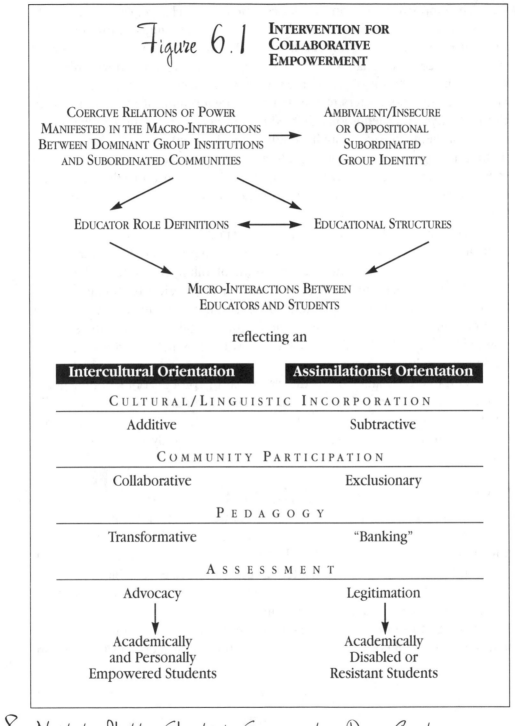

Figure 6.1   **INTERVENTION FOR COLLABORATIVE EMPOWERMENT**

COERCIVE RELATIONS OF POWER
MANIFESTED IN THE MACRO-INTERACTIONS
BETWEEN DOMINANT GROUP INSTITUTIONS
AND SUBORDINATED COMMUNITIES

AMBIVALENT/INSECURE
OR OPPOSITIONAL
SUBORDINATED
GROUP IDENTITY

EDUCATOR ROLE DEFINITIONS ←→ EDUCATIONAL STRUCTURES

MICRO-INTERACTIONS BETWEEN
EDUCATORS AND STUDENTS

reflecting an

Intercultural Orientation	**Assimilationist Orientation**
CULTURAL/LINGUISTIC INCORPORATION	
Additive	Subtractive
COMMUNITY PARTICIPATION	
Collaborative	Exclusionary
PEDAGOGY	
Transformative	"Banking"
ASSESSMENT	
Advocacy	Legitimation
Academically and Personally Empowered Students	Academically Disabled or Resistant Students

of, and active resistance to, dominant group values. At both extremes, the result has frequently been alienation from schooling and mental withdrawal from academic effort.

The educational effects of this pattern of macro-interactions are strikingly evident in many situations where formerly subjugated or colonized groups are still in a subordinated relationship to the dominant group. Examples abound from around the world. For example, most indigenous groups fall into this pattern (e.g. Australian Aboriginals, Maoris in New Zealand, Inuit and First Nations in Canada, Sami in Scandinavian countries, as well as indigenous populations in the United States and Latin America). Other examples are Burakumin in Japan who perform poorly in Japanese schools as a result of their low social status but perform well after immigration to the United States because educators are unaware of their low social status in their home country. Thus, educators tend to have the same high academic expectations of them as they do for other Japanese students (Ogbu, 1992). Similar patterns exist in Scandinavia where Finnish-background students in Sweden are reported to experience severe academic difficulties, a phenomenon not unrelated to the fact that Finland was colonized by Sweden for several hundred years (Skutnabb-Kangas, 1984).

Central to understanding the framework proposed in Figure 6.1, is the fact that coercive relations of power can operate only through the micro-interactions between educators and students. Thus, educators, students and communities can challenge this coercive process. Although educational and social structures will impose constraints on resistance, these structures can never stifle the pursuit of empowering interactions on the part of educators and students. In short, educators always have options in the way they negotiate identities with students and communities.

Educational Structures. Inter-group macro-interactions give rise to particular forms of educational structures that reflect the relations of power in the broader society. For example, the historical segregation of culturally diverse students from "mainstream" educational opportunities in many countries constituted one form of structural discrimination. As documented by Kozol (1991) for African American students and by Berman et al. (1992) for recent immigrants in California, similar patterns of segregation still characterize the education of many subordinated groups. Olsen and Minicucci (1992) discuss the implications of the Berman et al. (1992) findings with respect to the degree of integration/segregation of culturally diverse students in 27 California secondary schools:

On an integration/segregation continuum, the majority of the schools in our study are moving increasingly towards the use of sheltered English classes with a resultant formal curricular separation of limited English proficient students. Despite calling the LEP program 'transitional,' and despite recurring and persistent rhetoric about preparing the students to enter the mainstream, the evidence appears to run contrary to an integration orientation. LEP students are tracked into separate classes, spend the great percentage of the school day in these LEP classes, and appear to rarely be reclassified into the mainstream. Thus, it appears that through the use of English as a language of instruction students are being channelled away from their native language and culture, and they are simultaneously also being kept separate from their English speaking peers and denied access to the track which houses mainstream English speaking students. We would conclude from our small sample that secondary school LEP programs are thus segregatory. (1992, p. 18)

Other examples of educational structures that might systematically discriminate against culturally diverse students are:

- the medical model of special education that uncritically locates the source of academic difficulties within students rather than within the pattern of interactions that students experience in school (see Cummins, 1984, Harry, 1992; Ortiz & Yates, 1983; Rueda, 1989);

- ability grouping and tracking practices that deny students in low-ability groups access to quality instruction (Oakes, 1985);

- the use of culturally- and linguistically-biased IQ tests to give culturally diverse students a one-way ticket to special education or low-track programs (see Cummins, 1984; Harry, 1992).

- teacher education institutions that until recently have treated issues related to culturally diverse students as marginal and that sent new teachers into the classroom with minimal information regarding patterns of language and emotional development among such students and few pedagogical strategies for helping students learn;

- curriculum that reflects only the experiences and values of middle-class English-speaking students and effectively suppresses the experiences and values of culturally diverse students;

- the absence from most schools of professionals capable of communicating in the languages of culturally diverse students and their parents; such professionals could assist in functions such as: primary language instruction; primary language assessment for purposes of placement and intervention, and parent/school liaison;

- criteria for promotion to positions of responsibility (e.g. principals) that take no account of the individual's experience with or potential for leadership in the education of culturally diverse students.

These educational structures constitute a frame that sets limits on the kinds of micro-interactions that are likely to occur between educators and students. As one illustration of the impact of these structures, Jeanie Oakes (1985) has shown that tracking results in major differences in the quality of instruction that students receive; those in lower tracks receive instruction that is less challenging and motivating than those in higher tracks. She concludes that when schools are structured according to tracks the academic progress of those in average and low groups is retarded. Tracking also lowers educational aspirations, fosters low self-esteem and promotes dropping-out.

Educator Role Definitions. Societal macro-interactions will also influence the ways in which educators define their roles in relation to culturally diverse students and communities; in other words, they influence the mindset of assumptions, expectations and goals that educators bring to the task of educating students. The notion of *educator role definitions* is proposed as a central explanatory construct in the present framework. The framework suggests that culturally diverse students are empowered or disabled as a direct result of their interactions with educators in the schools. These interactions are mediated by the implicit or explicit role definitions that educators assume in relation to four institutional dimensions of schools. These four dimensions namely, language/culture incorporation, community participation, pedagogy, and assessment represent sets of educational structures that will affect, but can also be influenced by, educators' role definitions.

A concrete example will illustrate the ways in which educators' role definitions can combine with educational structures to the detriment of bilingual students' academic progress. The following psychological assessment was one of more than 400 assessments of culturally diverse students carried out in a western Canadian city (Cummins, 1984). It illustrates the assumptions that school psychologists and teachers frequently make about issues such as the appropriateness of standardized tests for culturally diverse students and the consequences of bilingualism for students' development.

Maria (not child's real name) was referred for psychological assessment by her grade 1 teacher, who noted that she had difficulty in all aspects of learning. She was given both speech and hearing and psychological assessments. The former assessment found that all structures and functions pertaining to speech were within normal limits and hearing was also normal. The findings were summarized as follows: "Maria comes from an Italian home where Italian is spoken mainly. However, language skills appeared to be within normal limits for English."

The psychologist's conclusions, however, were very different. On the Wechsler Preschool and Primary Scale of Intelligence (WPPSI), Maria obtained a Verbal IQ of 89 and a Performance IQ of 99. In other words, non-verbal abilities were virtually at the average level while verbal abilities were 11 points below the mean, a surprisingly good score given the clear cultural biases of the test and the fact that the child had been learning English in a school context for little more than a year. The report to Maria's teacher read as follows:

> Maria tended to be very slow to respond to questions, particularly if she were unsure of the answers. Her spoken English was a little hard to understand, which is probably due to poor English models at home (speech is within normal limits). Italian is spoken almost exclusively at home and this will be further complicated by the coming arrival of an aunt and grandmother from Italy.

> There is little doubt that Maria is a child of low average ability whose school progress is impeded by lack of practice in English. Encourage Maria's oral participation as much as possible, and try to involve her in extra-curricular activities where she will be with her English-speaking peers.

Despite the fact that the speech assessment revealed no deficiencies in Maria's spoken English, the psychologist has no hesitation ("There is little doubt...") in attributing Maria's academic problems to the use of Italian at home. The implicit message to the teacher (and parents) is clear: Maria's communication in L1 with parents and relatives detracts from her school performance, and the aim of the school program should be to expose Maria to as much English as possible in order to compensate for these deficient linguistic and cultural background experiences. In other words, the psychologist's assessment and recommendations reflect the assumptions of the *separate underlying proficiency* model of bilingualism (see Chapter 5).

How does this assessment (which was not atypical of the sample) represent institutionalized discrimination in action? In several ways:

- The structure of special education identification, assessment, and placement not only permits, but in many cases mandates the use of IQ tests which are characterized almost invariably by serious cultural and linguistic biases when used with culturally diverse students;

- The structure of psychologist training and certification frequently pays only lip-service to the implications of diversity for assessment and placement;

- The psychologist's role definition shows little sensitivity to the fact that the child's cultural background and linguistic talents differ significantly from those of the sample upon whom the test was normed. The psychologist is not conscious that the child's culturally-specific experiences (in L1) might have any implications for the administration or interpretation of the test. There is also no hesitation in drawing inferences about the negative effects of L1 use in the home nor in making recommendations about language use in school despite the fact that the psychologist has likely had no training whatsoever on issues related to bilingualism.

What are the probable consequences of this type of assessment? As a result of the assessment, there is an increased likelihood that Maria will be reprimanded for any use of Italian with other Italian students in school, thereby promoting feelings of shame in her own cultural background. It is also probable that the child's parents will be advised to use English rather than Italian at home. If parents adhere to this advice, then they are likely both to expose the child to poor models of English, and also reduce the quality and quantity of communication between adults and children in the home since their English is probably considerably less fluent than their Italian. The importance of adult-child home interaction for future academic achievement has been demonstrated repeatedly (e.g. Wells, 1986), and thus the advice to switch to English in the home has the potential to exert serious negative effects on children's development. Furthermore, it is likely to drive an emotional wedge between children and parents (including the recently arrived aunt and grandmother who will know no English) since parents may feel that communication of affection and warmth in Italian will reduce the child's future academic prospects. [2]

In summary, the example of Maria illustrates how students can become educationally disabled as a direct result of their interactions with well-intentioned educators. These interactions are mediated by the role definitions of educators which, in turn, are molded by a variety of influences; for example, the broader policy and legal structure within which educators operate, the institutional structure within which they have been trained, and the school and school district structures that determine priorities for action on a day-to-day basis.

Micro-Interactions as Reflections of Coercive or Collaborative Relations of Power

The framework proposes that the micro-interactions between educators and students form an interpersonal or an interactional space within which the acquisition of knowledge and formation of identity is negotiated.

In the past, schools have required that subordinated groups deny their cultural identity as a necessary condition for success in the "mainstream" society. The historical pattern of dominant-subordinated group interactions has been one where educators have constricted the interactional space in an attempt to sanitize deviant cultural identities. For educators to become partners in the transmission of knowledge, culturally diverse students were required to acquiesce in the subordination of their identities and to celebrate as "truth" the "cultural literacy" of the dominant group (e.g. the "truth" that Columbus "discovered" America). The constriction of the interactional space by educators reflected a process whereby they defined their role as "civilizing," "saving," "assimilating," or "educating" students whose culture and values they viewed as inherently deficient. Through these micro-interactions they reproduced the pattern of societal macro-interactions and limited students' possibilities to define and interpret their own realities and identities.

Adeline Becker (1990), for example, has documented how this process operated in an urban New England high school to shape the ethnic identity and academic engagement of Portuguese-background students. She interprets the 50% dropout rate among Portuguese-background students in the school as a function of the negative teacher attitudes towards Portuguese students and their culture which resulted in identity conflict and internalization of a sense of academic inferiority. Students simply lived down to their teachers' expectations regardless of which identity orientation (Anglo or Portuguese) they attempted to adopt.

It is important to note that students (and communities) do not passively accept dominant group attributions of their inferiority. Frequently, they resist this process of subordination actively through disruptive or oppositional behaviour. While for some students, resistance may contribute to academic development (Skutnabb-Kangas, 1988; Zanger, 1994), in many situations resistance has severe costs with respect to academic success and upward mobility, often culminating in students dropping out of school prematurely (Ogbu, 1992; Willis, 1977). In some situations, students may modify their cultural identity by "acting White" (Fordham, 1990) and buying educational success at the expense of rejection by their peers and ambivalence about their identity.

There is ample research evidence regarding the kinds of school structures, educator role definitions and instructional interactions that are effective in reversing the historical patterns of educational disempowerment experienced by culturally diverse students.

For example, Garcia's (1991) synthesis of research highlights the importance of support for primary language and literacy development as well as the importance of the way educators define their roles. He points out that educators in effective schools demonstrated a coherent pattern of high academic expectations for their students and perceived themselves as advocates for students. They also saw themselves as instructional innovators and had a strong commitment to school-home communication. They felt they had the autonomy to innovate and support from their principals to do so.

Stedman (1987) similarly highlights the importance of a positive orientation to cultural pluralism in schools that were effective in promoting academic achievement among low-income students. He argues that effective schools acknowledge the ethnic and racial identity of their students through having role models in high status positions and offering opportunities for students to develop their linguistic and cultural talents through programs such as bilingual education. Among the other factors stressed by Stedman are *parental participation* and *academically rich programs*. Parents are encouraged to become involved in their children's education and students are actively engaged in their own learning through cognitively challenging projects and tasks that capitalize on their prior experiences.

Finally, Lucas, Henze, and Donato's (1990) study of six successful high schools serving primarily Latino/Latina students in Arizona and California documented eight factors that appeared to distinguish these schools. These factors are as follows:

1. Value is placed on students' languages and cultures;

2. High academic expectations are communicated to bilingual students;

3. School leaders make the education of bilingual students a priority;

4. Staff development is explicitly designed to help teachers and other school staff to serve bilingual students more effectively;

5. A variety of advanced and basic courses and programs for bilingual students is offered;

6. School counselors are committed to and capable of providing appropriate guidance to bilingual students as a result of speaking students' language and coming from similar cultural backgrounds;

7. Parents of bilingual students are encouraged to become involved in their children's education;

8. School staff members share a strong commitment to create contexts both inside the school and in the community wherein a sense of empowerment can be generated among bilingual students.

The picture that emerges from these studies of school effectiveness for culturally diverse students has three specific and one general component that contribute to student academic success. The three specific components are:

• Affirmation of students' cultural identity and encouragement of L1 literacy and language development;

• Encouragement of active parental participation; and

• Cognitively-challenging instruction that provides opportunities for students to draw on their background experiences while working collaboratively to explore issues and topics that are relevant to their lives.

These specific interventions are implemented in a school context where issues related to the education of culturally diverse students have moved from the periphery to the center of concern for the entire school. Educators, both individually and collectively, have defined their roles in such a way that their interactions with culturally diverse students actively affirm students' identities. The educational structures established in the school reflect these role definitions.

The affective dimension of these interactions between educators and students is clear in student comments reported by Lucas and her colleagues:

> At all of the schools, students mentioned teachers who had given them special help and attention, often crediting them with providing personal counseling as well as academic support. Typical student comments included the following: 'The teachers here don't just teach; they care about you' and 'Teachers stay after school to explain what we didn't understand.' (p. 336)

For each of the four dimensions of school organization outlined in Figure 6.1, the role definitions of educators can be described in terms of a continuum with one end of the continuum promoting the empowerment of students while the other contributes to the disabling of students. In the sections that follow, the dimensions are described and examples of the discourses that have been mobilized to support both assimilationist and intercultural orientations are outlined.

Cultural/Linguistic Incorporation

As noted in Chapter 5, considerable research data suggest that for subordinated group students, the extent to which students' language and culture is incorporated into the school program constitutes a significant predictor of academic success (see for example, Beykont, 1994; Campos & Keatinge, 1988; Ramírez, 1992). Students' school success appears to reflect both the more solid cognitive/academic foundation developed through intensive L1 instruction and also the reinforcement of their cultural identity.

Educators' role definitions with respect to students' language and culture can be characterized along an "additive-subtractive" dimension. Educators who see their role as helping students to add a second language and cultural affiliation while maintaining their primary language and culture are more likely to create interactional conditions of empowerment than those who see their role as replacing or subtracting students' primary language and culture in the process of assimilating them to the dominant culture. Bilingual programs that aim explicitly to promote L1 literacy clearly communicate a strong additive orientation to students and have greater scope for creating conditions of empowerment than monolingual programs.

An additive orientation is not always dependent upon actual teaching of students' primary language. In many cases this may not be possible for a variety of reasons (e.g. low concentration of particular groups of bilingual students). However, even within a monolingual school context, powerful messages can be communicated to students regarding the validity and advantages of primary language development. For example, a teacher who decides to learn just one word per day of the various languages represented in her classroom communicates a strong message of respect for students' language and culture. Each day, one student can be invited to bring in a word that is particularly meaningful to him or her and all students in the class can learn this word and talk (in English) about its meaning and cultural connotations. In this way, students share their background experiences with other students and with the teacher and develop a greater awareness of how languages map out the world in different ways.

Along the same lines, Lucas and Katz (1994) have demonstrated that exemplary Special Alternative Instructional Programs (SAIPs), that use primarily English for instructional purposes, also make considerable use of students' primary language. The investigators studied language use patterns in nine SAIPs (operating in six states) that had been nominated as exemplary in terms of student outcomes. They found that although the programs were designed to provide instruction primarily in English, teachers made considerable use of students' L1 for instructional purposes:

> In practice, however, the classrooms were multilingual environments in which students' native languages served a multitude of purposes and functions. They gave students access to academic content, to classroom activities, and to their own knowledge and experience; gave teachers a way to show their respect and value for students' languages and cultures; acted as a medium for social interaction and establishment of rapport; fostered family involvement; and fostered students' development of, knowledge of, and pride in their native languages and cultures. (1994, p. 545)

Among the concrete ways in which teachers drew on the linguistic resources of their students were the following:

- Teachers set up activities that specifically called for students to use their L1 with each other; for example, a group writing assignment that used the L1 or, working in groups, translating stories from the L1 into English to tell to other students.

- Less fluent students were paired with more fluent students from the same L1 background so that the more fluent students could assist those who were less fluent.

- Bilingual dictionaries and L1 library books were provided to assist students comprehend instruction and to encourage development of L1 literacy skills. In addition, journal writing in L1 was encouraged in some schools.

Furthermore, when teachers or teaching assistants were fluent in students' L1, they used it for instructional purposes to clarify content and concepts originally presented in English or to teach content directly in the L1. Courses in L1 language arts were also offered in some sites and awards were given for excellence in languages that are not commonly studied (e.g. a senior award in Khmer language skill in one school).

Lucas and Katz conclude that "alternatives to bilingual education need not be English-only programs. There is no reason to assume that programs for students who speak many languages must use only English in ESL classes and content classes" (p. 557). They reinforce Elsa Auerbach's (1993) claim that the inclusion of students' L1 can reduce the degree of language and culture shock and strengthen students' self-esteem and identity. The *deep structure* of these programs is similar to that of genuine bilingual programs in that an additive orientation to students' language and culture is communicated to both students and parents. Thus, Lucas and Katz argue for going beyond the divisive debate on the merits or otherwise of bilingual education versus English-only programs; they suggest focusing instead on providing as much reinforcement for students' identity formation and academic development as the constraints of particular situations permit (e.g. availability of bilingual teachers, teaching assistants, L1 curriculum resources etc).

Lucas and Katz' conclusion is reinforced by the findings of an earlier year-long ethnographic study of an ESL classroom in which a variety of linguistic backgrounds were represented (Saville-Troike, 1984). It was found that opportunities to use the primary language were significantly related to the learning of English:

Most of the children who achieved best in content areas, as measured by tests in English, were those who had the opportunity to discuss the concepts they were learning in their native language with other children or adults. (p. 216) [3]

In summary, as documented in Chapter 5, the most powerful ways of incorporating students' language and culture into the curriculum are through two-way or developmental (late-exit) bilingual programs that aim explicitly to promote bilingualism and biliteracy. However, in situations where genuine bilingual programs are not possible, an additive orientation to students' language and culture can still be communicated to students and parents in a variety of ways. This reinforcement of students' identities is crucial for motivating students to engage with academic content. By contrast, when the implicit or explicit message given to students is that they should leave their language and culture at the schoolhouse door, many students will accurately perceive the schooling process to be coercive and may resist it actively by not learning. Pauline Gibbons (1991) has eloquently expressed a similar point:

A second language and culture is not learned by destroying the first. By ignoring the mother tongue, we run the risk of slowing down children's learning and encouraging, often unintentionally, the beginning of a one-way journey away from their families. (p. 69) [4]

Community Participation

Students from subordinated communities will be empowered in the school context to the extent that their parents are empowered through their interactions with the school. When educators and parents develop partnerships to promote their children's education, parents appear to develop a sense of efficacy that communicates itself to children with positive academic consequences (e.g. Ada, 1988a; McCaleb, 1994; Tizard, Hewison & Schofield, 1982). The positive impact of parental involvement and support, documented in the Ramírez (1992) and Beykont (1994) studies, illustrates the importance of pursuing these partnerships.

The teacher role definitions associated with community participation can be characterized along a *collaborative-exclusionary* dimension. Teachers operating at the collaborative end of the continuum actively encourage parents to participate in promoting their children's academic progress both in the home and through involvement in classroom activities. A collaborative orientation may require a willingness on the part of the teacher to work closely with classroom assistants or community volunteers in order to communicate effectively and in a non-condescending way with parents. Teachers with an exclusionary orientation, on the other hand, tend to regard teaching as *their* job and are likely to view collaboration with culturally diverse parents as either irrelevant or actually detrimental to children's progress.

Clearly, initiatives for collaboration or for a shared decision-making process can come from the community as well as from the school. Under these conditions, maintenance of an exclusionary orientation by the school can lead communities to challenge the institutional power structure. This was the case with the school strike organized by Finnish parents and their children at Bredby school in Rinkeby, Sweden. In response to a plan by the headmistress to reduce the amount of Finnish instruction, the Finnish community withdrew their children from the school. Eventually (after eight weeks) most of their demands were met. According to Skutnabb-Kangas (1988), the strike had the effect of generating a new sense of efficacy among the community and making them more aware of the role of an exclusionary orientation in the educational system in reproducing the powerless status of subordinated groups. A hypothesis that the present framework generates is that this renewed sense of efficacy will lead to higher levels of academic achievement among culturally diverse students in this type of situation.

Even simple initiatives that permit parents to participate actively in aspects of their children's education can have profound effects. For example, a two-year project carried out in six schools in an inner-city area of London, England, showed major improvements in children's reading skills simply as a result of sending books home on a daily basis with the children for them to read to their parents, many of whom spoke little English and were illiterate in both English and their L1 (predominantly Bengali and Greek) (Tizard, Schofield, & Hewison, 1982). The children attending the two schools that implemented the "shared literacy" program made significantly greater progress in reading than a comparison group in two different schools who received additional small-group reading instruction from a highly competent reading specialist. Of particular importance is the fact that the differences in favor of the shared literacy program were most apparent among children who were initially having difficulty in learning to read. Both groups made greater progress than a control group in two schools who received no special treatment. Teachers involved in the home collaboration reported that children showed an increased interest in school learning and were better behaved. The impact of this project in motivating students to read can be seen from the fact that the students in the two "shared reading" schools exhausted the supply of books in the school libraries that were appropriate for early elementary grades simply because they read so much.

Several reasons can be suggested for the success of this project. First, it changed fundamentally the relationship between the schools and community. Partnerships were established that enabled parents to play an important role in helping their children succeed academically. Second, the project motivated students to read more and the more students read, the stronger their reading skills become (Krashen, 1993; Fielding & Pearson, 1994). Third, it is likely that many students would have translated or paraphrased the story for their parent in their L1 since the parent would have had limited knowledge of English. This constitutes a cognitively demanding activity that may have increased students' overall ability to analyze the semantic and syntactic aspects of text.

Whatever the underlying reasons for the dramatic impact of this program, it surely points to the role of parents as largely untapped resources in accelerating students' academic skills development. Clearly, books can be sent home in students' L1 as an alternative to or in addition to books in English. The crucial aspect of this type of family literacy project is that students become motivated to read for pleasure outside of school because only in books will they find the academic language they need to succeed in school. [5]

In summary, when educators define their roles in terms of collaboration with culturally diverse parents and communities, they are challenging the all-too-prevalent coercive discourse that attributes students' academic difficulties to apathetic and uninvolved parents (e.g. Dunn, 1987). By refuting the myth of parental apathy, they expose the exclusionary structures that have prevented culturally diverse parents from productive involvement in their children's education.

Pedagogy

Three major orientations can be distinguished with respect to pedagogy. These differ in the extent to which the teacher retains exclusive control over classroom interaction as opposed to sharing some of this control with students. The dominant traditional instructional model in most western industrial societies has been termed a "banking" model (Freire, 1983; Freire & Macedo, 1987) on the grounds that teachers are expected to deposit information and skills in students' memory banks. This traditional model can be contrasted with progressive and transformative models of pedagogy. Progressive pedagogy historically is associated with the work of John Dewey (1963) who emphasized the centrality of student experience. Its most prominent current embodiment is in whole language approaches to language and literacy.

Traditional and progressive orientations have vied for ascendancy at regular intervals throughout this century. The focus on the transformative potential of education is a more recent phenomenon and is strongly influenced by Paulo Freire's work. In considering the implications of these orientations to pedagogy for culturally diverse students, I am summarizing a much more detailed discussion contained in Chapter 5 of the book *Brave New Schools: Challenging Cultural Illiteracy through Global Learning Networks* (Cummins & Sayers, 1995).

Each of the three orientations incorporates a set of instructional and social assumptions. Instructional assumptions are concerned with the conceptions of language, knowledge, and learning that underlie various forms of teaching while social assumptions focus on the ways in which relations of culture and power are addressed in the curriculum.

Most proponents of traditional and progressive pedagogies tend to focus more on instructional than on social dimensions. They tend to see their instructional recommendations as socially-neutral and non-ideological. By contrast, advocates of transformative pedagogy argue that all forms of instruction entail social assumptions, whether acknowledged explicitly or not. The forms of thinking and literacy that are encouraged in school anticipate the forms of civic participation that students are being prepared to undertake upon graduation. Transformative pedagogy explicitly aims to prepare students to participate fully in the democratic process and to uphold principles of human rights and social justice that are enshrined in the constitutions of most western industrialized countries (see Frederickson, 1994).

The instructional and social assumptions of traditional (banking), progressive, and transformative pedagogy are outlined in Figure 6.2.

Traditional Pedagogy. The basic premise of the traditional model is that the teacher's task is to impart knowledge or skills to students. This implies that the teacher initiates and controls the interaction, constantly orienting it towards the achievement of instructional objectives. The instructional content in this type of program derives primarily from the internal structure of the language or subject matter; consequently, it frequently involves a predominant focus on surface features of language or literacy and emphasizes correct recall of content taught. Content is transmitted by means of highly structured drills and workbook exercises, although in many cases the drills are disguised in order to make them more attractive and motivating to students.

Within this instructional orientation, language is decomposed into its component parts (e.g. phonics, vocabulary, grammatical rules) which are then transmitted in isolation from each other; learning is assumed to progress in a hierarchical manner starting with simple elements and progressing to more

Figure 6.2 **INSTRUCTION AND SOCIAL ASSUMPTIONS UNDERLYING TRADITIONAL, PROGRESSIVE AND TRANSFORMATIVE PEDAGOGY**

Traditional	Progressive	Transformative
Instructional Assumptions		
LANGUAGE		
Decomposed	Whole	Whole
KNOWLEDGE		
Static/Inert	Catalytic	Catalytic
LEARNING		
Hierarchical internalization from simple to complex	Joint interactive construction through critical inquiry	Joint interactive construction through critical inquiry
Social Assumptions		
CURRICULUM		
Transmission of "cultural literacy;" explicitly sanitized with respect to power relations	Celebrates differences but implicitly sanitized with respect to power relations	Focused on critical examination of student experience and social realities; explicit attention to power relations
STUDENT OUTCOMES		
Compliant/Uncritical	Liberal but Uncritical	Empowered/Critical

complex forms. Thus, explicit phonics instruction is a prerequisite for reading development; grammar, vocabulary, and spelling must be taught before students can start writing; and knowledge is viewed as static or inert, to be internalized and reproduced by students when required.

The social assumptions of traditional pedagogy are straightforward. Curriculum should present the "cultural literacy" of the society — in Hirsch's terms "what every American needs to know." However, by virtue of what it omits, this type of curriculum also operates to restrict access to alternative perspectives on historical and contemporary events (Macedo, 1993, 1994; Peterson, 1994). The curriculum is sanitized with respect to issues of historical and current power relations, and students are expected to emerge from schooling as "good citizens" who will comply with the expectations of the societal power structure.

With respect to the education of culturally diverse students, the major problems with this form of "banking" education are:

• It reinforces the cultural ambivalence of subordinated group students by providing no opportunity for students to express and share their experience with peers and teachers; in other words, students are silenced or rendered "voiceless" in the classroom (Giroux, 1991; Walsh, 1991). Their prior knowledge is untapped and there are few if any opportunities to reflect critically on social issues of direct relevance to their lives.

• It contravenes central principles of language and literacy acquisition in that it is impossible to learn language or develop literacy in the absence of ample opportunities for meaningful communicative interaction in both oral and written modes.

Cummins and Sayers (1995) summarize the limitations of traditional pedagogy as follows.

> In summary, traditional pedagogy aims to indoctrinate, both in its instructional and social goals. Facts are to be memorized, religious or cultural truths internalized, inquiry circumscribed, and contradictions obscured. The goal may appear laudable — to build a strong culture — but a culture whose identity is based on ignorance of all around it is living in a fool's paradise. (p. 150)

Progressive Pedagogy. Whereas traditional approaches decompose language — break it up into its component parts for easier transmission — progressive approaches insist that language can be learned only when it is kept "whole" and used for meaningful communication either in oral or written modes. Knowledge within traditional curriculum is viewed as fixed and inert whereas in progressive pedagogy it is seen as catalytic in the sense that new information acts as a catalyst for further inquiry. Learning in traditional pedagogy is largely memorization whereas in progressive pedagogy learning is constructed collaboratively through interaction with peers and teachers.

Within a progressive pedagogical approach, the teacher's encouragement for students to use both written and oral language actively allows students' experience to be expressed and shared within the classroom context. This expression and sharing of experience has the effect of validating students' identity. By contrast, "banking" approaches usually employ textbooks that reflect only the values and priorities of the dominant group, thereby effectively suppressing the experience of culturally diverse students.

Progressive approaches highlight the role of collaborative inquiry and the construction of meaning as central to students' academic growth. The classroom is seen as a community of learning where knowledge is generated by teachers and students together. The application of these instructional principles for second language learners is elaborated in Chapter 4. [6]

There is considerable research evidence supporting the general principles underlying a whole language, inquiry-based progressivist pedagogy (see Cummins & Sayers, 1995 for a review). Such an approach is not in any sense incompatible with a strong focus on providing explicit feedback to students on formal aspects of language. It can also accommodate the explicit teaching of learning strategies to help students become efficient and independent learners. [7]

While the instructional assumptions underlying progressive pedagogics are generally appropriate and supported by research, the social assumptions underlying progressive pedagogy are seldom articulated. With some exceptions, contemporary whole-language theorists have tended to focus on instructional rather than social realities. Their focus is on the child, either as an individual or within the classroom learning community. An unfortunate consequence of this, as Maria de la Luz Reyes (1992) has pointed out, is that without explicit attention to the social realities of diversity, many whole-language classrooms will be just as monocultural and blind to students' cultural realities as are more traditional classrooms. Similarly, issues of power and status are rarely the focus of instruction within whole-language classrooms. Any focus on multiculturalism is frequently limited to "celebrating diversity" — promotion of tolerance and acceptance that is aimed at increasing students' self-esteem but does little to challenge inequities of power and status distribution in the society.

In short, progressivist pedagogy usually focuses narrowly on the teaching-learning relationship and fails to articulate a coherent vision of the broader social implications of instruction. Tolerance and acceptance of cultural difference are often implied but critical reflection on students' own experience, and critique of social realities are not.

Transformative Pedagogy. The instructional assumptions of transformative pedagogy are similar to those of progressive pedagogy. However, they diverge with respect to social assumptions. Transformative pedagogy uses collaborative critical inquiry to enable students to relate curriculum content to their individual and collective experience and to analyze broader social issues relevant to their lives. It also encourages students to discuss ways in which social realities might be transformed through various forms of democratic participation and social action.

Thus, transformative pedagogy will aim to go beyond the sanitized curriculum that is still the norm in many schools. It will attempt to promote students' ability to analyze and understand the social realities of their own lives and of their communities. It will strive to develop a critical literacy which Ira Shor (1992) has defined as follows:

> Habits of thought, reading, writing, and speaking which go beneath surface meaning, first impressions, dominant myths, official pronouncements, traditional clichés, received wisdom, and mere opinions, to understand the deep meaning, root causes, social context, ideology, and personal consequences of any action, event, object, process, organization, experience, text, subject matter, policy, mass media, or discourse. (p. 129)

In short, critical literacy reflects the analytic abilities involved in cutting through the surface veneer of persuasive arguments to the realities underneath and analyzing the methods and purposes of particular forms of persuasion. Clearly, the ability to think critically in these ways is crucial for meaningful participation in a democratic society. If consent can be manufactured effortlessly through media persuasion, then democracy merges into totalitarianism.

A transformative orientation to pedagogy inevitably means that educators must be willing to explore the ways in which dominant groups both historically and currently have maintained their power. In order to challenge the operation of coercive relations of power in their own lives, students and communities must understand how it works. [8] The ways in which a transformative pedagogy might operate in the classroom context can be illustrated by Alma Flor Ada's (1988a, 1988b) adaptation of Paulo Freire's pedagogical approach.

Ada's Critical Literacy Framework. Ada distinguishes four phases in what she terms "the creative reading act." [9] Each of the phases distinguished by Ada is characterized by an interactional process (either between the teacher and students or among students working in groups) that progressively opens up possibilities for the articulation and amplification of students' critical thinking. The texts that are the focus of the interaction can derive from any curricular area or from newspapers or current events. The process is equally applicable to students at any grade level. Ada (1988b, p. 103) stresses that although the phases are discussed separately, "in a creative reading act they may happen concurrently and be interwoven."

- *Descriptive Phase.* In this phase the focus of interaction is on the information contained in the text. Typical questions at this level might be: Where, when, how, did it happen? Who did it? Why? These are the type of questions for which answers can be found in the text itself. Ada points out that these are the usual reading comprehension questions and that "a discussion that stays at this level suggests that reading is a passive, receptive, and in a sense, domesticating process" (1988b, p. 104). Students' comprehension of the text is quite limited in that they have processed or acted on the text only to the extent that they are capable of reproducing the basic information it contains. Minimal cognitive action is involved. If the process is arrested at this phase, the knowledge will remain inert rather than becoming a catalyst for further inquiry. Instruction remains at a safe distance from any challenge to the societal power structure.

- *Personal Interpretive Phase.* After the basic information in the text has been discussed, students are encouraged to relate it to their own experiences and feelings. Questions that might be asked by the teacher at this phase are: Have you ever seen (felt, experienced) something like this? Have you ever wanted something similar? How did what you read make you feel? Did you like it? Did it make you happy? Frighten you? What about your family? Ada

(1988b) points out that this process helps develop children's self-esteem by showing that their experiences and feelings are valued by the teacher and classmates. It also helps children understand that "true learning occurs only when the information received is analyzed in the light of one's own experiences and emotions" (p. 104). An atmosphere of acceptance and trust in the classroom is a prerequisite for students (and teachers) to risk sharing their feelings, emotions, and experiences. It is clear how this process of sharing and critically reflecting on their own and other students' experiences opens up identity options for culturally diverse students. These identity options are typically suppressed within a transmission approach to pedagogy where the interpretation of texts is non-negotiable and reflective of the dominant group's notions of cultural literacy. The personal interpretive phase deepens students' comprehension of the text or issues by grounding the knowledge in the personal and collective narratives that make up students' histories. It is also developing a genuine cultural literacy in that it is integrating students' own experience with "mainstream" curricular content.

- *Critical Analysis Phase.* After children have compared and contrasted what is presented in the text with their personal experiences, they are ready to engage in a more abstract process of critically analyzing the issues or problems that are raised in the text. This process involves drawing inferences and exploring what generalizations can be made. Appropriate questions might be: Is this perspective valid? Always? When? Do these actions benefit everyone alike? Are there any alternatives to this situation? Would people of different cultures (classes, genders) have acted differently? How? Why? Ada emphasizes that school children of all ages can engage in this type of critical process, although the analysis will always reflect children's experiences and level of maturity. This phase further extends students' comprehension of the text or issues by encouraging them to examine both the internal logical coherence of the information or propositions and their consistency with other knowledge or perspectives. When students pursue guided research and critical reflection, they are clearly engaged in a process of knowledge generation; however, they are equally engaged in a process of self-definition; as they gain the power to think through issues that affect their lives, they simultaneously gain the power to resist external definitions of who they are and to deconstruct the sociopolitical purposes of such external definitions.

- **Creative Action Phase.** This is a stage of translating the results of the previous phases into concrete action. The dialogue is oriented towards discovering what changes individuals can make to improve their lives or resolve the problem that has been presented. Let us suppose that students have been researching (in the local newspaper, in periodicals such as National Geographic, the Greenpeace magazine etc.) problems relating to environmental pollution. After relating the issues to their own experience, critically analyzing causes and possible solutions, they might decide to write letters to congressional representatives, highlight the issue in their class/school newsletter in order to sensitize other students, write and circulate a petition in the neighborhood, write and perform a play that analyzes the issue, etc. Once again, this phase can be seen as extending the process of comprehension insofar as when we act to transform aspects of our social realities we gain a deeper understanding of those realities.

The representation of Ada's framework in Figure 6.3 highlights the fact that comprehension is not an all-or-nothing phenomenon; rather, it can take

Figure 6.3

COMPREHENSIBLE INPUT AND CRITICAL LITERACY

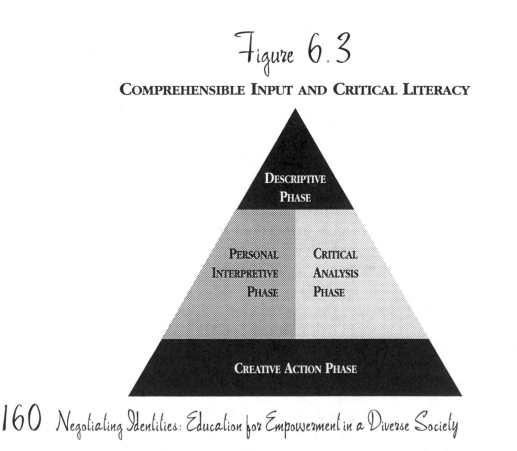

place at different levels and the process outlined by Ada represents phases in the progressive deepening of comprehension and expansion of conceptual horizons. Thus, the more we process input or information, the more potential there is for deepening our understanding of the phenomena in question. In other words, for purposes of academic language development, the notion of comprehensible input merges into the notion of critical literacy. Critical literacy is required to make literature and complex social issues comprehensible. Furthermore, the more critically literate students become, the more they generate the power to define their own identities and realities rather than being subject to the kinds of external definitions that historically have served to disempower subordinated groups.

Assessment

In the past, assessment has played a central role in legitimating the instructional disabling of culturally diverse students. Biased standardized tests have located the "problem" within the student, thereby screening from critical scrutiny the subtractive nature of the school program, the exclusionary orientation of teachers towards subordinated communities, and "banking" models of teaching that suppress students' experience and inhibit them from active participation in learning.

This process is virtually inevitable when the conceptual base for the assessment process is purely psychoeducational. If the psychologist's task (or role definition) is to discover the causes of a student's academic difficulties and the only tools at her disposal are psychological tests (in either L1 or L2), then it is hardly surprising that the child's difficulties will be attributed to psychological dysfunctions. The myth of bilingual handicaps that still influences educational policy was generated in exactly this way during the 1920's and 1930's.

A number of studies suggest that despite the appearance of change with respect to nondiscriminatory assessment, the underlying structure has remained essentially intact. Mehan, Hertweck and Meihls (1986), for example, reported that psychologists continued to test children until they "found" the disability that could be invoked to "explain" the student's apparent academic difficulties. The Cummins (1984) study, discussed earlier, also revealed that although no diagnostic conclusions were logically possible in the majority of assessments, psychologists were most reluctant to admit this fact to teachers and parents. In short, the data suggest that the structure within which psychological assessment takes place orients the psychologist to locate the cause of the academic problem within culturally diverse students themselves.

The alternative role definition that is required to reverse the traditional "legitimating" function of assessment can be termed an "advocacy" role. Educators must be prepared to become advocates for the student in critically scrutinizing the societal and educational context within which the student has developed. This implies that the conceptual basis for assessment should be broadened so that it goes beyond psychoeducational considerations to take account of the student's entire learning environment. To challenge the disabling of culturally diverse students, the assessment must focus on the extent to which children's language and culture are incorporated within the school program, the extent to which educators establish genuine partnerships with culturally diverse parents, and the extent to which students are encouraged to use language (both L1 and L2) actively within the classroom to amplify their experiences in interaction with other students and adults. In other words, the primary focus should be on remediating the educational interactions that culturally diverse students experience.

It is worth noting that assessment and pedagogy are closely linked in that classroom teachers have considerable opportunity to observe children undertaking a variety of cognitive and academic tasks when the instruction is individualized and interactional. This information can and should play an important role in assessment/placement decisions. An excellent resource for authentic assessment procedures that can contribute to both instruction and placement decisions is O'Malley and Pierce's recent book *Authentic Assessment for English Language Learners: Practical Approaches for the K-12 Classroom*.

By contrast, within a "banking" instructional model student learning activities are teacher-imposed rather than expressive of students' own experience; consequently, this form of instruction limits the extent to which students' knowledge and abilities can find expression in the classroom in a similar way that most standardized tests exclude students' culturally-specific knowledge and abilities. Under these conditions of silencing, there is much less opportunity for teachers to observe students' academic strengths and weaknesses.

In summary, an advocacy approach to assessment of culturally diverse students will involve a willingness to locate the "problem" in the societal power relations between dominant and subordinated groups, in the reflection of these power relations between school and communities, and in the suppression of students' experience and identities within classrooms oriented only towards transmission of information and skills. These conditions are a more probable cause of the threefold over-representation of Latino/Latina students in Texas in the learning disabled category than any intrinsic processing deficit unique to Latino/Latina students (Ortiz & Yates, 1983).

In most industrialized countries the training of psychologists and special educators does not prepare them for this advocacy role since advocating for bilingual students frequently will involve a challenge to the societal and educational power structure. Thus, typically, rather than challenging a socio-educational system that tends to disable bilingual students, educators accept a role definition and an educational structure that makes discriminatory assessment virtually inevitable.

Conclusion

Alternative visions of society have emerged in the debate during the past two decades in regard to the education of culturally diverse students in North America. At issue is the extent to which the educational system will take seriously notions such as *equity* and *justice* and promote academic achievement for all students regardless of race, class or income; or will the educational system continue its traditional function of reproducing the power structure such that the existing division of status, resources and income is reinforced?

In spite of considerable rhetoric endorsing equity and justice, little has changed in terms of educational outcomes. Culturally diverse students are still massively over-represented in low-achieving categories.

In order to understand why so little has changed in the big picture, a theoretical framework was proposed for analyzing culturally diverse students' academic difficulties and for predicting the effects of educational interventions. I have argued that the patterns of micro-interactions that culturally diverse students experience in the educational system are a function of the power relations operating between dominant and subordinated groups in the wider society. The power structure in the wider society strongly influences the culture of the school which is expressed in the educational structures implemented in the school and in the ways educators define their roles with respect to culturally diverse students and communities. Thus, it is not surprising that most educational reforms have remained at a surface level where they do not seriously challenge the societal power structure.

Genuine reform, at a deep structure level, requires that the culture of the school change in ways that potentially challenge coercive relations of power. Individual educators are by no means powerless; they have many opportunities within the school to challenge the operation of the societal power structure. Specifically, they can become advocates for the promotion of students' linguistic talents, actively encourage culturally diverse parents to participate in developing students' academic and cultural resources, and implement pedagogical approaches that encourage students to use oral and written language to reflect critically on and amplify their experience. When educators define their roles in terms of promoting social justice and equality of opportunity, then their interactions with culturally diverse students are more likely to embody a transformative potential that challenges coercive relations of power as they are manifested in the school context. [10]

The outcome of this process for both educators and students can be described in terms of *empowerment*. Conditions of collaborative empowerment are created when educators attempt to organize their interactions with culturally diverse students in such a way that power is generated and shared through these interactions. This involves becoming aware of, and actively working to change, educational structures that limit culturally diverse students' opportunities for educational and social advancement. Teaching for empowerment, by definition, constitutes a challenge to the societal power structure. Interventions that fail to challenge the power structure simply erect a cosmetic facade that obscures the continuing reality of disempowerment.

Genuine educational reform requires that innovations permeate and transform the entire culture of the school. If innovations arc restricted to a single classroom and affect only a small number of teachers and school staff, the culture of the school will remain largely unchanged. Neither educational structures nor collective role definitions will be affected. By contrast, when most educators in the school "buy into" and take ownership of the approach or innovation, it becomes part of the school's mission. The culture of the school becomes infused with this mission; structures and collective role definitions change to accomplish a set of explicitly articulated goals related to culturally diverse students and communities (Hopkins, 1987; OECD/CERI, 1991; Olsen et al., 1994).

In the next chapter, portraits of schools and educators that have created conditions of collaborative empowerment are sketched. Not only have most of these schools moved towards the intercultural end of the continua of Figure 6.1, they have done so in such a way that their innovations become part of the collective identity of the entire school. As a result, the interactional spaces in these schools, where minds and identities meet, generate power for both educators and students. [11]

Endnotes to Chapter 6

1. Currently 26% of children under 6 years of age are living in poverty in the United States. In total, 14.5 million U.S. children are living in poverty. Cross-national comparisons from 1991 show that 20.4 percent of U.S. children live in poverty compared to 9.3 percent in Canada, 9 percent in Australia, 8.4 percent in the United Kingdom, 4.6 percent in France, 3.8 percent in the Netherlands, 2.8 percent in West Germany and 1.6 percent in Sweden (Bracey, 1995).

   Most of these children living in poverty will attend schools that are funded to a much lower level than schools attended by affluent children. In critiquing former President Bush's *America 2000* educational reform program (reinvented by President Clinton as *Goals 2000*), Harold Howe II (1991) points out that the proposed reforms fail to acknowledge the impact of poverty on "school failure, job failure, emotional imbalance, and social rejection." His criticism applies equally to the Clinton Administration's *Goals 2000* document:

   > There is not even a whisper in the document to suggest that the troubles of children and youth are closely related to the rapid growth of poverty in our society over the last two decades. The number of children who experience poverty in the U.S. ...is headed for one child in four in 2000. That means that, before the close of this century, fully one-fourth of all children in this country will be beleaguered by some combination of inadequate housing, lack of family support, poor health care, and inattention to personal and social development — a level of social trauma that is not approached by any other major industrialized nation in the world. ...The unstated expectation of America 2000 is that this growing army of poverty-stricken children and young people will take the new tests, meet the new standards, benefit from the new model schools, and use the leverage of choice to find schools that will best serve their interests and needs. That expectation is a pipe dream. (1991, p. 201)

2. Rodriguez (1982) provides an autobiographical account of the emotional schism brought about by teachers' advice to parents to switch from Spanish to English in the home:

   > One Saturday morning three nuns arrived at the house to talk to our parents...I overheard one voice gently wondering, 'Do your children speak only Spanish at home, Mrs. Rodriguez?' ...With great tact the visitors continued, 'Is it possible for you and your husband to encourage your children to practice their English when they are at home?' Of course, my parents complied. What would they not do for their children's well-being? And how could they have questioned the Church's authority which those women represented? In an instant, they agreed to give up the language (the sounds)

that had revealed and accentuated our family's closeness. The moment after the visitors left, the change was observed. '*Ahora,* speak to us *en inglés*', my father and mother united to tell us. (p. 20-21)

Rodriguez goes on to describe the effect of this language switch for the family's interaction at home:

The family's quiet was partly due to the fact that, as we children learned more and more English, we shared fewer and fewer words with our parents. Sentences needed to be spoken slowly when a child addressed his mother or father. (Often the parent wouldn't understand.) The child would need to repeat himself. (Still the parent misunderstood.) The young voice, frustrated, would end up saying, 'Never mind' — the subject was closed. Dinners would be noisy with the clinking of knives and forks against dishes. (p. 23)

Rodriguez (1982) argues that this schism between children's lives in home and school, their private and public selves, is necessary and that bilingual programs are potentially detrimental to bilingual children because they create the illusion that it is possible for children to become integrated into American society without fully giving up their cultural identity. An examination of the research data on bilingual education from virtually any country in the world shows that this argument is totally without foundation. It exemplifies the arrogance of many of those opposed to bilingual education (e.g. Rosalie Pedalino Porter, Arthur Schlesinger Jr. among many others) who seem to believe that their subjective opinions outweigh vast quantities of opposing empirical evidence.

3. Other countries have similarly sought ways of incorporating students' L1 into what are essentially English language programs. For example, the New Zealand Department of Education (1988) has suggested a variety of strategies such as:

• Provide signs in the main office and elsewhere that welcome people in the different languages of the community;

• Encourage students to use their L1 around the school and to write contributions in their L1 for school newspapers and magazines;

• Provide opportunities for students from the same ethnic group to communicate with one another in their L1 where possible (e.g. in cooperative learning groups on at least some occasions);

• Provide books written in community languages in both classrooms and the school library;

• Provide opportunities for students to study their L1 in elective subjects and/or in extra-curricular clubs;

• Encourage parents to help in the classroom, library, playground, and in clubs;

- Invite second language learners to use their L1 during assemblies, prize givings, and other official functions;

- Invite people from culturally diverse communities to act as resource people and to speak to students in both formal and informal settings.

In the Australian context, Pauline Gibbons (1991, pp. 67-69) has suggested additional ways in which students' primary language and cultural identity can be reinforced in the classroom. Some of her ideas are paraphrased below:

- Build mother tongue stories into the program, using tapes at listening posts or making available books in the mother tongue. Older children or parents may help produce tapes.

- Display the children's mother tongues in the classroom. Label objects around the classroom and display the children's writing.

- Build up a stock of bilingual books based on the children's own writing. Children who are literate in their mother tongue, or parents, may help with translation. If the English and the mother tongue are on facing pages, all children will have access to the text.

- Invite children to teach you and the class a little of their language, such as a song, a greeting, colors or how to count. Each morning for a week say 'good morning' to the class in one of the class languages, and encourage all children to reply.

4. David and Yvonne Freeman (1994) provide several concrete examples of an intercultural orientation in practice in their book *Between Worlds: Access to Second Language Acquisition*. These include student explorations of their own communities and family histories as well as in-depth study of the history of particular cultural groups. For example, in one sixth-grade class, students examined the significant contributions made by Mexican Americans in a variety of spheres of endeavor. The impact on both Anglo and Mexican American students is described as follows:

> When Anglo students in Rusty's class read about the rights promised Mexicans living in the United States by the Treaty of Guadalupe Hidalgo, the treaty written when the war between Mexico and the United States ended in 1848, they also feel the indignation of their Hispanic classmates over the broken promises. Students study the changing geography of the Southwest between 1810 and 1848, and they begin to understand the strong roots that Spanish-speaking peoples claim in this country. Studying about political activists like César Chavez and Gloria Molina, as well as writers and artists, gives Hispanic students a pride in their culture and people. (1994, p. 282)

5. A useful resource for parental involvement initiatives is Sudia Paloma McCaleb's (1994) book *Building Communities of Learners: A Collaboration Among Teachers, Students, Family and Community*. The projects and initiatives documented in the book were inspired by Alma Flor Ada's pioneering work in the Pajaro Valley School District (described in Chapter 1).

Another outstanding project also inspired by Alma Flor Ada's work is the *The Family Connection: Hmong Parent Education Project* carried out with the support of Title VII funds in Merced County, California (Eccles, Kirton & Xiong, 1994). The project has translated a variety of children's literature into Hmong, produced Hmong "Big Books" and published an extensive collection of stories and accounts of life in Laos written and illustrated by Hmong parents in the Merced County area. Most of these books are cerlox bound and have a "story cloth" set of illustrations on the left facing page and Hmong and English versions of the story on the right facing page.

Frances Eccles describes how parents discovered their voice in the unfamiliar medium of written language:

> In working with our Hmong parents, most of whom had never been to school and didn't know how to read and write their own language, much less English, we found that they thought they could not write, and that they had nothing to say that anyone would want to read…Once the parents realized they did indeed have stories to tell, and that they could tell their stories to a tape recorder and someone else could transcribe them we were off and running.
>
> The easiest stories to elicit were stories from their own lives and personal experience. So we developed some questions to help them organize their writing. (1994, p. 1)

Writing of personal histories was facilitated by questions about home and family life as a child and teenager in Laos as well as questions related to cultural conventions and the experience of war and migration to the United States. These oral histories were transcribed and published in both Hmong and English with parents themselves illustrating "story cloths" that depicted events in the stories.

Questions were also asked about topics that would be suitable for children's stories (e.g. things that scared the parents as children) and books on these topics were produced and are used extensively in the district's bilingual programs. North American folktales (e.g. The City Mouse and the Country Mouse) were also translated into Hmong and discussed among the parents in relation to their own experiences. A variety of imaginative lesson plans for use by teachers in school and activities for both parents and children at home have been developed by the project. These activities focus directly on the texts written by the parents.

Crucial to the success of the project has been the involvement of a bilingual/bicultural Parent Education Facilitator (Blong Xiong) and the fact that parents see quick and powerful results (their books in print, in the school library, and being used in classrooms). The project directors also point out that parents like learning about North American cultures and about the literature used in school, and they enjoy stories of all kinds because theirs is a culture of learning through oral tradition.

Materials developed by the project can be ordered from: Bilingual Education, Merced County Office of Education, 632 West 13th Street, Merced, CA 95340.

Of related interest is the fact that resources related to Hmong history, culture, language, and current events are now available on the World Wide Web. The Hmong Home Page address is: http://www.stolaf.edu/people/cdr/hmong.

6. The importance of creating classroom and schoolwide communities of learning that focus on acceleration of student progress rather than remediation is reinforced by the success of the Accelerated Schools Project, initiated by Stanford University professor Henry Levin (1993). This project, currently implemented in more than 300 schools across North America, rejects remediation for low-income students and instead argues that what works for so-called gifted and talented students will work for all students. Curriculum and instruction build on students' experiences, interests, motivations, culture, and observed abilities. Language use is emphasized across the curriculum and the development of higher-order literacy skills is fostered from an early age. A focus on experiential learning (i.e. learning-by-doing rather than learning-by-listening), problem-solving, peer tutoring and cooperative learning are also central to instruction in Accelerated Schools. There is also a strong focus on parents as partners in a shared educational enterprise, with parents expected to contribute significantly to their children's engagement in learning.

Accelerated schools (at both elementary and middle school level) have shown substantial increases in student achievement in places as diverse as San Francisco, Los Angeles, Seattle, New Orleans, Missouri and Illinois (Levin, 1993). Levin cautions, however, that usually about six years is required for a school to make the full transformation from a conventional to an accelerated school because major changes in school organization are required. Central among these changes is a shift from "top-down" to "bottom-up" decision making with teachers taking collective responsibility for decisions which they will implement and evaluate.

7. Several critics of whole-language approaches (e.g. Delpit, 1988; Kalantzis & Cope, 1993) have argued convincingly that some children require more explicit forms of instruction and corrective feedback than is the case in many whole-language classrooms. Specifically, there is a need for explicit instruction in how to use language powerfully to achieve social goals. This would entail developing competence in the conventions of different genres (e.g. report writing, formal letters etc.) and an awareness of how language is used in a wide variety of social contexts. In Lisa Delpit's words, teachers must learn not only how to "help students to establish their own voices, but to coach those voices to produce notes that will be heard clearly in the larger society" (1988, p. 296).

Reyes (1992) has also criticized the "one size fits all" assumptions of some whole-language classrooms, arguing that there is a need to affirm more explicitly culturally diverse students' cultural knowledge and to promote multicultural awareness.

These critiques of whole-language or progressive pedagogy are important but they appear to apply more to the way whole language has been interpreted and implemented inappropriately in certain contexts rather than to any central theoretical assumptions underlying whole-language pedagogy. Many educators whose views are generally consistent with whole-language approaches would also endorse strongly an explicit focus on critical literacy and on developing students' language awareness. This would include providing relevant explicit instruction and corrective feedback on formal aspects of language in order to ensure that students' voices will be heard and understood in the wider society. This orientation would also strive to affirm students' primary language and culture and challenge educational structures that devalue these and other aspects of students' identity (see, for example, Freeman & Freeman, 1992, 1994).

In short, it does not seem difficult to avoid the excesses occasionally identified in the implementation of whole-language and process writing approaches by insisting on the importance of explicit instruction to guide students' critical inquiry and their use of both written and oral language.

8. Two excellent resources produced by the editors of the periodical *Rethinking Schools* are: *Rethinking Columbus: Teaching About the 500th Anniversary of Columbus's Arrival in America* (1991) and *Rethinking Our Classrooms: Teaching for Equity and Justice* (1994). These can be ordered (for $4 and $6 each respectively) from Rethinking Schools, 1001 E. Keefe Avenue, Milwaukee, WI 53212 (fax: 414/964-7220; tel. 414/964-9646). Both publications focus on how critical literacy can be promoted in the classroom as a central component of a multicultural anti-racist curriculum.

The urgency of promoting critical literacy can be gauged from Donaldo Macedo's (1993, 1994) provocative and sobering account of how educational systems frequently promote "literacy for stupidification" and sanitize the curriculum through "the pedagogy of big lies."

9. I have slightly modified the labels given by Ada for the four phases in order to try and highlight certain aspects of the process. Although presented here in a linear format, the phases should not be thought of as requiring a linear or sequential approach. In other words, the process of collaborative critical inquiry can begin at any of the four phases and be incorporated in any manner into the instructional process. For example, as emphasized in Chapter 4, an experiential or personal interpretive phase in which the teacher elicits students' personal experiences relevant to the text or topic should normally precede the descriptive phase. Ada's scheme is not in any sense formulaic but should be re-invented by individual teachers according to their perceptions and circumstances. The essential components are that students' experience and critical inquiry constitute the curriculum as much as any "text" since in the absence of students' experience and critical inquiry no text can become truly meaningful.

10. In view of the fact that educational failure is concentrated among culturally diverse communities, it is surprising that issues of diversity remain at the periphery of much of the restructuring process in California and elsewhere. This is true even for schools that are attempting to engage in a participatory and democratic restructuring process rather than a "top-down" process. This pattern is illustrated by the findings of a major research project conducted by the advocacy group *California Tomorrow* involving 73 Californian schools that were in the process of restructuring. The sample included a variety of restructuring models based on the work of James Comer (1980), Henry Levin (1988), Theodore Sizer

(1984) as well as other initiatives funded through California's 1991 school restructuring legislation (SB 1274). The study revealed a silence about issues of culture and identity and "heavy barriers to bringing diversity and equity issues into the school's plans to better serve their students" (Olsen et al., 1994, p. 31). In spite of genuine commitment, the agenda for the reform process was largely determined by the concerns of dominant group educators and the voices of culturally diverse educators and parents were rarely heard around the table. Parents and instructional aides who were capable of adding to the knowledge base about issues of language, culture and race in the lives of the students were excluded from significant participation in the restructuring process in a large number of schools. The report suggests some of the reasons why dialogue about diversity and equity was missing:

> Four-fifths of California's teachers are white. Most do not come to work with firsthand knowledge of the communities and cultures of their students. Most speak only English…Teacher education programs are far behind the times in providing teachers with the knowledge about second language acquisition, about the impact of racism in students' lives, and about the diverse cultural backgrounds of the students in the public schools. We found more direct, lively dialogue and consideration of issues of race, culture and language in schools where prior to restructuring, there had been a tradition of strong bilingual programs or multicultural education and community embeddedness. …Generally, however, it appeared to us that in many schools, people were unaware that there is a perspective, a knowledge base that is missing around their table. They do not know that they do not know (1994, p. 30).

11. One set of voices conspicuously absent from educational reform debates are the voices of students. We would do well to heed the views of students such as nine-year-old Jessica Rosciglione and her seven-year-old sister, Julia, who express succinctly and eloquently much of what I have labored over in this book. Both girls are bilingual in Italian and English and spent the initial years of their life in Italy before moving to Toronto. Their mother, Jane O'Hare, interviewed them as part of a class project at the Ontario Institute for Studies in Education. Here are some of their likes, dislikes, and suggestions regarding schooling:

> I wish we could work with younger kids and older kids, so we'd help younger kids and older kids would help us;

> I wish we could decide some of the topics instead of the teacher telling us what to do. We're always doing animals;

> I wish school was half a day and they'd give us lots of homework;

> I wish school was like an Open House so that parents and grandparents could come in and help and teach us some of the things they've learned;

> I wish I knew or could know about the other kids' families or backgrounds and stuff like that to know what they're like;

I wish we could teach each other our languages;

I wish we could learn what's going on in the world, like: *Why do people have wars? Why do we have a food bank? Why are rich people — people at the top — mean to people at the bottom? Why do people sell drugs? Why do people take drugs? Why do people smoke? Why are some people poor?*

I don't like it when the teacher tells us to be quiet all the time — maybe we have good ideas that we'd like to share with the class;

I don't like it when the teacher tells us to be silent when I'm talking to my friend because maybe he or she doesn't understand something and I'm trying to explain it.

Chapter 7
Collaborative Empowerment at the Preschool, Elementary, and Secondary Levels

This chapter presents portraits of programs that have succeeded, to a significant extent, in creating contexts for collaborative empowerment in the interactions between educators and culturally diverse students. These portraits demonstrate that transformation of culturally diverse students' educational opportunities is not only possible, but is happening, in schools throughout North America. They also illustrate that what is fundamental is not what a particular program is called, but the extent to which genuine change occurs in the role definitions of educators and in the structures that frame the interactions between educators and students. The portraits in the text derive from the United States but relevant international examples are sketched in the endnotes. [1]

The Preschool Level

Among advocates for culturally diverse children and families, there is widespread agreement that the network of 23 preschool centers operated by the Foundation Center for Phenomenological Research, a non-profit organization based in Sacramento, California, was one of the most outstanding North American examples of early childhood education (e.g. Chang & Sizai, 1993). The Foundation Center's network of centers was de-funded by the California State Department in June 1995. [2] The Foundation Center's programs served children from low-income and migrant agricultural working families. The programs were based on the Montessori Method, delivered in children's home languages, and staff came predominantly from the communities being served. The Foundation

Center trained almost 100 of its staff as credentialed Montessori teachers and became the largest officially designated Montessori school system in the United States. This represents a remarkable achievement in view of the fact that many staff members had minimal education before joining the centers as teaching assistants. The Montessori training program was offered through Spanish, teachers' dominant language. Antonia López, Co-Director of the Foundation Center, explained the rationale for training teachers from the community:

> When we first started, we found that most of the existing teachers were not from the same culture as the children. The teachers were frustrated because they weren't getting the results they wanted. There was an invisible distance created by barriers of language and culture. Children were acting out and teachers were having difficulty forming relationships with parents…We realized that in order to have an emotionally safe environment, we needed to find a way to bring people from the community into the center as staff. But we did not want them to simply become teacher's aides — children are already too accustomed to seeing members of the community in secondary, subservient roles. (Chang & Sizai, 1993, p. 31) [3]

Because of the fact that the centers were staffed by community members, issues of cultural conflict never arose. In Antonia López' words:

> Everything about how the centers run is embedded in the culture of the people — what is an acceptable noise level, what are appropriate adult-child interactions, how they talk about problems, what they say at parent meetings. Because the staff come from the communities, we don't have to worry about "cultural conflicts" or to plan inservices on cultural awareness. They relate to the families and respond to them naturally. Staff is often not even conscious of what they do that is culturally appropriate. (Chang & Sizai, 1993, p. 28)

In addition to use of the Montessori Method and exclusive use of children's primary language for instructional purposes, the program focused on children's nutrition and on supporting family health care. Only organic foods were served in the centers on the grounds that families working in agricultural settings are already exposed to excesses of noxious chemicals without also eating pesticide-treated food. A comprehensive program of family health education was in place at all the centers and all members of the child's family underwent free health screening on a regular basis. This resulted in the detection of serious life-threatening illness such as hypertension, diabetes and major hearing impairments in about 25% of the fathers of children in the preschool programs (López, 1988).

Although no formal evaluation has been conducted of the Foundation Center's preschool programs, anecdotal accounts suggest a program that was exceptional in promoting children's social and conceptual development. Lily Wong Fillmore, one of the most credible voices in American education, expressed eloquently what many people (including this author) have felt on visiting one of the Foundation Center's programs:

> There are few honest-to-god epiphanies in the education business or in life, for that matter. I experienced one a couple of months ago in Winters, California. I visited a child development center located in a Winters public housing project. The Center, which is sponsored by a group called the Foundation Center for Phenomenological Research, serves the children of seasonal and migrant farm workers. The children range in age from two to six. The program is just about the best I have ever seen: it is exactly what I would have chosen for my own children. Indeed, it is the kind of child development program Yuppie couples seek out before they even consider having a child. ...It has a family health services program that can easily be a model for early education programs throughout the country. Parents and children attend clinics and health education programs that are designed to keep the entire family in good shape and to establish good health as a family affair. The facilities are beautifully designed and maintained...The physical environment is bright and attractive. Paintings and drawings are hung at child-eye-level. They are meant to be seen, touched, and enjoyed by the children...

> Was this program a miracle? How was it achieved? The teachers at this Center are mostly women from the same background as the parents of the children in the Center. The lead teacher had just one year of formal schooling before joining the staff of the Winters Child Development Center. After eight years on the job, she is a highly skilled professional educator. That's the genius of this program... [Many of the children coming out of the Foundation Center's programs] have been judged to be 'gifted' after they leave the Center. From what I saw, they certainly are.

Here then is the kind of program that Latino children, indeed all children, need. It is a program that begins with the assumption that children and their parents want and deserve the best education that can be provided. But good education such as I have described must be very costly, you must be thinking.

I too was a bit worried that this program was too good to be true. It had to be terribly expensive. It could never be replicated on a wide scale, I thought. This turned out to be the biggest surprise of all. While the not-so-hot-programs that one finds across the country cost around $23 per child per day for a three and a half hour program, the programs run by the Foundation Center operate on just $19 per child per day for an 11-hour a day program, including two hot meals and two snacks. (1993, pp. 3-6)

The Foundation Center was able to offer this outstanding program by paring administrative costs to the bone. While California early childhood education centers can spend up to 15 percent of their budgets on administration, the Foundation Center spent only 7-9 percent (Chang & Sizai, 1993, p. 34). [4]

The Elementary School Level

Three programs are reviewed briefly here. Two are two-way bilingual programs operating at opposite ends of the continent, while the third exemplifies the kind of transformative pedagogy discussed in Chapter 6.

The Dual Language Programs in Healdsburg, California. Two bilingual education programs operated in the late 1980s in the Healdsburg Union School District of Northern California. More than one-third of the district's student population is of Spanish-speaking background. These programs are the Bilingual-Bicultural program, also known as Project Puente, and the Two-Way Bilingual Spanish Immersion program. Both programs are intended to serve students who are in the process of learning English as well as those who are fluent English speakers. In the Bilingual-Bicultural program, initial literacy is supported in each student's primary language whereas in the Bilingual Spanish Immersion program initial literacy is introduced in Spanish and formal instruction in English literacy is begun around the middle of the grade 3 year.

These programs were documented in the context of an international Case Studies project of cultural diversity in education initiated by the Organization for Economic Cooperation and Development [OECD] (1991). [5] The

Healdsburg programs were judged as outstanding among the 23 programs from around the world studied by the OECD. They illustrate the educational benefits for all sectors of the community when "us-versus-them" divisions are overcome and rational language learning goals are adopted for all children.

A major goal of these programs is the development of oral fluency and literacy in Spanish and English for both English- and Spanish-speaking students. In the early eighties, the then coordinator of bilingual education for the district (Arturo Vásquez), started laying the groundwork within the Healdsburg community for the implementation of programs that would achieve this goal. As expressed by Pease-Alvarez:

> Vásquez enlisted the support of the Healdsburg community and parents as he became a key figure in community activities. He joined the Rotary Club and organized a sister-cities program with Cuernavaca [Mexico]. He gave presentations on bilingual education to Kiwanis, church groups, and a variety of other organizations. In addition, he developed a good relationship with the staff of the local newspaper which has continued to spotlight the accomplishments of the bilingual program to this day. He enlisted parent support through his many community activities and by organizing meetings to inform parents about bilingual education and later about Spanish immersion education. (1989, p. 4)

As a result of these initiatives, parents interested in establishing a two-way immersion program formed a Healdsburg chapter of Advocates for Language Learning. Parents raised money to pay for books and staff development and worked with district administrators to establish policies for admittance into the program. A large majority of these parents were of Anglo background. A concern for program administrators has been the relatively weaker role played by Spanish-speaking parents in decision-making processes related to the immersion program (Pease-Alvarez, 1989; Vásquez, Pease-Alvarez, & Shannon, 1994). However, administrators in both programs have successfully sought out sources of funding to enhance Latino/Latina parent involvement in the schools.

Both the bilingual and Spanish immersion programs are considered highly successful both within the district and externally. For example, the bilingual program (Project Puente) was designated an exemplary program on the basis of (among other things) strong standardized achievement test performance in both English and Spanish. Parents, school board members, and school administrators have actively supported both bilingual programs.

The bilingual programs have influenced other district classrooms through their adoption of promising instructional practices such as cooperative learning, whole language, literature-based reading, and process writing. Teachers reported that they felt a sense of professional empowerment in being encouraged to implement innovative approaches to curriculum.

Teachers in both programs noted increased interaction between the English- and Spanish-speaking students in the community and attributed this to the inclusive nature of the bilingual programs:

> every teacher...could recount occasions when Latino and Anglo students interacted with one another on the playground or outside of school. The students and parents who were interviewed also described close friendships that had formed between Latino and Anglo students. (Pease-Alvarez, p. 17)

Pease-Alvarez (1989) suggests that the success of these programs is at least in part due to the social context of the community and the relative lack of divisiveness across ethnic boundaries:

> No doubt this is due in part to the relatively small number of Latinos who live in and around the Healdsburg community and perhaps, as one individual feels, to the fact that they do not occupy positions of power. However, respondents repeatedly alluded to the liberal attitudes of white residents of the Healdsburg community. ...As one Chicano teacher claims, 'Even the most rednecked ones are not as rednecked as they are in other places.' (1989, p. 41)

In conclusion, the bilingual programs in Healdsburg illustrate the educational benefits that can be achieved for all students when the community as a whole recognizes and values the linguistic resources of its bilingual population. The fact that teachers in both programs are fluent in Spanish reduces cultural discontinuities and misunderstandings and makes fluency and literacy in two languages a natural goal for all students. There are currently in the United States close to 180 two-way bilingual immersion programs of the type implemented in Healdsburg. The vast majority of these appear highly successful in developing bilingual and biliteracy skills for minority and majority student populations alike (Christian & Montone, 1994; Crawford, 1995; Dolson & Lindholm, 1995).

The inner-city setting in New York City from which our second example of two-way bilingual education is drawn contrasts markedly with the rural Healdsburg situation but the underlying changes in school structures and educator role definitions are very similar.

The Dual Language Program of Manhattan's District 3. This two-way bilingual program was initiated in Public School 84 in 1984 and by 1993 had expanded horizontally to eight other schools in the district and vertically beyond elementary school to middle school (Foster & Swinney, in press; Morison, 1990). The program currently operates in some of the richest and some of the poorest schools in the district.

In order to desegregate the bilingual program and to provide linguistic role models in both languages, schools strive to attain a 50/50 ratio of Spanish and English dominant students. The program operates on an alternative day basis with English and Spanish being used on succeeding days for all content instruction. The program philosophy is student-centered with considerable emphasis placed on cooperative learning and hands-on activities designed to foster both learning and cross-cultural understanding. The separation of Spanish and English is central to the language policy of the Dual Language Program.

At the middle school level, the traditional middle school structure does not allow for an alternate day design. Thus, the curriculum is organized in thematic units with specific goals for each language. About 35 percent of the instructional time is spent through Spanish and 65 percent through English.

Morison describes the development of reading and writing in the program as follows:

> Older children have been writing plays and poetry in two languages with the help of a poet-consultant from the Teachers and Writers Collaborative…The question of whether or not children will become confused learning to read in two languages simultaneously is no longer even discussed. After five years of experience, it is taken for granted that learning to read is one process. Each class library has collections in both Spanish and English, and the teacher reads to the children every day. The children eagerly follow along, especially when big books are used. The teacher also records experiences so that children can see their words being put to print. The children also write little

books of their own, on letters of the alphabet, colors, collective stories, and so on. In the beginning, second-language reading lags behind, but that is expected and no pressure is applied to hasten the balance. (1990, p. 167)

Considerable emphasis is placed on reading literature in the two languages (with the focus on Caribbean and Latin American literature in the Spanish component) and artists and writers from the community work directly with students and teachers to enrich the program. With their help, many classes in the dual language program have written and performed their own theatrical works in Spanish.

The picture that emerges from the program descriptions provided by Morison (1990) and Foster and Swinney (in press) is of a dual language program dedicated to building on the bilingual nature of the community and enabling all students to use both languages of the community in authentic and powerful ways. The potential of such a program to unite communities across cultural and linguistic boundaries is expressed by Morison: "As a result of word of mouth and other publicity, we are inundated with requests for information and tours, especially from white middle-class parents who are attracted by the enrichment offered by such a program" (1990, p. 168).

The Bilingual Bicultural Mini School in East Harlem. The achievements of this program were featured in the periodical *Electronic Learning* in September 1995 (Siegel, 1995). The school is a "mini-school" of 560 students located within another school. The mini-school was founded in 1973 in response to Spanish-speaking parents' requests for a bilingual program that enhanced students' knowledge of their own language and cultural heritage together with teaching them English and other core subjects. Students in the school come from many South and Central American countries and from the Caribbean. All of the teachers in the school are bilingual. The school transitions students into greater amounts of English instruction over the course of elementary school but maintains a strong focus on developing students' language and culture. In the words of Lourdes Arroyo, the school's director: "We strive to make them feel proud and knowledgeable about their own history, though not at the expense of learning about American history" (p. 27). The focus of language learning is two-way: English dominant students in the school learn Spanish just as Spanish dominant students learn English.

What attracted *Electronic Learning* to the school was its innovations in using technology to promote collaborative critical inquiry among its students. The school was one of 11 winners of the Apple Computer Partners in Education Grant for 1994-5. The hardware and software they received permitted them to implement their proposal which called for an extensive revision of the entire curriculum, using El Barrio (East Harlem) as its focus.

Students' work for the 1994-95 year was displayed for three days at the end of May at the school fair. Prominent among the project exhibits was a huge model of East Harlem itself. Technology facilitated the process of cultural exploration and self-definition that students engaged in over the course of the year:

> Third graders in their social studies class looked at what defined the neighborhood as a community. In fourth-grade science, students tested water quality in the school; in fifth-grade math they created graphs measuring immigration flow into the neighborhood and compared the results to other eras. In each grade, technology fit like another puzzle piece into the overall plan. Students produced *HyperStudio* living histories of El Barrio, learned *Lego Logo* to move the elevated train across the model of the neighborhood, and videoed El Barrio's landmarks. (Siegel, 1995, p. 28)

Among the other projects carried out by students in the school were:

- A project on "The Trees of East Harlem" (Los Arboles del Barrio) that used *HyperStudio* to create text, drawings, photographs, and sound relating to six different trees found in East Harlem. Students also produced a 1995 calendar on this topic which they sold to raise money for the school.

- A telecommunications project carried out by the third/fourth-grade class with 15 other schools in the area monitoring the water quality of Harlem Meer, a body of water in the northern stretch of Central Park. Students collect water samples on a regular basis which they test and send the results on-line to the Central Park Conservatory.

- A survey carried out by grade 6 students on the countries of origin of students in their school which they integrated with U.S. census data.

- A survey of different ethnic groups' home remedies integrated into a *HyperStudio* database.

What is remarkable about the achievements of the Bilingual Bicultural Mini School is not the technology that they used but the pedagogical vision that unleashed students' and teachers' creative intellectual energies. Students and teachers engaged in collaborative critical inquiry to gain insights into their identities as individuals, as a neighborhood community, and as a school community.

Opponents of bilingual education might argue that the successes of this school have very little to do with its bilingual bicultural program. Yet, how much real communication would be going on in the school, or between teachers and parents, if all the teachers were monocultural and monolingual and students were discouraged from using Spanish in the classroom? To what extent could students have planned and implemented their complex projects if communication among them had been limited to their weaker language? To what extent could students have carried out parent and community surveys if they had not developed the Spanish literacy to record their responses and data? Finally, would it even have been possible for educators to conceive of integrating the curriculum with community and encouraging students to take pride in their "neighborhood as laboratory" if the school culture had focused on assimilation and excluded students' language and culture from the school? Why should students take pride in their neighborhood or community when the culture of the school communicates clearly to them that the language of that community has no place within the walls of the school?

The pedagogical innovations undertaken at the Bilingual Bicultural Mini-School serve as a model of what can be achieved when bilingual students are encouraged and enabled to use their entire linguistic repertoire for purposes of collaborative critical inquiry. An implication is that any program — transitional bilingual, two-way bilingual, ESL, mainstream — will achieve its potential for accelerating students' academic development only when collaborative critical inquiry becomes the central pedagogical focus of the entire school (Cummins & Sayers, 1995). [6]

The Secondary School Level

The first example of collaborative empowerment at the secondary level comes from an analysis of educational changes implemented in a school in a Navajo reservation community (McLaughlin, 1992). The second example focuses on the transformative journey undertaken by one Latino teacher and his students in Oxnard, California (Jasso & Jasso, 1994; Terrazas, 1995).

A Navajo-English Applied Literacy Program. Dan McLaughlin first came to "Mesa Valley" (a pseudonym) as a teacher of secondary level gifted-and-talented students. A large majority of students designated as gifted and talented were children of school staff members (and presumably non-Navajo) and were making good academic progress. By contrast, students in the mainstream program were falling further and further behind as they progressed from one grade level to the next. In order to remedy this situation, the school abolished the gifted-and-talented program and instituted a program for all students based on specifying products that students would produce for particular audiences. Thus, curriculum was conceived as product plus audience (C = P + A). The approach was seen as congruent with Navajo cultural learning style, characterized by McLaughlin as "practice privately and in small groups first, then perform." In McLaughlin's terms:

> The climate of community control and community participation at the school was such that we also felt intuitively the need to create products for viable audiences. The need was to "hook in" not only the students but also their parents and other community members. Because most people in the community spoke only Navajo, inserting the students' first language into instruction was an obvious first requirement. (1992, pp. 245-246)

The curriculum focused on four areas: Navajo Research, English Research, Computers, and Performance which students rotate through in nine-week cycles over the course of the year. All of the activities incorporate cognitive challenges. As described by McLaughlin:

> In 12th grade, for example, students divide equally into the project's four classes. In Navajo Research, they develop an editorial-style article in Navajo, first articulating research questions, next interviewing at least two experts (with contrasting points of view) on their research topic, then evaluating and synthesizing opinions, and finally writing editorial articles for publication in the bilingual community newspaper. Seniors in English Research follow the same set of procedures, only in English, to develop editorial-style articles for the same newspaper. In computers, with the Navajo-smart word processors, students learn to use different word-processing and page layout programs, which they may encounter at work or in higher education. In Performance, they analyze a topic of critical importance to the indi-

vidual, the school, the community, the Navajo Tribe, and prepare comprehensive videotape products to be aired over the community's low-power television station. (pp. 246-247)

In summary, the Navajo-English Applied Literacy program provided students with an opportunity to use their lived experiences as a basis for acquiring language, literacy and critical thinking skills. In very much the way that Alma Flor Ada's critical literacy framework suggests (see Chapter 6), students were enabled to relate community social issues to their own experience, analyze alternative perspectives on these social issues, and generate new syntheses in written or video form that extended the horizons of community dialogue. The fact that students' first language was validated within the high school, on an equal basis with English, appears to have been a central component of the program's success. [7]

The portraits of empowerment pedagogy to this point have been characterized by a strong whole school commitment to validating students' language and culture, encouragement of parent and community participation, and approaches to pedagogy and assessment that promote critical and independent learning among students. The innovations infused the culture of the school at a deep structure level.

The final example focuses on innovations that were instituted by one teacher in one classroom and viewed with a certain ambivalence by other staff members. The example illustrates very clearly how the creation of contexts for collaborative empowerment almost inevitably constitutes a challenge to the traditional power structure that has operated in the school and wider society.

Students for Cultural and Linguistic Democracy. One gets a glimpse of what a high school education could and should be like from two chapters in the book *Reclaiming Our Voices: Bilingual Education, Critical Pedagogy & Praxis* (Frederickson, 1995). Both accounts document the events and dialogue leading up to the formation of Students for Cultural and Linguistic Democracy (SCaLD) in a high school in Oxnard, California. Adriana and Rosalba Jasso describe the personal transformations they experienced as students in Bill Terrazas Jr.'s high school classroom:

We had heard before about a different classroom at our high school, and we were about to step inside it for the first time in our junior year. Mr. Terrazas was a different teacher, you felt special in his class, like a "somebody." You could honestly say it was your class. We were surrounded by butcher paper hanging from the walls with bright colors, beautiful drawings, and big letters. There were no desks or rows, instead there were big round tables. You could choose your own seat and you were responsible for your own work and production.

The most exciting thing we can remember is going into the classroom and having one of those deep and powerful dialogues. In these powerful dialogues we also shared and examined our own lives... As students we were taking control of our lives, getting to know ourselves, and we were able to share our feelings with others. If we had known that sharing and looking closely at our cultures, our lives, and society was so transforming, we would have done it sooner!...

Our classroom was full of human knowledge; all of us knew something different and we were confident enough to share it with each other. We had a teacher who believed in us; he didn't hide our power, he advertised it. He gave us the opportunity we truly needed to reclaim our voices. He too was sharing his oppressive life experiences, his human knowledge, his cultural truth — this is what we appreciated the most. He shared information about oppression, discrimination, and exploitation of oppressed peoples in the United States. We had never heard this history before. (1995, p. 255)

Bill Terrazas Jr. describes the same reality from the perspective of a teacher who became more a colleague of his students in a search for insight and identity than an "instructor" who has information, skills, and values to transmit:

These huge [butcher] sheets are filled with students' writings, projects, research, and dialogue questions on their life experiences, social issues of importance to them, text book information, cultural art, cultural history of the common people, and the life experiences of famous leaders from social justice movements like Marcus Garvey, Malcolm X, Dolores Huerta, and César Chavez. We use tons of butcher paper. We always display our critical work, because all our investigations connect with real life situations and knowledge that can dramatically affect and change the living conditions of someone in class. (pp. 286-287)

Terrazas goes on to describe critical incidents in the cultural and social explorations of students in the school. He concludes his account as follows:

Many of my students return to visit me after being in my classes. In every case they never mention the grammar, vocabulary, writing, or reading lessons we studied. Instead, they always remember the critical dialogues we voiced in class. All of them have said that their classroom experiences changed their life and their way of looking at the world. At times, this baffles me. This wasn't what the university teacher training programs had taught me to do, nor to expect. I had learned how to design a lesson plan, to organize a good lecture, to select appropriate worksheets and assignments. I had learned how to keep my students quiet, managed, and passive. To listen silently. With my students I have learned another view of education, another approach to educating. I no longer practice a curriculum made for failure and poverty. (pp. 307-308) [8]

Conclusion

The portraits of "schools in action" outlined in this chapter are intended to illustrate in a concrete way the theoretical framework discussed in previous chapters. To me, these portraits show clearly how culturally diverse students' academic success or failure is crucially dependent on the ways in which identities are being negotiated in the classroom and school. They show also that *empowerment* is generated only through interactions that critically affirm students' identities and extend their conceptual horizons. The creation of power in these interactions is at the core of genuine educational reform.

One reason why much educational reform has remained at a safe surface level, endorsing the rhetoric of equity and grasping at a few instructional panaceas, is that genuine reform of the kind sketched in this chapter is not safe; it threatens structures of privilege and status within the society. Faced with the escalating rhetoric of diversity as the enemy within, it takes courage for educators to assert the rights of children to develop their home languages and the importance for the nation of fostering these multilingual resources; it takes courage to cross cultural and linguistic boundaries to create structures for genuine parent and community participation and partnership; it takes courage to lift the veil obscuring the social realities around the classroom and unleash students' power to analyze these realities and their own place within them.

The next chapter focuses on the discourse of disempowerment. As discussed in Chapter 2, opponents of bilingual education have attempted to rationalize English-only programs as being in children's best interests. Few would acknowledge explicitly that their goal is to preserve a societal power structure that historically has excluded subordinated groups from full participation. To them, bilingual education is self-evidently inferior to English-only programs since it exposes children to less of "the language of equal opportunity."

One can understand how members of the general public and many media commentators might confine their analysis to this "sound-bite" level. Academics, however, are trained in research procedures and analysis techniques. Their *raison d'être* within the society is to generate knowledge and insight. It is thus important to examine more closely the academic arguments against bilingual education. If there truly is a case to be made that bilingual education impedes children's educational progress, then this would undermine the argument proposed here that the discourse against bilingual education and cultural diversity is a thinly disguised attempt to preserve the societal power structure.

Endnotes to Chapter 7

1. An outstanding example of community-initiated preschool education is the national experiment in Maori language revitalization currently underway in New Zealand (Aotearoa). The indigenous Maori community constitutes about 13 percent of the New Zealand population. Sociolinguistic surveys conducted during the 1970s in New Zealand showed that the language was in danger of virtually disappearing within one generation (Benton, 1988). These data acted as a catalyst for community and government action to revitalize the Maori language through the institution of preschool programs conducted exclusively through Maori. As of 1992, these programs numbered more than 600 and served more than 10,000 children (16.6% of all Maori children under 5) (Waite, 1992). Their rapid growth has continued in recent years and as of April 1995 they numbered 865 throughout the country (Cazden, 1995).

   These programs are called *Kohanga Reo* (language nests) and they have increased pressure for the establishment of more extensive bilingual and Maori language immersion programs at the elementary and secondary level. While such immersion programs, termed *Kura Kaupapa Maori*, have expanded during the past decade, in 1992 only 0.4% of Maori elementary students were in Maori immersion programs, 3.6% were in bilingual schools, and 9.2% were in bilingual classes within primarily English-speaking schools (Waite, 1992).

   Smith (1992) has analyzed the establishment of *Kura Kaupapa Maori* as a form of resistance to the dominant ideology of Eurocentric schools that have systematically excluded Maori language, traditions, and belief systems:

   > Kaupapa Maori schooling is an intervention strategy entirely different from the unsuccessful strategies attempted by Pakeha [European-origin New Zealanders] in the past. It is clearly Maori in design, content and practice. Its establishment *outside of the system* questions the right of Pakeha to dominate education to the exclusion of Maori-preferred interests in educa-

tion. Kura Kaupapa schooling asserts the right to overtly validate Maori knowledge, language, custom and practice. Implied is an analysis of (and a response to) the unequal power relations that led State schooling to serve only dominant Pakeha interests... Maori people have resisted assimilation by Pakeha culture through both individual and collective actions. Within the existing schooling crisis, Maori resistance can be gauged through disproportionate levels of pupil absenteeism, truancy, early school leaving, disruptive school behavior, underachievement, and at times overt cultural expression. Kura Kaupapa Maori has moved Maori resistance to another level and to another site. (pp. 100-103)

The outcomes of this social experiment in attempting to reverse language shift and resist social subordination remain to be seen over the next decade. Data from other parts of the world suggest that schools alone are limited in their power to revitalize endangered languages (Fishman, 1991). However, the progress made during the past 15 years by Maori communities is truly remarkable and the outcomes of this struggle for social equality and language rights cannot be prejudged.

The Maori initiatives were highly influential in inspiring even more ambitious language revival efforts in another part of the Pacific, Hawaii. The *Punana Leo* program begins at the preschool level in much the same way as the Maori *Kohanga Reo* and currently has expanded into seven schools with 750 students in grades K-9. According to Crawford (1995), "the total immersion approach postpones English instruction until the 5th grade. Yet, over the long term, students outscore their English-speaking counterparts on standardized tests, according to William Wilson of the University of Hawaii" (pp. 192-193). However, no formal evaluation of the program has been conducted.

2. The advantages and potential disadvantages of recruiting staff from the communities being served were elaborated on by Antonia López in an interview with the periodical *Montessori Life:*

> 'The advantages were clear: a staff native to the culture could offer language and cultural compatibility, access to community support, development of local role models, long-term commitment to children and families, and the opportunity for genuine community development.'

> The disadvantages were also very real.'Most staff members come to us with limited educational backgrounds. But the greatest challenge is the self-doubt compounded by cultural chauvinism and resistance to change, varying degrees of cultural "self-hate" resulting from their acceptance of the dominant culture's negative attitude about language and cultural minorities and low-income people.' (Montessori Life, 1990, p. 21)

Another outstanding early childhood education program that has emulated many of the Foundation Center's initiatives is the Even Start program in the Lincoln Unified School District (LUSD) in Stockton California that serves a low-income Cambodian-origin community. I am indebted to Beverly Chelseth, Preschool and Multilingual Services Coordinator of the LUSD for the opportunity to visit this program.

3. The California State Department's decision in June 1995 not to renew any of the Foundation Center's contracts was rationalized on the grounds that Marilyn Prosser, executive director of the Center, had been charged with misuse of funds by the Federal Bureau of Investigations (FBI). These charges followed a two-year investigation initiated as a result of anonymous allegations of corruption, money laundering, and attendance fraud. None of these initial allegations were mentioned in the FBI indictment.

   The conflict between the Foundation Center and the Child Development Division of the California State Department of Education goes back more than a decade. Twice the Foundation Center successfully brought suit against the Child Development Division for harassment. In both cases, the State was forced to settle out of court in the Foundation Center's favor.

   The allegations against the Foundation Center were the subject of several newspaper articles during 1994. These articles raised the concerns of some sectors of the community as to why public monies should be supporting a "cadillac" program for low-income minority students (with classical music, organic food and toothpaste, and aesthetic surroundings). The fact that, as a result of administrative streamlining, this program was operated at a smaller per-pupil cost than other State-funded programs did not seem to matter. The not-so-subtle implication in much of this debate was that low-income minority children are second-class citizens who deserve only a second-class education.

   The charges against the Foundation Center lack credibility in the extreme. As Rosa Zubizarreta (personal communication, June 1995) points out: "How is it possible to provide the admittedly world-class programs that the Foundation Center runs, on the same low funding that all other State-supported pre-school centers receive, and possibly be 'stealing money from the till?'" The quality of the Foundation Center's programs was never contested by the State; indeed it would be hard to contest their quality in view of the fact that in the late 1980s they were judged one of the two foremost early childhood programs in the world by a New Zealand television documentary.

4. The importance of early childhood education that strongly promotes the child's home language has been demonstrated in the interview study of more than 1,000 families (from various language backgrounds) coordinated by Lily Wong Fillmore (1991b) in the early 1990s. As noted in Chapter 5, a majority of families whose children attended monolingual English daycare or preschool programs reported that their children's L1 skills declined. By contrast, preschool programs, such as those of the Foundation Center, that utilized children's L1 exclusively were associated with significantly less language loss.

   The policy implications of these data with respect to the optimal language of preschool programs were debated in the pages of *Education Week* by Porter (1991) and Wong Fillmore (1991c). Porter invoked the principle of "time-on-task" to argue for maximizing preschool children's exposure to English while Wong Fillmore suggested that the predominance of English-only preschool provision was a major contributor to a breakdown of family communication (see also Soto [in press] for additional data on bilingual families and early childhood education).

A Swedish study (Sirén, 1991) of 600 families in the Stockholm area similarly showed extremely rapid language shift from the home language to Swedish among preschool children. Factors that slowed the rate of language loss were consistent parent L1 use and L1 support in the preschool (see Cummins, 1993, for a more detailed summary of Sirén's findings).

In the Canadian context, Merylie Wade Houston has outlined a wide variety of strategies for supporting bilingual children's home languages within the preschool. A first step, she argues, is provision of books in the home language. This can be achieved by linking up with the local public libraries which often have collections in languages other than English (at least in multilingual cities like Toronto and Vancouver):

> Even the small local branches had children's books in the languages reflected in the surrounding neighborhoods. Ours, for instance, offered Greek and Cantonese. The librarians believed the books were there to be read... They were willing to lend our [preschool] program bags full of books every two weeks. They even asked us to tell them exactly which languages we needed, so that when they spent the little funding they had for new acquisitions, they would be sure to be getting what the community wanted. (1995, p. 33)

Houston also suggests coordinating with community associations, churches, synagogues, and mosques to solicit donations of L1 books. Families can also be asked to make connections with relatives here or in other countries to obtain L1 books that may have been outgrown by older children. The rationale for reflecting the family's language in the preschool and communicating a positive orientation to the family's language is outlined by Houston as follows:

> If children hear their parents switch to English whenever they are outside the home, whether or not they speak it well, then they may grow up thinking that their home language is second class, that their parents don't belong in their new school world and that they themselves are not as good as the other children. Teachers have a crucial role to play here. It doesn't matter if you don't speak a second language. It is your *attitude* towards language that counts. Because your opinion is so very important to the children's development of values, it is essential that you respect and value their language by reflecting it in your classroom. One of the easiest and most effective ways to do this is through books. (p. 33)

A final note in regard to early childhood education and promotion of children's L1 concerns the position adopted by the National Association for the Education of Young Children (NAEYC) at its annual conference in November 1995. According to a NAEYC Information Services media release, NAEYC's position is as follows:

Children's educational experiences should afford them the opportunity to learn and to become effective, functioning members of society. Language development is essential for learning, and the development of children's home language does not interfere with their ability to learn English. Because knowing more than one language is a cognitive asset,...early education programs would encourage the development of children's home language while fostering the acquisition of English. (NCBE Dateline, November 30, 1995)

5. The OECD Case Studies project examined the schooling of culturally and linguistically diverse students in 23 countries in North America, Europe, and Australia. The project was coordinated by Alan Wagner and included Jim Cummins, Kenji Hakuta, David Hopkins, and Euan Reid as consultants who took responsibility for drafting sections of the final report.

6. On the international scene, one other elementary school that has been extensively documented is the Richmond Road school in Auckland, New Zealand/Aotearoa. See Cazden (1989) and May (1994) for detailed accounts of the success of this multilingual, multicultural school.

7. The cultural congruity between community, students and the school that is facilitated when the L1 is incorporated into the school program and accrued high status is also evident in accounts of the success of Calexico High School in promoting Latino and Latina students' academic achievement. The school population is 98% Spanish-speaking, and Spanish is used predominantly in the community which is very close to the Mexican border. About half the residents are farm laborers who follow the crops much of the year. When school starts many leave their children with relatives or other family members.

Despite the fact that most low-income bilingual communities experience high dropout rates and low achievement levels, this is not the case in Calexico. According to a report reprinted from *California and the West* in the CABE Newsletter (July/August, 1991, Vol. 14, No. 1):

> For five years running — from 1986 through last year — Calexico High School has had the lowest dropout rate of any predominantly Latino school in California, state figures show. In 1990, the dropout rate at Calexico High stood at a relatively low 11% — nine percentage points below the statewide dropout rate of 20.2%...the statewide dropout rate among Latinos [is] 29.2%...more than double the 14.4% rate for Anglos. In Calexico, not only are dropout rates low, the rate of students continuing their education after graduation is high. Two-thirds of the 1990 Calexico High graduates went on to either a community college or a four-year university...
>
> Much of the credit for Calexico's success is given to the district's extensive bilingual program — built around the premise that students learn best in their native tongue...Dennis Parker is manager of the Office of Instructional Strategies at the [state] department and has worked as a state consultant to the Calexico schools from 1981 to 1986. He sees two main

reasons Calexico's bilingual program succeeds where others fail. "First, they have more instruction in Spanish than other bilingual programs, as high as 80% in the early grades," Parker said. "After they become fluent in English, they still receive instruction in Spanish 15% to 20% of the day in their classes. Second, English is introduced gradually, and to make it more comprehensible they use more pictures, more hands-on activities. (California Association for Bilingual Education: "Calexico Defies Odds on Dropout Rate," 1991, pp. 1 & 20)

Other commentators talked about the "unity of an entire Hispanic community so fired up about the pursuit of education" and the fact that "all the teachers at Calexico understand the culture of the people — they speak and understand Spanish."

8. While changes are occurring in teacher pre-service education in California and elsewhere, it is not clear that the scope of change extends much beyond transmitting strategies for more effective teaching of English and content subjects to bilingual students. One illustration of how teacher education can extend itself into the transformative domains highlighted by Bill Terrazas Jr. has been described by Lois Meyer of San Francisco State University in an article entitled "Barrio buddies: Learning through letters about kids, cultures, communities, and self-confrontation." In a course entitled "Linguistic and Cultural Diversity in the Elementary School" which all teacher candidates were required to take for the first time in Fall 1992, Meyer initiated various forms of contact between the teacher candidates and inner-city culturally diverse children. The teacher candidates were predominantly White monolingual students whose experience of diversity varied greatly but in many cases was limited. Meyer describes the course as follows:

I arranged for each teacher candidate in my two sections to be paired or "buddied" with one or two children in a fourth or fifth grade classroom at Marshall School...[in the] Mission District, an immigrant Latino barrio that has seen a recent influx of Southeast Asian and Cantonese-speaking families. Since my students were not bilingual, the selected buddy classrooms were English language development classes... Three components became central to the semester's work:

1) *Buddy Letters:* The university students' primary task was to develop a relationship through letters and finally in person with their buddy(ies), and to document their reflections and learnings in a Buddy Book. The hope was that through the exchange of letters they would learn about the personal histories and experiences of individual children from diverse racial/ethnic backgrounds, at the same time that they reflected upon and shared with their buddy their own personal story...

2) *The University Adventure:*...The university students, in consultation with the buddy teachers, were to organize a field trip which brought their buddies to San Francisco State University at the end of the semester...

3) Reflections on readings, presentations and discussions:...Many of my students' most passionate and revealing reflections were written in response to course readings or class sessions that jarred their previous assumptions about the children's lives and communities. As they gained more knowledge from multiple perspectives about their buddies, my students began to analyze themselves as cultural beings, including their own assumptions, stereotypes, biases, and fears concerning cultural perspectives and linguistic practices different from their own, and their assumptions about the purposes and practices of schools. (1994, p. 94)

Meyer describes in detail the conflicting range of emotions the university students went through over the course of the semester as a result of their contacts with their buddies and in reaction to readings such as California Tomorrow's *Crossing the Schoolhouse Border* (Olsen, 1988) and Rethinking Schools' *Rethinking Columbus* (1991). Most developed new perspectives and profound insights on issues of diversity, racism, and second language learning. A few students, however, were infuriated by what they regarded as "offensive" readings (e.g. *Rethinking Columbus*).

Meyer's article makes fascinating reading not only as documentation of a highly creative innovation in teacher education but also as a reminder of how many middle-class students and members of the general public are still almost totally isolated and insulated from the realities of cultural diversity and inner-city life. Teachers are likely to find it much more difficult to connect with inner-city students when they have no direct experience or understanding of diversity than when they understand their students' realities and are willing to learn from their students. Meyer's article illustrates how powerful the learning experience can be when these "two solitudes" come together in a process of negotiating identities.

Chapter 8

Disinformation in the Information Age: The Academic Critics of Bilingual Education

The term "disinformation" refers to the systematic spreading of false information in order to confuse and disorient the opposition. Although the term is usually associated with the activities of groups such as the CIA and former KGB (and more recently, tobacco companies), the phenomenon of disinformation is no less evident in debates on domestic political issues such as the education of bilingual students. In some cases disinformation is spread deliberately; in other cases, the false information is genuinely believed by those spreading it but they have avoided ample opportunities to correct their ignorance or misinformation by means of selective inattention to awkward facts or inconsistencies. This latter form of disinformation is very evident in controversy surrounding bilingual education.

My goal in this and the final chapter is to try to put the volatile debate on bilingual education into a larger context where the underlying issues and the choices facing educators can be seen more clearly. Both advocates and opponents of bilingual education invariably claim that they are motivated by what is in the best interests of bilingual children rather than by political considerations. Not surprisingly, each side accuses the other of political rather than educational motivation.

It is immediately obvious that the issues here are neither linguistic nor instructional. The question of whether a particular program is "bilingual" or "English-only" is not the critical issue in determining its likely effectiveness.

Among applied linguists around the world there is no controversy about the educational legitimacy of bilingual education for both minority and majority students. The research data from North America and elsewhere reviewed in Chapter 5 show clearly that there is little relationship between the amount of instructional time spent through the majority language and academic achievement in that language. In the case of well-implemented bilingual programs, the relationship is often inverse: students from subordinated backgrounds who experience greater amounts of L1 instruction in the early grades show stronger academic achievement over time than those whose instruction has been primarily through their L2 (e.g. Dolson & Lindholm, 1995; Ramírez, 1992; Rosier & Holm, 1980; Thomas & Collier, 1995). Anybody who denies this pattern has either not read the research or has chosen to ignore it because it is politically inconvenient.

Thus the evidence is very clear that bilingual education, in general, is a legitimate and useful way of promoting academic skills for all children, and that, in particular, two-way bilingual immersion programs provide optimal conditions for academic development in both languages. However, bilingual education is no panacea. In some cases, it may not be feasible to implement bilingual programs (e.g. lack of bilingual teachers in some contexts). In other situations, the implementation of bilingual programs may have been undermined for political reasons with the result that it fails to achieve its goals. Finally, some bilingual programs represent only surface-level interventions that entail little or no change in the way educators define their roles or in the overall organizational structure of the school. Pedagogy remains transmission-oriented rather than transformational. Under these circumstances, students' academic progress will be less than ideal.

In other words, the fact that a particular program is labelled "bilingual" is no guarantee of its effectiveness. By the same token, as outlined in Chapter 6, some programs that have little or no formal L1 instruction can promote students' academic development in effective ways when the entire school program is oriented to creating contexts of empowerment for students, parents and educators. Despite the absence of formal L1 instruction, these programs will usually find ways to encourage students to develop bilingual and biliteracy skills and take pride in their cultural background. At a deep structure level these programs challenge coercive relations of power in similar ways to genuine bilingual programs, although their ability to promote full biliteracy skills is obviously more limited.

Thus, in the context of the present theoretical framework, the central issue in examining a particular program's effectiveness is the extent to which power is being generated in the interactions among educators, parents and students rather than whether the program is labelled "bilingual" or "English-only." However, it is important to analyze the arguments against bilingual education because they inadvertently reveal much about the true agenda within which they are embedded. Understanding this agenda is crucial for educators who are committed to creating contexts of empowerment in their classrooms and schools.

Most of the arguments against bilingual education reduce to the following: there is minimal evidence that bilingual education is effective in comparison to alternative programs, and English-only immersion programs represent a more promising alternative that is supported empirically by the results of Canadian French immersion research.

This line of argument was first articulated by Noel Epstein (1977) but its elaboration into a coherent position was carried out by Keith Baker and Adriana de Kanter (1981) in their detailed review of research evidence on bilingual education. Much of the initial skepticism regarding the effectiveness of bilingual education derived from the findings of the American Institutes for Research (AIR) report that transitional bilingual programs appeared to be no more effective than English-only programs in promoting academic development among bilingual students (Danoff et al., 1978). Claims of empirical support for English immersion programs have been made by Russell Gersten and John Woodward (1985a, 1985b). A monograph by Lloyd Dunn (1987), an article by Nathan Glazer (Glazer and Cummins, 1986), several articles in an edited volume by Gary Imhoff (1990), and Rosalie Pedalino Porter's book *Forked Tongue: The Politics of Bilingual Education* have all supported English immersion over bilingual education.

Early Critiques: Epstein and the AIR Report

The first serious educational challenges to the rationale for bilingual education came in 1977 with the publication of Noel Epstein's monograph *Language, Ethnicity and the Schools* and the AIR study on the impact of ESEA Title VII Spanish/English bilingual programs (Danoff et al., 1977, 1978). Epstein pointed out that research evidence in support of bilingual education was meagre and also that the rationale for bilingual education was by no means as clear-cut as advocates suggested. The success of French immersion programs in Canada, he argued, showed that "the language factor itself can neither account for nor solve the educational difficulties of these minority students" (1977, p. 59).

As is clear from previous chapters, Epstein's questioning of the "linguistic mismatch" rationale for bilingual education is clearly valid and appropriate. However, his report fails to adopt a theoretical perspective in that it does not consider the assumptions underlying alternative positions. Had he done this he would have seen that there is abundant evidence refuting the "maximum exposure" assumptions which he endorses implicitly in advocating experimentation with English immersion programs. Epstein also failed to consider the major differences in sociocultural context between French immersion programs for majority students in Canada and the situation of language minority students in the United States. However, as an initial critical inquiry into the relation between policy and research in the area of bilingual education, Epstein's monograph represents an intelligent, if flawed, critique. It raised important questions and challenged bilingual educators to clarify the rationale for bilingual education, which was not as self-evident as many had assumed.

Suspicions that the "real" purpose of bilingual education had more to do with promoting cultural pluralism and language maintenance received a boost when the AIR study reported that, according to teacher judgements, less than one-third of the students enrolled in bilingual classrooms were there because of their need for English instruction (although both Title VII [bilingual program] and non-Title VII Spanish-speaking students were functioning at approximately the 20th percentile on measures of English academic functioning). In addition, the results of comparative analyses showed that students in Title VII programs were doing no better academically than non-English background students in regular programs.

The AIR study has been criticized by numerous researchers (e.g. Gray, 1977; O'Malley, 1978; Swain, 1979). The major criticisms are that:

1. Data from effective and ineffective programs were aggregated with the result that negative results from programs experiencing serious implementation difficulties as a result of factors such as bilingual teacher unavailability, curriculum inadequacy, district lack of support, and so on, would have obscured any positive impact of high quality bilingual programs. For example, only half of the Title VII teachers in the study were proficient in English and Spanish, and only 26% had bilingual teaching credentials.

2. Related to this was the fact that the Title VII and non-Title VII treatments were not clearly separated in that many of the non-Title VII teachers and aides were bilingual (while many of the Title VII staff were not) and some of the students in non-Title VII programs had received bilingual education, although for a shorter period of time, on average, than Title VII students. These students may have been exited from bilingual programs on the basis of their English proficiency, which further confounds the comparison since these students are likely to be better language learners than those who were retained in the bilingual program. The treatments were defined on the basis of funding rather than instructional content and thus no inferences can be made about the impact of bilingual education since there are no data on the extent to which "bilingual education" was going on in the Title VII classrooms.

In short, the AIR study tells us nothing about the effects of bilingual education, except to point to large variation in the quality and outcomes of all programs for Latino/Latina students.

The Baker and de Kanter Report

A detailed review of the literature on "The Effectiveness of Bilingual Education" was undertaken by two staff members of the Office of Planning, Budget and Evaluation in the U.S. Department of Education and published in 1981. The major conclusions of this literature review were as follows:

- Schools *can* improve the achievement level of language-minority children through special programs.

- The case for the effectiveness of transitional bilingual education is so weak that exclusive reliance on this instructional method is clearly not justified… Therefore…each school district should decide what type of special program is most appropriate for its own setting.

- There is no justification for assuming that it is necessary to teach non language subjects in the child's native tongue in order for the language-minority child to make satisfactory progress in school…

- Immersion programs, which involve structured curriculums in English for both language and non language subject areas, show promising results and should be given more attention in program development. (de Kanter and Baker, *Education Times*, October 5, 1981)

There have been many critiques and rebuttals of the Baker/de Kanter report. It is sufficient to quote the review written by the American Psychological Association (1982) to indicate that the report's conclusions have been largely rejected by researchers, despite its impact in legitimating the Reagan administration's policy in regard to bilingual programs.

> The Department of Education draft report entitled "Effectiveness of Bilingual Education: A Review of the Literature" does NOT (emphasis original) support the conclusion that bilingual education is ineffective, inappropriate, or unnecessary. In fact, it does not even attempt to address such questions. In debates on bilingual education in which the issues are defined in such terms, the study can be ignored — because it is irrelevant…

> The scientific quality of the report is questionable. Inconsistencies are apparent in the application of the methodological standards utilized. The evaluation question addressed by the study was limited, and an arbitrary and narrow definition of 'acceptable data' was utilized. (pp. 8-9)

Similar assessments have been expressed in other critiques of the report (e.g. Willig, 1981/82). It is also worth noting that Willig's (1985) meta-analysis of essentially the same data as Baker and de Kanter (quoted in Chapter 5) reached a very different conclusion supportive of bilingual education.

The Baker/de Kanter report exemplifies well three strategies that Noam Chomsky (1987) has identified as central to the process of "manufacturing consent:" (a) limiting the framework of discourse; (b) denying/distorting empirical realities; and (c) ignoring logical contradictions.

The report limits the framework of discourse to "transitional bilingual education versus structured immersion" in the sense that all programs considered were categorized as one or the other of these options. Most North American researchers have been extremely critical of quick-exit transitional bilingual programs as much inferior to developmental or two-way bilingual immersion programs that aim to promote bilingual and biliteracy skills. Yet, this option does not exist within the framework of discourse established by Baker and de Kanter. Thus, none of the data can be interpreted as supportive of this option.

Baker and de Kanter also distort empirical realities as a result of their categorization of vastly different forms of bilingual education as "transitional bilingual education" (TBE). In fact, the "structured English immersion" program in McAllen, Texas (Peña-Hughes & Solís, 1980) that Baker and de Kanter describe as "promising" involved more L1-medium (Spanish) instruction (50-60 minutes a day) than a large number of so-called transitional bilingual programs in the United States. As Willig (1981/82) points out, the director of this program considered it a bilingual program.

A tendency to play games with labels as a way of denying empirical support for bilingual education is also evident in Baker and de Kanter's review of Legaretta's (1979) evaluation of a 50/50 Spanish-English morning/afternoon program. Baker and de Kanter acknowledge that this is one of the best designed research studies that they reviewed but suggest that the success of the program is more appropriately attributed to the fact that it is "an alternate immersion program" (1981, p. 15).

Finally, Baker and de Kanter ignore obvious logical inconsistencies in their interpretation of the research data. Virtually all the evaluation results reviewed in their report are consistent with the interdependence principle in that bilingual students instructed through their L1 for all or part of the school day performed at least as well academically in English as equivalent students who were instructed totally in English. These data refute the "time-on-task" or "maximum exposure" assumption upon which Baker and de Kanter base their call for structured English-only immersion. In extrapolating from the Canadian immersion data, they also fail to emphasize that L1 instruction is regarded by Canadian researchers and educators as a crucial component of immersion programs and that these programs are varieties of bilingual education, taught by bilingual teachers, and designed to promote full bilingualism. [1]

Gersten and Woodward: A Case for Structured Immersion

Gersten and Woodward (1985a) claim to have found empirical evidence that structured immersion that uses the "direct instruction model" (i.e. DISTAR) produces large academic gains among bilingual students. Their initial discussion of the rationale for immersion programs reveals a very surprising ignorance of the Canadian research upon which they base their arguments. For example, they note the fact that Baker and de Kanter:

called public attention to the promising research findings from Canada on *structured immersion*. With structured immersion, all instruction is done in the commonly used language of the school (English in the U.S., French in Canada)...Difficult new words are pre-taught, sometimes using the child's native language...Santiago, in the March 2, 1983, *Education Week*, said that 'the immersion method has only been tried with middle class children.' His statement is not accurate; the bulk of the Canadian research was with low-income students. (1985, p. 75-76)

There are many inaccuracies here. First, in French immersion programs, children's L1 (English) is usually introduced about grade 2 or 3 and its use increased as children go up the grades so that by grade 5 about half the instructional time is spent through English. Thus to say that all instruction is done in French is simply wrong.

Second, French immersion programs are based explicitly on the premise that language is acquired through *use*. Vocabulary is rarely, if ever, pre-taught.

Third, although researchers have argued that French immersion programs are appropriate for low-income students and should not be restricted only to middle-class children (e.g. Genesee, 1987, Cummins, 1984, Swain and Lapkin, 1982), the vast majority of children in French immersion programs come from middle-class backgrounds and very little research data are available on the performance of working-class children in these programs. [2]

Gersten and Woodward are no more convincing in their presentation of empirical data supportive of structured immersion. They describe results of two programs that used DISTAR with bilingual students, one group of Spanish-speaking background near the Mexican border in Texas (Uvalde), and the other predominantly of Asian origin in California (Pacific City). In the Uvalde evaluation no comparison group was available and thus the evaluation data would be dismissed according to the criteria set up by Baker and de Kanter (Santiago, 1985). When tested at the end of grade 3, after three years of DISTAR, the children were reported to be performing close to national norms on the language (i.e. usage, tense, punctuation, etc.) and math subtests of the Metropolitan Achievement Test. However, scores on the reading comprehension subtest were considerably lower, at the 34th percentile, just slightly above the median district score in previous years (30th percentile). After leaving the program, students' reading comprehension scores dropped to the 15th and 16th percentile in grades 5 and 6 (Becker & Gersten, 1982; Krashen, 1991a). Krashen (1991a, p. 8) points out that while "this performance was better than a comparison group, it is still dismal. Children at this grade level who have had proper bilingual education do much better" (Krashen & Biber, 1988).

Gersten (1985) reports longitudinal data from the Pacific City program that suggests better progress in English in the early grades for bilingual students in a DISTAR-based immersion program than for students in a transitional bilingual program. However, the numbers of students involved in this evaluation were extremely small; the first cohort involved only 12 immersion program students and nine bilingual program students while the second involved only 16 and seven in each group. These numbers scarcely constitute an adequate sample upon which to base national educational policy. A more adequate assessment of structured immersion can be found in the Ramírez report. There was little evidence in this large-scale investigation that students in structured immersion would ever catch up to grade expectations. This is in contrast to the pattern observed for students in late-exit programs (Ramírez, 1992).

Glazer: Stirring the Melting Pot

Nathan Glazer's views on bilingual education were outlined in a journal called *Equity and Choice* which asked both him and me to respond to a series of questions on bilingual education (Glazer and Cummins, 1985). While admitting a role for "taking cognizance of native language, using it for part of the school day [and] continuing it after transition to English for purposes of maintaining facility," he expresses concern that some bilingual programs are "keeping children in classes conducted primarily in their native language as long as possible" (p. 47).

In response to a question on the best methodology for teaching English as a second language, Glazer responded as follows:

"I don't think (probably) there is one 'best' way. But all our experience shows that the most extended and steady exposure to the spoken language is the best way of learning any language" (1985, p. 48).

Glazer clearly had not read the large body of research that refutes the "maximum exposure" assumption upon which he based this response. There is a certain arrogance in regarding one's uninformed personal opinion as more relevant to policy decisions affecting the lives of millions of children than the findings of empirical research.

Glazer's answer to the subsequent question regarding how long it takes children to achieve sufficient proficiency in English to succeed academically in English instructional contexts reveals a similar ignorance of the research. This did not stop him from articulating his opinion: "How long? It depends. But one year of intensive immersion seems to be enough to permit most children to transfer to English-language classes" (p. 48). In fact, the data show that 5-10 years is usually required for ESL students to attain grade-appropriate levels in English cognitive/academic skills, although fluent conversational skills may develop considerably sooner (Collier, 1987, 1992; Cummins, 1981b; Klesmer, 1994; Ramírez, 1992).

Like many of the other opponents of bilingual education, Glazer's primary concern is with the dangers of creating a distinctive Latino/Latina enclave within American society (1985, p. 51). These fears, legitimate or not, in no way justify spreading disinformation about bilingual education.

Dunn: "Teachers are not Miracle Workers"

Some of Dunn's (1987) naive and patronizing views on the genetic inferiority of Mexican American and Puerto Rican students and their alleged lack of effort on behalf of their children have been discussed in Chapter 3. Here we are concerned with his views on bilingual education and his proposal for English immersion programs "with supplemental services" as the most appropriate policy option for Puerto Rican and Mexican American students. He argues that because they suffer from a "lack of intellectual, scholastic, and language aptitude...it is clear that these children are not, as a group, able to cope with the confusion of two languages in the regular grades" (p. 76). Dunn does acknowledge the research data "on the need to develop proficiency in one's native language before undertaking English as a second language" (p. 73) and thus suggests that some bilingual children might not be ready for English immersion until they are beyond 6 years of age. However, his main thrust is to argue against L1 promotion on the grounds that "20 years of experimentation with so-called 'bilingual education' has not worked well, and will not, even with further tinkering, and therefore...it is time to abandon this movement in favor of alternate procedures that are likely to be more effective" (p. 66).

What evidence does Dunn cite to dismiss bilingual education in favor of English immersion?

He refers to the AIR (1977) and Baker and de Kanter (1981) reports as indicating lack of impact of bilingual education. Dunn notes Willig's (1981/82) documentation of "serious problems" with these two reports but argues that "it seems safe to conclude that their conclusion is sound" (p. 70). He suggests that the conclusion of these reports should come as no surprise since "the scholastic ability of most Puerto Rican and Mexican American children is too limited to succeed well in two languages and to handle switching from one to the other efficiently" (p. 70). The only "evidence" presented for English immersion as an alternative is his own experience in teaching immigrant students in western Canada in the 1930's.

Dunn does acknowledge the existence of what he terms the *Spanish Bilingual-Bicultural Maintenance Approach*, i.e. developmental or two-way bilingual immersion programs. As discussed above, these programs involve immersing bilingual students in their L1 in the early grades in order to develop a strong conceptual foundation that will provide a basis for acquiring academic skills in English. Dunn chooses to ignore the considerable research on these programs (reviewed for example in Cummins, 1984), instead dismissing them as follows:

> Under the 'maintenance theory' (or excuse), in extreme cases, some Mexican American pupils are taught almost exclusively in Spanish by Mexican American activist teachers, who repeatedly point out to the pupils that they are an oppressed group, and therefore obligated to assist in social change. With this focus, it is not surprising that these children are not prepared to switch over to English at the end of elementary school, and have not adequately mastered the regular elementary school subject matter. (p. 67)

Once again, we see an abdication of responsibility to consider the research data on bilingual education. The extremism of Dunn's rhetoric, combined with his racist perspective on the genetic inferiority of Latinos/Latinas, is ironic in light of his statements that those who believe that IQ tests are biased are manifesting an "emotional and irrational defense reaction" (p. 62) and those who oppose English immersion are demonstrating "irrational extremism" (p. 71).

Forked Tongue: Double-Talk on Bilingual Education

Rosalie Pedalino Porter served as Director of Bilingual and English-as-a-Second-Language programs in Newton, Massachusetts and the first two chapters of her book describe what she terms the Newton district's "struggle against bureaucratic vindictiveness" in its attempts to institute an alternative program that involved minimal bilingual instruction. What is communicated to the reader in these chapters is a strong sense of outrage and bitterness against the "self-serving" "defensiveness and paranoia of the bilingual education establishment" (p. 56). According to Porter, the continued implementation of bilingual programs is a function not of research on their effectiveness but of "the impulse for preserving jobs and budgets for the bilingual establishment" (p. 73).

Porter maintains, however, that she is not in any way opposed to bilingualism as such; in fact she singles out Canada "for its innovative language-education approach that has allowed hundreds of thousands of children to become functional bilinguals, with fluency in two languages for both social and academic purposes" (p. 86). In the case of second language learners of English, however, she insists on maximizing the time spent "on task" learning English.

Porter's attack on bilingual education is full of inaccuracies and contradictions. While she insists that exposure to English is a decisive factor in determining academic success for bilingual students, she nevertheless endorses two-way bilingual programs that will normally have far less exposure to English than either English immersion or transitional bilingual education. She suggests, for example, that "two-way programs are the best opportunity for families that are seriously committed to genuine bilingualism for their children" (p. 156) but she never addresses the fact that the documented academic success of Spanish-speaking students in such programs, despite reduced exposure to English, refutes her cherished "time-on-task" principle. [3]

She also appears to believe that typical transitional bilingual programs in the United States involve almost exclusive L1 instruction in the early grades. She suggests, for example, that "the teaching of all subjects in the native language of the child for the first few years of schooling has become a non-negotiable condition for the TBE [transitional bilingual education] framework" (p. 71). In fact, large-scale studies have shown that in typical transitional bilingual education programs only about 25% of instructional time is spent through the medium of L1 (e.g. Tikunoff, 1983). Teachers typically switch to L1 for clarification of instruction. In many cases the instructional time devoted to L1 is minimal; for example, in a longitudinal study of instructional practices in bilingual classes involving Chinese- and Spanish-background students, Wong Fillmore, Ammon, McLaughlin & Ammon (1985) reported that the L1 of students was used for no more than 10% of the instruction (see Wong Fillmore and Valadez [1986] for a detailed review of research on time allocation in bilingual classes).

The level of scholarship in Porter's book can be seen most clearly in her discussion of Canadian French immersion programs. I note some relatively inconsequential inaccuracies before discussing the misuse of the French immersion data to argue for English immersion in the United States:

- In the first sentence under the heading of "The French Immersion Experiment" Porter claims that "the Canadian Ministry of Education generously supported the establishment of various experimental programs for English-speaking children to learn French" (p. 108-109). In fact, there is no "Canadian Ministry of Education" since education is a provincial responsibility.

- Two sentences later, she suggests that "over 100,000 children have participated over the past seventeen years." This is a gross underestimate since over the past few years the number of students enrolled in French immersion at any one time has been close to 300,000 and considerably more than that, in total, have participated since the inception of the program (in the mid-sixties).

- Porter describes "Inuit" as a language that does not have a written symbol system (p. 66). In fact, Inuktitut is the language of the Inuit (Eskimos) and a syllabic writing system has been in use for more than 100 years.

Many more inaccuracies in Porter's book are documented by Baker (1992a), Cummins (1991a) and Krashen (1991a, 1991b). At a more consequential level, Porter, like Gersten and Woodward, and Rossell, appears to believe that Canadian French immersion programs serve predominantly working-class students. Furthermore, she makes the bizarre suggestion that Canadian researchers have systematically concealed this "fact" in order to further their own career advancement:

> "The linguists, educators, and researchers whose career advancement is linked to the success of immersion education argue protectively that this program is only appropriate for middle-class children who, secure in their majority language and status, are learning a less-valued language. They have clung to this bias despite the fact that the large percentage of children in the Canadian immersion programs are from low-income working-class families" (p. 117).

It is significant, but not surprising, that there is no citation to back up this "fact." As noted above, the vast majority of students in French immersion programs continue to come from middle-class families.

The importance to Porter's argument of insisting that most students in French immersion programs are from low-income working-class backgrounds is that she wants to be able to generalize the French immersion results directly to the United States context and argue that low-income bilingual students should be provided with English immersion. She fails to realize that the French immersion programs are bilingual programs involving two languages of instruction, taught by bilingual teachers with the goal of promoting bilingualism, whereas English immersion programs in the United States are usually conceived as monolingual programs, taught by monolingual teachers with the goal of producing monolingualism.

In summary, Porter's account of the bilingual education data in the United States and elsewhere is confused to the point of incoherence. While criticizing transitional bilingual education programs on the grounds that they reduce the amount of exposure to English, she nevertheless endorses two-way bilingual programs that reduce the amount of exposure to English to a considerably greater extent. She appears to believe that most children in Canadian French immersion programs are from working-class backgrounds despite the virtual absence of low-income inner-city working-class students in these programs. [4]

Rossell: Deconstructing Structured Immersion

Christine Rossell's (1990, 1992; Rossell & Ross, 1986) analyses of the bilingual education data are similar to those of Porter, and Gersten and Woodward, insofar as she bases much of her argument for structured immersion on the success of French immersion programs in Canada. For example, Rossell and Ross claim that immersion was more effective than bilingual education in six studies, four of which were Canadian immersion studies. One of the U.S. studies (Gersten, 1985) has been considered above and the other was Peña-Hughes and Solís' (1980) report on the McAllen, Texas, program which included 50-60 minutes of Spanish instruction per day, more than most early-exit transitional programs (see Krashen, 1991; Willig, 1981/82).

Rossell's (1990) interpretation of the French immersion data is only slightly more sophisticated than Porter's or Gersten and Woodward's and the same counter-arguments apply. The success of bilingual programs, taught by bilingual teachers, intended to develop bilingualism should provide little comfort for those who endorse monolingual programs, taught by monolingual teachers, intended to develop monolingualism.

Rossell (1990), like other opponents of bilingual education, originally endorsed the "time-on-task" principle as the central theoretical construct underlying her call for structured immersion. She is more forthright, however, than Porter (1993) in admitting that the Ramírez report findings refute this principle: "Large deficits in English language instruction over several grades apparently make little or no difference in a student's achievement" (1992, p. 183). She argues also that the report provides no support for the facilitative effect of primary language instruction. [5]

Richard Rodriguez: Hunger of Memory

Richard Rodriguez' autobiography, *Hunger of Memory* exerted a strong negative impact on support for bilingual education after it appeared in 1982. Rodriguez based his opposition not on any form of empirical evidence or scientific logic but on a logic woven from the pain of his own experience. The trauma which he recounts of passing from the private world of warm intimate sounds to the cold public world of English was discussed briefly in Chapter 6. Rodriguez' argument against bilingual education is that it holds out a romantic but unrealistic promise of an easier passage from private to public worlds, a passage that would avoid sacrificing the intimacy and warmth of the private for the cold utility and necessity of the public.

Applying cold scientific criteria to this argument, it is clear that there is no evidence to support the position advocated by Rodriguez. The enormous legacy of school failure among Spanish-speaking children illustrates the difficulty of this passage from private to public about which he writes so eloquently. Extrapolation from his own (N=1) successful emergence from the trauma of early schooling to generalized statements about program alternatives clearly has no scientific credibility. Also, the growing evidence, documented in previous chapters, that bilingual children's prospects for academic success are greatly enhanced when their cultural identity is validated rather than eradicated cannot lightly be dismissed.

I find Rodriguez' account interesting, however, because of the insights he provides about the psychology of dominant-subordinated relationships within American society. Some of these insights summarized in an essay on bilingual education published in *The New York Times* (November 10, 1985, p. 83) are worth quoting in detail:

> The official drone over bilingual education is conducted by educationists with numbers and charts. Because bilingual education was never simply a matter of pedagogy, it is too much to expect educators to resolve the matter. Proclamations concerning bilingual education are weighted at bottom with Hispanic political grievances and, too, with middle-class romanticism…

> …in private, Hispanics argue with me about bilingual education and every time it comes down to memory. Everyone remembers going to that grammar school where students were slapped for speaking Spanish. Childhood memory is offered as parable; the memory is meant to compress the gringo's long history of offenses against Spanish, Hispanic culture, Hispanics…Bilingualism becomes a way of exacting from gringos a grudging admission of contrition — for the 19th century theft of the Southwest, the relegation of Spanish to a foreign tongue, the injustice of history…

> The child's difficulty [in language acquisition] will turn out to be psychological more than linguistic because what he gives up are symbols of home. I was that child! I faced the stranger's English with pain and guilt and fear. Baptized to English in school, at first I felt myself drowning — the ugly sounds forced down my throat — until slowly, slowly…suddenly the conviction took: English was my language to use.

> Bilingual enthusiasts bespeak an easier world. They seek a linguistic solution to a social dilemma. They seem to want to believe that there is an easier way for the child to balance private and public, in order to believe that there is some easy way for themselves…The debate is going to continue. The bilingual establishment is now inside the door. Jobs are at stake. Politicians can only count heads; growing numbers of Hispanics will insure the compliance of politicians.

Publicly we will continue the fiction. We will solemnly address the issue as an educational question, a matter of pedagogy. But privately, Hispanics will still seek from bilingual education an admission from the gringo that Spanish has value and presence. Hispanics of middle class will continue to seek the romantic assurance of separateness. Experts will argue. Dark-eyed children will sit in the classroom. Mute" (1985, p. 63).

Rodriguez provides here a painfully clear depiction of the price exacted for participation in mainstream institutions: namely the eradication of children's home language and culture and the internalization of shame. Rodriguez also correctly, I believe, identifies the central issues as sociopolitical, rather than educational in a narrow sense. He describes the desire of Latinos/Latinas to reverse the historical pattern of subjugation, and their use of bilingual education as a wedge to attain this goal. The resistance by the dominant society to allowing subordinated minorities "inside the door" is also clearly implied in Rodriguez' account. In short, he provides an experiential account of dominant-subordinated power relationships and their consequences for children in the early years of schooling that fits closely with that offered, from a very different perspective, in the present analysis.

Where my perspective differs from that of Rodriguez is that I believe that subordinated groups' use both of bilingual education and constitutional provisions for educational equity as a wedge to get "inside the door" is an appropriate and useful strategy, whereas he appears to question it, almost in a fatalistic way, on the grounds that the power structure is so well entrenched that it is a romantic dream to believe that the private and public worlds can be productively merged without destruction of the private.

Also, unlike Rodriguez (apparently), I also believe that there is a role for empirical evidence in discussions of educational policy. Thus, I find convincing evidence (including Rodriguez' own biographical account) that the mute Latino/Latina child is considerably more likely to be found in English-only or structured immersion classes ("drowning — the ugly sounds forced down my throat") than in classes where the child's language and culture are validated, classes to which the parents have access, and where children's experiences are amplified through collaborative critical inquiry.

Conclusion

It is difficult to avoid the conclusion that there is a sociopolitical agenda at work in the opposition of academic critics to bilingual education. Several of those cited in this chapter demonstrate huge gaps in their knowledge of research about bilingual education (e.g. Dunn, Gersten/Woodward, Glazer, Porter). Gersten and Woodward's claim that four out of five studies carried out on French immersion programs involved working-class students illustrates this pattern, as does Porter's accusation that Canadian researchers have conspired to hide this reality from the unsuspecting public.

Others insist on averting their eyes from the outcomes of bilingual programs that work (e.g. developmental and two-way bilingual immersion programs) on the basis of convenient but questionable methodological criteria (e.g. Baker/de Kanter, Rossell). For example, Rosier and Holm's case study of the Navajo-English bilingual program at Rock Point may not have had an adequate control group by strict psychometric criteria, but it did show significant increases in English academic achievement in comparison to both pre-bilingual program results and other schools in the Navajo reservation. As an individual case, it also refuted the "time-on-task" principle insofar as less instruction through English was associated with greater English achievement, the opposite of what this principle would have predicted. The accumulation of individual cases either supporting or rejecting particular theoretical propositions has clear relevance for policy decisions. As noted earlier, the results of virtually every bilingual program ever evaluated are consistent with the interdependence principle and inconsistent with the "time-on-task" or "maximum exposure" principle. In order to maintain their credibility, it thus becomes necessary for opponents of bilingual education to avert their eyes from these data. Limiting the framework of discourse to transitional bilingual education versus structured immersion programs is one effective strategy for accomplishing this goal.

Related to this is the aversion to theory that characterizes opposition to bilingual education. The interdependence principle was formulated and published as a hypothesis in 1978. I have yet to see a serious critical examination or attempt at refutation of this principle by opponents of bilingual education. The reasons are obvious. A focus on theory would immediately reveal the vulnerability of the "time-on-task" principle since it is refuted by virtually all the research data. Admission that this principle is without foundation was forthcoming from Rossell (1992) only when she was invited to contribute to a volume specifically focused on the Ramírez report data. [6]

In view of the overwhelming evidence against the "time-on-task" assumption, it is legitimate to inquire why certain academics have failed to question this assumption and what function their silence serves. In other words, the lack of both empirical support and theoretical coherence in arguments against bilingual education suggests that it is these arguments themselves that require explanation.

Although spurious, arguments about the self-evident validity of intensive exposure to English for bilingual students have served to undermine many bilingual programs, leading to the implementation of relatively ineffective "quick-exit" models rather than the considerably more effective programs aimed at biliteracy. Because such quick-exit programs seldom require or encourage any personal or collective role redefinitions on the part of educators, subtle forms of discrimination in many schools have been preserved (e.g. low expectations). In fact, discriminatory structures have probably been preserved even more effectively because there is the appearance of change to meet "the needs" of bilingual students. The hysterical/paranoid reaction that even these minimal changes evoke from groups such as *U.S. English* reinforces the illusion that real educational change has occurred.

As Rodriguez (1985) notes from a different perspective, to the extent that typical transitional bilingual education programs have brought about any real change, it has been less in the sphere of promoting educational equity than in letting subordinated groups "inside the door" and promoting a consciousness among culturally diverse communities of issues related to equity and power. The issue of bilingual education has become symbolic of past injustice and current institutionalized racism.

Within this context, the psychoeducational concerns of policy-makers, educators and academics about bilingual education hindering the acquisition of English simply mask the more pressing concern that bilingual education programs have increased the status and power of the Spanish-speaking minority at a time when demographic changes are already posing a threat to the dominance of the Euro-American majority in several parts of the country. Thus, it becomes important to eliminate these programs in order to preserve the current power structure (see, for example, John Tanton's memorandum quoted in Chapter 2, Note 6).

Academic opponents of bilingual education have played an important role in this process. They have attempted to legitimate the eradication of all forms of bilingual education by arguing that these programs hinder students' learning of English and academic progress. In this way, the status quo (submersion under the guise of structured immersion) can be reinstated while preserving the myth that bilingual students' needs are being met.

If, as I have suggested, many of those who vehemently oppose bilingual education are more concerned with preserving the current power structure, with its very unequal distribution of status and resources, than with what is in the best interests of bilingual children, then the escalation of anti-bilingual rhetoric in recent years is totally predictable. The more empirical evidence is produced that certain types of bilingual programs result in personal and academic growth among bilingual students, the more vehement will be the denial of this evidence and the rejection of these programs by the socially powerful establishment.

The last chapter attempts to reframe the issues, arguing that far from being a threat to the coherence of society, effective bilingual programs can contribute significantly to challenging coercive relations of power that constitute the real threat to future generations.

Endnotes to Chapter 8

1. Baker (1992a, 1992b) has adopted a more favorable stance on the effectiveness of bilingual education in recent years. However, he claims that these programs are superior to all-English programs only in the early stages of learning English. He rejects both the "time-on-task" theory and the "facilitation" theory (which he attributes to me although I have never used the term) arguing instead for a theory based on the "mental fatigue" that afflicts learners totally immersed in an L2 environment. Bilingual programs work in the early stages of learning because they introduce much needed periods of rest from constant exposure to the new language. In support of this argument he cites the findings of the Ramírez report and a research study conducted by Burkheimer et al. (1990).

   While Baker's thesis that L1 instruction in the early grades may reduce the stress and fatigue that second language learners are likely to experience is plausible, it appears overly simplistic by itself to account for the complexity of the outcomes of different types of bilingual programs. It essentially denies the reality of cross-lingual conceptual transfer (interdependence) and the importance of sociocultural and sociopolitical factors. It would appear to have difficulty explaining the excellent academic performance of both language majority and minority students in two-way bilingual immersion programs in which 90% of initial instruction is through the minority language (e.g. Dolson & Lindholm, 1995; Thomas & Collier, 1995).

2. Gersten and Woodward (1985b) reiterated their claim that Canadian immersion programs involved predominantly working-class students in their response to Santiago's (1985) rebuttal of their original article, stating that:

there were four studies other than the St. Lambert study, all of which involved children from working-class families. The results of structured immersion with these students were comparable to those found with the middle-class children in the St. Lambert study (1985b, p. 83).

They seem to believe that only five studies of French immersion were carried out in Canada (up to 1985), and four of these involved working-class students. In fact, Swain and Lapkin's (1982) bibliography in their book on immersion contains more than 500 citations, most of these empirical studies.

3. In contrast to Porter's perspective, most bilingual education advocates argue that transitional bilingual education programs have had mixed results because many have failed to provide an adequate L1 conceptual foundation in the early grades as a result of insufficient time devoted to L1 promotion. By contrast, two-way bilingual immersion programs that do involve intensive L1 instruction in the early grades have been remarkably successful. For example, the two-way program implemented in the San Diego City Schools which had 30 minutes of English in grades K-1 and 60 minutes in grades 2-3 reported the following results:

> …though native-Spanish-speaking project students are not exposed to English reading and writing as early as they would be in the regular English-only instructional program, they eventually acquire English language skills which are above the norm for students in regular English-only instructional programs and, in addition, develop their native-language skills (San Diego City Schools, 1982, p. 183).

Dolson and Lindholm (1995) present longitudinal evaluation data from the River Glen two-way bilingual immersion program in San Jose, California. The program involved 90% Spanish instruction in grades K and 1, 80% in grades 2 and 3, and 50% in grades 4 through 5. Thirty percent of instruction in middle school (grades 6 through 8) was through Spanish. Almost two-thirds of the school population is low-income, based on participation in the Free School Lunch program, and 72% are of Latino/Latina origin. Performance of the Latino/Latina students in grades K though 5 was compared to a Spanish-speaking comparison group in a high quality late-exit transitional program, and a sample of middle class English speaking grades 1-4 students served as a comparison group for the English L1 students.

With respect to conversational skills development, a large majority (more than 90%) of the grades 3-5 Spanish-speaking students were rated as fluent in English in spite of the limited quantity of English instruction in the school day. Almost 80% of the English-speaking students were rated as fluent in Spanish by grade 5. All students made much better than average progress in content areas such as science, math, and social studies taught in Spanish. Spanish reading and language scores for both groups were also extremely high (greater than 95th percentile at grade 5). Dolson and Lindholm summarize the results in English reading as follows:

> In English reading achievement by third grade, English-speaking students scored average to above average. By fifth grade, 85% of the English speakers were scoring above the 50th percentile, and over 50% of the students above

the 75th percentile. The English-speaking students' performance was also slightly higher than English-speaking counterparts in the regular English-only instructional program. Among the Spanish speakers, performance in English reading increased steadily across the grade levels. However, their reading achievement in English did not approach average until seventh grade... Comparisons of the Spanish-speaking two-way bilingual immersion students with Spanish-speaking students in a high quality transitional bilingual education program in the district indicated that the bilingual immersion students scored higher in every area: Spanish reading, language, and mathematics, and English reading and mathematics... In analyses of the students' cross-cultural attitudes, we find that the students have very positive attitudes toward speakers of other languages, toward the second language, and toward students who are different from them. (1995, p. 91-92)

4. The debate on Porter's book took an unexpected turn when Keith Baker (formerly a strong opponent of bilingual education) delivered a scathing critique in the pages of *TESOL Quarterly*. Among his comments after reviewing a host of inaccuracies and misrepresentations in Porter's book:

> Porter violated the most basic trust between reader and author of scholarly works. Porter's level of scholarship falls far short of the most minimal standards of acceptable research. Porter's unmerited scholarly pretensions led to large numbers of people on the far right and in the English-only movement who share Porter's biases giving the book wide publicity as evidence of both the ineffectiveness and political corruption of the bilingual education movement. Neither conclusion is justified... My view is that the research clearly shows bilingual education programs are superior to all-English programs, such as those advocated by Porter, in the early stages of learning English, but I still would not say that a federal mandate is justified. (1992a, pp. 401-402)

Porter (1993), in response, cited Baker's "inexplicable reverses" and "sudden about face" and accused him of character assassination. The vehemence of this exchange clearly reflects a personal as well as an academic conflict. Keith Baker was the first director of READ (the Institute for Research in English Acquisition and Development), which is largely funded by the English Only movement (Crawford, 1995, p. 75). Porter succeeded him in this position.

5. Rossell (1990) analyzes considerable amounts of data from the Berkeley Unified School District comparing the results to outcomes in Fremont and San Jose. She claims to find no effect for participation in a bilingual program. Most of these analyses are uninterpretable because of uncontrolled differences across the comparison groups. The reader is referred to Krashen's (1991) review of these analyses which, he claims, indicate some positive findings related to participation in bilingual programs:

In another analysis Rossell compared California Test of Basic Skills (CTBS) scores for bilingual and ESL pull-out students after "reclassification." Rossell concluded that these data show no difference between the two groups. For each subtest of the CTBS, however, the regression coefficient for participation in bilingual education was positive, and in the case of math, it reached the .05 level for a two-tailed test, which Rossell did not indicate. (Krashen, 1991, p. 4)

One other researcher, Herbert Walberg, has expounded on the inappropriateness of bilingual education along much the same lines as other opponents considered in this chapter. He suggests that socioeconomic factors can explain the poor school performance of bilingual students and that second language acquisition research would suggest that these students should receive maximum exposure to English:

For many immigrant children who are not proficient in English, the problems of second-language and academic learning are more acute largely because they come from deprived socioeconomic backgrounds. More than others, these children need maximum exposure to English in school in order to learn it, because they might be deprived of such exposure at home and in their neighborhoods. Because bilingual education deters the very factors that promote English mastery and other academic accomplishments, it can hardly be held out as their hope. (1990, p. 159)

I would respond by suggesting that Walberg look at and try to explain the outcomes of two-way bilingual programs such as the Dual Language Program in Manhattan's District 3 (Morison, 1990 — see Chapter 7) or the San Jose two-way bilingual immersion program evaluated by Dolson and Lindholm (1995, note 3 above). Neither low-income status nor significantly reduced exposure to English instruction inhibited academic achievement in English among these students.

6. Opponents of bilingual education have typically either ignored the research evidence or considered it only in terms of questions that *logically* cannot be answered. For example, the central question of whether bilingual education is effective assumes that "bilingual education" can reasonably be thought of as one phenomenon and also that we have a clear understanding of what "effectiveness" implies.

Neither of these conditions is met. Hence the issues become mystified with the result that opponents of bilingual education can claim that the research evidence is mixed or insufficient for policy decisions. For example, it is clear that there are a large variety of bilingual education program models, and, within models, pedagogical practices and student populations vary enormously. Thus, to aggregate all this variation under the rubric "transitional bilingual education" with no theory for disentangling the effects of program variation is to ensure that there will be so much noise in the data that virtually no conclusions regarding "effectiveness" will be possible.

The problem is compounded by the absence of any theory in most of the evaluations and reviews regarding the meaning of "effectiveness," specifically the expectations or predictions regarding what different types of bilingual program should achieve and how long they should take to do it. For example, if the theory or expectation (implicit or explicit) of how a bilingual program should work dictates that students should be capable of transferring to an English-only program within a year, then a bilingual program that does not achieve this goal is ineffective. On the other hand, the theory might specify that it can take most of the elementary school years for bilingual students to deepen their academic knowledge of both L1 and English in order to transfer successfully to an all-English program. Within the context of this latter theoretical prediction, the "effectiveness" of transitional bilingual programs could not be adequately assessed until students had completed most of their elementary schooling in the program.

Chapter 9
Babel Babble: Reframing the Discourse of Diversity

Literacy is dangerous and has always been so regarded. It naturally breaks down barriers of time, space, and culture. It threatens one's original identity by broadening it through vicarious experiencing and the incorporation of somebody *else's* hearth and ethos. So we feel profoundly ambiguous about literacy. Looking at it as a means of transmitting our culture to our children, we give it priority in education, but recognizing the threat of its backfiring we make it so tiresome and personally unrewarding that youngsters won't want to do it on their own, which is of course when it becomes dangerous... The net effect of this ambivalence is to give literacy with one hand and take it back with the other, in keeping with our contradictory wish for youngsters to learn to think but only about what we already have in mind for them (James Moffett, 1989, p. 85).

Genuine critical literacy threatens established systems of privilege and resource distribution because it reduces the potency of indoctrination and disinformation. Critical literacy enables us to read between the lines, to look skeptically at apparently benign and plausible surface structures, to analyze claims in relation to empirical data, and to question whose interests are served by particular forms of communication.

Many social, cultural, and religious institutions throughout the world tend to be wary of both critical literacy and cultural diversity because they bring other perspectives into mind. At issue is the question of whether being willing to look at current issues and historical events from the perspective of the Other will undermine or enrich our original perceptions. North American academics and policy-makers who argue stridently against multicultural and bilingual education view cultural diversity as the enemy within and want to minimize what they see as its destructive effects on the collective psyche of the nation. They want to ensure that students remain within predetermined cultural and intellectual boundaries. They want to retain control of what can be thought as a means of ensuring the smooth functioning of a democratic society in the service of the current power structure. Their dilemma, of course, is that the economic and diplomatic realities of our interdependent global society in the 21st century demand enormous critical literacy and problem-solving abilities and the constant crossing of cultural and linguistic boundaries.

In this final chapter, I suggest that the enemy within is neither cultural diversity nor critical literacy but a politics of greed and exploitation that is willing to jeopardize not only the lives of individual children but also the coherence of entire societies for its own coercive ends. Core notions that define our societies, such as "liberty and justice for all," have given way to policies that are promoting increased economic polarization and marginalization. The chapter analyzes how coercive relations of power operate to manufacture consent for programs and policies that are not for "the common good" nor in the best interests of the society as a whole. The scapegoating of immigrants and cultural diversity since the late 1980s has reignited *Us versus Them* divisions and fears in order to obscure and distract attention from the increasingly obvious redistribution of wealth in North American societies. Indoctrination and disinformation are the tools whereby consent is manufactured for this process.

How can disinformation be identified? As outlined in the previous chapter, disinformation is achieved by distorting empirical data, limiting the framework of discourse, and ignoring logical contradictions (Chomsky, 1987). It can be identified by examining the empirical data. In the debate on the merits or otherwise of bilingual education, the evidence for disinformation is very clear. For example, on the surface, the claim that bilingual children need English-only instruction to maximize time-on-task appears plausible and well-intentioned. But when this claim is analyzed against the empirical data, it immediately falls apart. There is no evidence in the United States or elsewhere that less instructional time through the majority language reduces students' achievement in that language. If bilingual education were harmful, why would elite groups around the world demand it for their children? At this point, there is overwhelming evidence that the best prospects for academic enrichment of all children are pro-vided in programs, such as two-way bilingual immersion programs, that aim to develop biliteracy rather than just literacy in one language.

(3) Similarly, claims that "bilingualism shuts doors" (Schlesinger) or "causes personal problems for the individual and society" (Gingrich) are belied by the glossy full page Berlitz advertisements for language courses that have been in virtually every airline magazine I have read during the past five years. The alleged problems of bilingualism for society are also belied by the fact that "the Central Intelligence Agency now has difficulty meeting its needs for critical language skills, even in commonly taught languages such as Spanish" (The Stanford Working Group on Federal Programs for Limited-English-Proficient Students, 1993, p. 12). A more appropriate inference from the data would be that American society suffers from a lack of bilingualism rather than an excess. Despite the enormous potential linguistic resources of the United States, the situation has changed little since The President's Commission on Foreign Language and International Studies pointed out that "Americans' scandalous incompetence in foreign languages" "diminishes our capabilities in diplomacy, in foreign trade, and in citizen comprehension of the world in which we live and compete" (1980, p. 12).

(4) A process of disinformation is also evident in the attempt to invoke Canadian French immersion programs as research support for English-only immersion in the United States. The extraordinary ignorance of these programs shown by many academics who oppose bilingual education (e.g. the claim that no more than five empirical studies of French immersion have been carried out and four of these involved low-income children) is matched only by their arro-gance in posing as experts without having read even a fraction of the relevant research. If not an attempt at disinformation, how can we explain arguments for monolingual English-only education based on the success of bilingual pro-grams, whose goal is bilingualism and biliteracy, and which are taught by bilin-gual teachers?

I suggested in the previous chapter that these patently flawed arguments serve to reinforce a coercive power structure that historically has denied sub-ordinated communities full access to societal resources. In this chapter, I try to place the xenophobic discourse against cultural diversity into the larger con-text of which it is a part. I argue that the scapegoating of immigrants and the demonization of bilingual education is part of an exercise to divert public atten-tion away from the massive transfer of wealth from middle-class and poor to the rich that took place in the United States during the 1980s and continues to this day. I also suggest that coercive relations of power have reached a point of diminishing returns, even for those socially advantaged groups whose interests they are intended to serve. The fiscal and social costs of maintaining the current structure of privilege and resource distribution far outstrip the costs that would be involved in shifting to more collaborative relations of power.

Why should educators care about this larger social reality? How is it relevant to the task of teaching English and academic skills to bilingual students?

In the first place, we all have a vested interest in the future of our society, with respect to both its economic health and social cohesion. Our incomes and quality of life (and those of our children and grandchildren) are very much tied to how effectively our society functions and the extent to which our educational systems give students a stake in contributing to their society. If they don't develop the abilities and interest to participate productively in the social and economic life of their society, the chances are that they will drain resources from their society. If schools continue to fail in their attempts to educate students whose communities have been subordinated economically and socially for generations, everyone in society will pay the price. I have argued in this volume that the source of this educational failure is a coercive power structure that is reflected, often inadvertently, in many schools and other societal institutions. Thus, educators who aspire to create contexts of empowerment with their students as the only route to educational success, must understand how disempowerment has all too frequently been created within our classrooms.

Secondly, as educators, we have considerable power to affect change in the lives of those we interact with. As Poplin and Weeres (1992) point out in the quotation that opens this volume, students respond very positively when they sense that their teachers care about them and want to connect with them as people. For teachers, their best experiences were also when they connected with students and were able to help them in concrete ways. These human relationships that form the core of successful schooling determine the social and economic horizon that students see when they look beyond the school.

Our interactions with students in the classroom embody an image of the society they will graduate into and the kind of contributions they are being enabled to make within this society. As educators we are faced with choices and constraints with respect to what and how we teach, the nature of our personal goals in teaching, and the kind of aspirations we have for the students we teach. Classroom interactions collectively shape both our students' future possibilities and those of our society. Thus, understanding the forces that influence the interactional choices we make in our classrooms and thinking critically about the constraints that are imposed on those choices is central to how we define our roles in our schools and the society beyond the school.

Because all sectors of our society have strong vested interests in what happens in schools, claims and counter-claims in the media about appropriate directions for education are broadcast loudly into classrooms. Although invariably phrased in terms of what is in the best interests of children, these claims and counter-claims also embody social agendas; they reflect alternative visions of society. The discourse on either side of these debates is intended to mold schools into conformity with particular social, cultural, or religious images.

⑥   Educators are committed to helping children learn. However, their choices with respect to issues of language, culture, pedagogy, and parent involvement also reflect the societal discourses that swirl around their classrooms in relation to these issues. If educators are to achieve their goal of helping children learn, it is imperative to analyze critically the societal discourses that are vying for their allegiance. To what extent are different claims supported by verifiable data? Whose interests do these claims serve? What forms of instruction are in the best interests of children and serve the common good of our society? What kinds of knowledge, skills, and values will best serve students as they graduate into the 21st century? Is this the kind of education I would want for my own child?

In the sections that follow, I present my own perspectives on these issues and elaborate the kind of education that I would want for my own children. These perspectives are part of a discourse that values cultural diversity, critical thinking, and social justice. They represent an explicit vision of a society founded on principles of collaborative relations of power, as articulated in Chapter 1. The claim is that the common good of society will be better served by educators and by educational systems that are oriented explicitly to challenging coercive relations of power.

As with any other set of discoursal claims, these arguments should be analyzed critically by readers. Are the data presented convincing? If not, where are the gaps or inaccuracies? Whose interests do these arguments serve? Ultimately, individual educators must define their roles and make their own choices about their instructional and social goals in the classroom. However, making well-informed choices should be an explicit process that takes account of the empirical data and critically examines alternative perspectives. Only through this form of critical analysis will educators challenge the structures in schools and society that serve to disempower them as much as their students.

Graduating into the 21st Century

Public schools serve the societies that fund them and they aim to graduate students with the knowledge, skills, and values that will contribute most effectively to their societies. In an era of rapid and intense change, it is often difficult to predict the kinds of "human resources" our societies will need in the future. However, some patterns are beginning to emerge and their implications for education are immense. In the sections below, I describe the changing cultural, economic/scientific, and existential realities that should be reflected in classroom interactions if they are to prepare students to contribute effectively to their societies in the 21st century. [1]

Cultural Realities. Schools intent on preparing students for the realities of the 21st century must take account of the fact that cultural diversity is the norm in both the domestic and international arenas. [2] Around the world we see unprecedented population mobility and intercultural contact resulting from factors such as economic migration, displacement caused by military conflicts and famine, as well as technological advances in transportation and communication. Increased intercultural contact within industrialized countries as a result of decades of migration is matched by growing intercultural contact between countries, reflecting increased global economic and political interdependence.

This escalation of intercultural contact, both domestically and internationally, has major implications for our schools. In the first place, it suggests that the transmission of cultural myopia in schools is a recipe for social disaster. The prophets of doom who warn about the infiltration of the Other in the guise of multicultural curricula and bilingual education have closed their eyes to the urgent need for school programs that promote sensitivity to, and understanding of, diverse cultural perspectives. If we are to learn anything from the racial and ethnic tensions in North American cities and the brutal armed conflicts abroad that have characterized the 1990s, surely it is that our schools have a crucial role to play in helping us live and grow together in our global village. Educators concerned with preparing students for life in the 21st century must educate them for global citizenship. The potential to achieve this goal is obviously greater in a classroom context where cultural diversity is seen as a resource rather than in one where it is either suppressed or ignored.

In the second place, if we take seriously the concerns about the competitiveness of American business in an increasingly interdependent global economy, highlighted by Reagan/Bush era educational reformers, then it is the monolingual/monocultural graduate who is "culturally illiterate" and ill-equipped to prosper in the global economy. Students who grow up and are educated in a monocultural cocoon risk becoming social misfits, totally unprepared for the worlds of work or play in the 21st century. Hirsch got it wrong: students require not just cultural literacy, but intercultural literacy (Cummins & Sayers, 1995). A recent survey of eight major U.S.-based multinational corporations reported that they are placing added value on college graduates with <u>bilingual</u> <u>skills</u>. These corporations are especially interested in less commonly taught languages such as Chinese, Japanese, and Russian. [3] In short, bilingual and multilingual individuals are likely to be more attractive to employers involved in international trade as well as those faced with providing service to a linguistically diverse clientele in societal institutions (hospitals, seniors' homes, airports, schools, etc.).

It doesn't take a genius to see that nurturing the linguistic and cultural resources of the nation is simply good common sense in light of the cultural realities of the 21st century. Even minimal investment in bilingual programs for both majority and minority students and a focus on infusing multicultural awareness across the curriculum can contribute significantly both to the nation's economic competitiveness and to its ability to collaborate internationally in resolving global problems. Australian historian and TIME magazine's Art critic, Robert Hughes, expressed it well in his best selling book *Culture of Complaint*:

> To learn other languages, to deal with other customs and creeds from direct experience of them and with a degree of humility: these are self-evidently good, as cultural provincialism is not...In Australia, no Utopia but a less truculent immigrant society than this one, intelligent multiculturalism works to everyone's social advantage, and the conservative crisis-talk about creating a "cultural tower of Babel" and so forth is seen as obsolete alarmism of a fairly low order... In the world that is coming, if you can't navigate difference, you've had it. (1993, pp. 88-100)

Economic/Scientific Realities. As discussed above, national economies are increasingly implicated in the global economy. A product may be conceived in one country, designed in another, manufactured in yet another, and then marketed and sold throughout the world. The capacity to communicate across cultural and linguistic boundaries is crucial to business success in this environment, as is access to and ability to manipulate information. Thus, the competitiveness of a business or a country in the global marketplace depends on its human resources: the knowledge, learning, information and intelligence possessed by its people; what Secretary of Labor in the Clinton administration, Robert Reich (1991), has called *symbolic analysis skills*. These include abstract higher-order thinking, critical inquiry, and collaboration — defined as the capacity to engage in active communication and dialogue to get a variety of perspectives and to create consensus when necessary.

Even for relatively unskilled jobs in the fast-growing service sector, where high levels of literacy are not required for adequate job performance, employers have raised educational standards for applicants. This trend appears to be related to the perception that the "trainability" of workers is essential for businesses to adapt in a flexible manner to a rapidly changing economic environment.

In short, many workers today employ literacy skills in the workplace that are far beyond what their parents needed. In a context where information is doubling every five years or so, employers are looking for workers who know how to get access to current information, who can think critically about what information is relevant and what is not, and who know how to collaborate creatively in problem-solving activities across cultural, linguistic, and racial boundaries. What few workplaces need are workers whose heads are full of inert and soon-to-be-obsolete information.

Two implications for education are clear. First, passive internalization of inert content, which, as noted earlier, research suggests is still a common mode of learning in many North American classrooms (e.g. Goodlad, 1984; Ramírez, 1992), does not promote the kind of active intelligence that the changing economy increasingly requires in the work force. To address the economic needs of the societies that fund them, schools must promote students' capacities for collaborative critical inquiry.

Second, the failure of schools to educate all students carries enormous economic (and social) costs. If students do not graduate from school with the symbolic analysis skills to contribute productively to the economy, then they are likely to be excluded from the economy. Individuals who are excluded from the economy don't just fade away and disappear. They frequently end up on welfare or in jail. There is a huge correlation between dropping out of school and ending up in prison — more than 80 percent of prisoners in U.S. prisons are high school dropouts, each costing taxpayers a minimum of $20,000 a year to contain, much more than it would have cost to educate them (Hodgkinson, 1991). The U.S. incarcerates its population at a rate far higher than any other industrialized country (e.g. ten times that of the Netherlands and six times that of Australia) and this pattern has escalated dramatically in recent years at enormous cost to taxpayers. Natriello et al. (1990) in their aptly titled book *Schooling Disadvantaged Children: Racing Against Catastrophe* estimated conservatively that the cost to the nation of the dropout problem is approximately $50 billion in foregone lifetime earnings alone: "Also associated with this cost are forgone government tax revenues, greater welfare expenditure, poorer physical and mental health of our nation's citizens, and greater costs of crime…" (p. 43). As one example of the returns on educational investment, it has been estimated that every dollar spent on Head Start programs will save $7 in reduced need for special education, welfare, incarceration and so on (Schweinhart et al., 1986).

In short, compared to the alternatives, education is one of society's most cost-effective investments. To push low-income culturally diverse students out of school at current levels in urban centers across the nation is financially absurd (not to mention socially unjust in the extreme). Thus, to address the economic realities of the 21st century, schools must look rationally at which programs for culturally diverse students are most likely to succeed in developing high levels of literacy. To exclude from consideration genuine bilingual and multicultural programs, whose success has been demonstrated repeatedly, purely on the ideological grounds that they are "un-American" is irrational and simply panders to the neurotic paranoia of the patriotically-correct (to borrow Robert Hughes' phrase).

Existential Realities. By "existential realities," I am referring to the increasing sense of fragility that characterizes our relationship to both our physical and social environment. For example, a perusal of virtually any newspaper anywhere in the world will quickly show the extent of environmental deterioration and the enormity of the global ecological problems that our generation has created for our children's generation to resolve. Similarly, the "new world order" of peaceful co-existence that seemed at hand with the end of the Cold War has been overtaken by eruptions of brutal conflicts around the world. Violence in our schools and streets signal the enormous pressures just beneath the surface of our social fabric. Increased incarceration responds to symptoms rather than to underlying causes and consequently has done little to curb crime. In fact, it has probably contributed to crime since it drains dollars from schools and other social programs.

Despite these changed existential realities, many schools appear dedicated to insulating students from awareness of social issues rather than communicating a sense of urgency in regard to understanding and acting on them. In most schools across the continent, the curriculum has been sanitized such that students rarely have the opportunity to discuss critically, write about, or act upon issues that directly affect the society they will form. Issues such as racism, environmental pollution, genetic engineering, and the causes of poverty are regarded as too sensitive for fragile and impressionable young minds. Still less do students have the opportunity to cooperate with others from different cultural and/or linguistic groups in exploring resolutions to these issues.

A major reason why schools try to maintain a facade of innocence in relation to social and environmental issues is that such issues invariably implicate power relations in the domestic and international arenas. Promoting a critical awareness of how power is wielded at home and abroad is not a task that society expects educators to undertake. In fact, renewed demands for a core curriculum and for imposition of "cultural literacy" can be interpreted as a way of controlling the information that students can access so as to minimize the possibility of deviant thoughts. As Donaldo Macedo (1993, 1994) argues, in the shadows of the list of facts that every American should know is the list of facts that every American must be *discouraged* from knowing. Prominent among these is the history of imperialism and colonialism of Western powers from 1492 to the present (see, for example, *Rethinking Schools*, 1991).

In short, this analysis suggests that issues related to the organization of society, specifically the division of resources and power, be taken off the taboo list of what is appropriate to explore in school. Students whose communities have been marginalized will increasingly perceive the omission of these fundamental issues as dishonest and hypocritical, and this will reinforce their resistance to achievement under the current rules of the game. By contrast, a focus on critical inquiry, in a collaborative and supportive context, will encourage students to engage in learning in ways that will promote future productive engagement in their societies. The research, critical thinking, and creative problem-solving skills that this form of education entails will position students well for full participation in the economic and social realities of their global community. By contrast, excluding students from the learning process at school is pushing us toward a society where everyone loses because every dropout carries an expensive price tag for the entire society.

This analysis of the cultural, economic/scientific, and existential realities that students will graduate into in the 21st century suggests that priorities for our schools should be:

- Promoting bilingual or multilingual skills and intercultural sensitivity among all students;

- Promoting not just basic functional literacy but critical literacy that would include capacities for abstract higher-order thinking and collaborative problem-solving; in other words, collaborative critical inquiry should be the predominant learning focus in our schools;

- Creatively exploring ways to help all students graduate with high academic achievement; since subordinated group students are massively overrepresented among dropouts and low-achievers, this essentially means restructuring schools to challenge and reverse the causes of subordinated group underachievement;

- Promoting an awareness of, and concern for, the common good in our societies; this will entail collaborative critical inquiry into domestic and international social justice issues related to the distribution of resources, status and power in our societies.

These educational directions represent direct inferences from an analysis of clearly observable social trends. Why is it that so few schools across the North American continent are actively pursuing these directions? Why is it that even suggesting directions such as these is likely to be castigated as "radical?" Why do so many working- and middle-class Americans feel such frustration and anger about issues such as immigration and diversity (as illustrated in the overwhelming support for Proposition 187 in California)?

To answer these questions we need to examine some data about how the power structure operates to deflect challenges and minimize dissent.

Coercive Relations of Power in Action

The Polarization of Income. Consider some of the data outlined in *Philadelphia Inquirer* reporters Donald Barlett and James Steele's (1992) book *America: What Went Wrong?* Chapter 1 of their book is entitled "Dismantling the Middle Class" and the statistics show clearly how this has been achieved:

• In 1989, the top 4% in income earned as much as the bottom 51%. Thirty years earlier, in 1959, the top 4% earned as much as the bottom 35% — a 16 point difference. According to Barlett and Steele "The wage and salary structure of American business, encouraged by federal tax policies, is pushing the nation toward a two-class society" (p. ix).

• During the 1980s, salaries of people earning $20,000 to $50,000 increased by 44% while salaries for those earning $200,000 to $1 million increased by 697%; if you were fortunate enough to earn more than $1 million, the icing on the cake was that you received a whopping salary increase of 2,184%! In Barlett and Steele's terms: "Viewed more broadly, the total wages of all people who earned less than $50,000 a year — 85 percent of all Americans — increased an average of just 2 percent a year over those ten years. At the same time, the total wages of all millionaires shot up 243 percent a year" (p. 4).

• As a result of the Tax Reform Act of 1986 those earning up to $50,000 saw tax cuts of between 6% and 16% while those earning more than $500,000 saw tax cuts of between 31% and 34%. This represented an average 1989 tax savings per return of $300 for those earning $20,000 to $30,000 compared to an average savings of $281,033 for those earning $1 million or more.

• During the 1950s the corporate share of U.S. income tax collected was 39% compared to 61% for individuals; in the 1980s the corporate share had dropped to 17% while individuals' share rose to 83%.

• The percentage of workers receiving fully paid health insurance fell from 75 percent to 48 percent between 1982 and 1989.

Barlett and Steele argue that as a result of the way the rules of the game have been rigged "the already rich are richer than ever; there has been an explosion in overnight new rich; life for the working class is deteriorating, and those at the bottom are trapped" (p. 2). They summarize the data as follows:

Indeed the growth of the middle class — one of the underpinnings of democracy in this country — has been reversed. By government action. Taken as a whole, these are the results of the rules that govern the game: (20)

• They have created a tax system that is firmly weighted against the middle class.

• They have enabled companies to trim or cancel health-care and pension benefits for employees.

• They have granted subsidies to businesses that create low-wage jobs that are eroding living standards.

• They have undermined longtime stable businesses and communities.

• They have rewarded companies that transfer jobs abroad and eliminate jobs in this country.

• They have placed home ownership out of reach of a growing number of Americans and made the financing of a college education impossible without incurring a hefty debt.

Look upon it as the dismantling of the middle class. And understand that, barring some unexpected intervention by the federal government, the worst is yet to come. For we are in the midst of the largest transfer of wealth in the nation's history. (pp. 2-3)

Noam Chomsky (1995) is even more blunt in his assessment of the causes of crime and violence in American society. He points to the fact that "we're the only industrial nation that doesn't have some sort of guaranteed health insurance...Despite being the richest society we have twice the poverty rate of any other industrialized nation, and much higher rates of incarceration" (pp. 128-129). In pointing to the powerful state protection for the rich (illustrated in Barlett and Steele's data), he suggests that:

(22) The United States has, from its origins, been a highly protectionist society with very high tariffs and massive subsidies for the rich. It's a huge welfare state for the rich, and society ends up being very polarized. Despite the New Deal, and the Great Society measures in the 1960s, which attempted to move the United States toward the social contracts of the other industrialized nations, we still have the high-

est social and economic inequality, and such polarization is increasing very sharply. These factors — high polarization, a welfare state for the rich, and marginalization of parts of the population — have their effects. One effect is a lot of crime. (p. 129)   23

One of the major sources of subsidies for the rich is the Pentagon, which is why, according to Chomsky, it hasn't declined substantially with the end of the Cold War. In fact the U.S. is still spending almost as much on the military as the rest of the world combined. [4] In addition to the Pentagon, Chomsky highlights straight welfare payments to the rich in the form of home mortgage tax rebates, about 80% of which go to people with incomes over $50,000 (who represent just 15% of the population, according to Barlett and Steele). He justifies labelling these welfare payments on the grounds that "it's exactly the same if I don't give the government $100 or if the government does give me $100" (p. 131). Another example of social welfare for the rich is business expenses as tax write-offs which far outweigh welfare payments to the poor.

In summary, the economic hardship that many middle-class people are feeling has come from the transfer of resources from middle-class and poor families to the wealthy. This combined with the Savings and Loan bailout of hundreds of billions of dollars and the obscene level of military expenditures during the 1980s and 1990s has resulted in hard times for ordinary people. They feel angry about it and want to blame someone.

Finding Scapegoats. The escalation of rhetoric against immigration, bilingual education, and cultural diversity in general is a convenient way of accomplishing two goals: First, it directs people's anger against a potential threat to the established power structure. The projected rapid growth of minority populations, particularly Spanish-speakers, is a source of concern; if these groups retain some cultural and linguistic distinctiveness, it is feared that they may be less subject to persuasion (control) than other Americans. If they were ever to exercise their right to vote in substantial numbers then, in columnist James Reston's view, they might "not only influence but hold the decisive margin in state and local elections" (The Journal, Milwaukee, WI, February 5, 1981). In order to prevent this catastrophic scenario, it is imperative to reverse the infiltration of alien languages and cultures into American institutions as rapidly as possible. [5]

Second, directing people's anger against immigrants, bilingual educators, welfare mothers, single parent families, and the like, serves to divert attention from the massive transfer of wealth from middle-class and poor to the rich. It very effectively obscures the real operation of the power structure. Once again, Chomsky lucidly identifies how this scapegoating process works:

> The building up of scapegoats and fear is standard. If you're stomping on people's faces, you don't want them to notice that; you want them to be afraid of somebody else — Jews, homosexuals, welfare queens, immigrants, whoever it is. That's how Hitler got to power, and in fact he became the most popular leader in German history. People are scared, they're upset, the world isn't working, and they don't like the way things are. You don't want people to look at the actual source of power, that's much too dangerous, so therefore, you need to have them blame or be frightened of someone else. (1995, p. 134)

Resolving Contradictions. The roots of the contradictions identified earlier become more intelligible in light of this analysis of coercive relations of power. To reiterate the contradictions:

• Our societies urgently need more people with fluent bilingual skills, yet we demonize bilingual education, the only program capable of delivering bilingualism and biliteracy.

• Our economy increasingly requires people with symbolic analysis skills who are capable of collaborative critical inquiry, but we still insist that schools "get back to basics" (as though they ever left).

• In order to increase economic performance and decrease the escalating costs of incarceration, we need to enable more low-income young people to graduate from high school with the possibility of more than a below-the-poverty-line job; only in this way will they have a stake in contributing to our society; yet we resist the kind of educational reforms that would promote contexts of empowerment for low-income students, preferring instead to warehouse them indefinitely in prisons built at enormous cost to the taxpayer.

• Finally, our society desperately needs to restore some sense of coherence and community to its people, founded on notions such as social justice and the common good; yet, any attempt to desanitize the curriculum and look at historical and current issues of social justice from multiple perspectives is still vehemently resisted.

The reason our school systems are discouraged or prevented from pursuing these directions that respond rationally to the changing social realities of the 21st century is that, in one way or another, these directions potentially threaten the coercive power structure that manufactures consent for grossly inequitable resource distribution in our societies. If bilingualism or intercultural literacy were encouraged, it would legitimate the presence of the Other within societal institutions; if critical literacy were encouraged, it might undermine the process of manufacturing consent through indoctrination and disinformation; if we seriously contemplated reversing underachievement among low-income inner city youth, it would require "an investment in education comparable to what has been spent on building a high-tech military machine" (Wirth, 1993, p. 365) — in other words, a significant transfer of wealth from the rich to the poor. Finally, it is virtually unthinkable in most societies around the world to invite educators to desanitize the curriculum and examine the ways in which power has been, and is, wielded for coercive ends. [6]

To what extent can educators, operating within these constraints, realistically create contexts of empowerment that would challenge the impact of coercive relations of power on themselves and their students? Chomsky is pessimistic:

> It's just not going to be allowed, because it's too subversive. You can teach students to think for themselves in the sciences because you want people to be independent and creative, otherwise you don't have science. But science and engineering students are not encouraged to be critical in terms of the political and social implications of their work. In most other fields you want students to be obedient and submissive, and that starts from childhood. Now teachers can try, and do break out of that, but, they will surely find if they go too far, that as soon as it gets noticed there'll be pressures to stop them. (1995, p. 141)

I am somewhat more optimistic than Chomsky about what educators, individually and collectively, can achieve. This is elaborated in the final section.

Towards Collaborative Relations of Power in the Classroom

In the dismal scenario sketched above, there are two beacons of hope. One is the fact that power structures are not monolithic. There are many individuals and institutions within North American societies that are committed to challenging inequality and exploitation. In fact, at one level, the United States has committed itself to educational equity more vigorously than most other Western nations. Since the mid-1960s considerable resources have been expended on research to try to understand the causes of school failure and on intervention aimed at reversing a legacy of educational exclusion. This public commitment has been matched by the enormous dedication of many educators who go far beyond their job descriptions to promote contexts of empowerment in their classrooms. However, as documented above, at another level, a very different process is operating that attempts to neutralize potential challenges to the coercive power structure.

A reason for some optimism at this point is that the operation of coercive relations of power has reached a point of diminishing returns. The contradictions are becoming more obvious. Fiscal deficits are unlikely to be reduced when more police are required to combat crime and more prisons are being built to contain undereducated young people; business is unlikely to thrive when fewer people have the disposable income to buy its products; and so on. I am optimistic enough to believe that, in the coming years, coercive power structures will become visible to a greater number of people, thereby providing more scope for educational and other institutions to pursue an agenda of social justice and collaborative empowerment.

A second source of optimism lies in the power that schools, communities, and individual educators have to create contexts of empowerment even under unfavorable conditions. [7] Scattered throughout this volume are examples of this process. School systems are increasingly showing an interest in two-way bilingual immersion programs that explicitly, and very successfully, challenge the *Us versus Them* ideology promoted by groups such as U.S. English. Periodicals such as *Rethinking Schools* create a community of inquiry among educators that counteracts processes of indoctrination and disinformation. In many cases, culturally diverse communities themselves are mobilizing to demand respectful and high quality education for their children. [8]

As emphasized throughout this volume, individual educators are never powerless, although they frequently work in conditions that are oppressive both for them and their students (see, for example, Kozol, 1991). While they rarely have complete freedom, educators do have choices in the way they structure the micro-interactions in the classroom. They do determine for themselves the social and educational goals they want to achieve with their students. They are responsible for the role definitions they adopt in relation to culturally diverse students and communities. Even in the context of English-only instruction, educators have options in their orientation to students' language and culture, in the forms of parent and community participation they encourage, and in the way they implement pedagogy and assessment.

In short, through their practice and their interactions with students, educators define their own identities. Students, likewise, go through a process of defining their identities in interaction with their teachers, peers, and parents. This process of negotiating identities can never be controlled from the outside, although it will certainly be influenced by many forces. Thus, educators individually and collectively, have the potential to work towards the creation of contexts of empowerment. Within these interactional spaces where identities are negotiated, students and educators together can generate power that challenges structures of injustice in small but significant ways. Each student who graduates into the 21st century with well-developed critical literacy skills, intercultural sensitivity, and an informed commitment to the ideals of "liberty and justice for all," enshrined in the American constitution, represents a challenge to coercive relations of power.

When classroom interactions are fueled by collaborative relations of power, students gain access to ways of navigating difference that our domestic and international communities are sadly lacking at the present time. Bilingual students who feel a sense of belonging in their classroom learning community are more likely to feel "at home" in their society upon graduation and to contribute actively to building that society. Schools that have brought issues related to cultural and linguistic diversity from the periphery to the center of their mission are more likely to prepare students to thrive in the interdependent global society in which they will live. The goal for all of us as educators is to strive to make our classrooms and schools microcosms of the kind of caring society that we would like our own children and grandchildren to inherit. I strongly believe that this is an attainable goal.

Endnotes to Chapter 9

1. The analysis presented here is elaborated in more detail in Cummins and Sayers (1995). The analysis in the chapter as a whole elaborates on a keynote presentation I gave at the 1995 California Association for Bilingual Education conference in Anaheim entitled *Resisting Xenophobia: Proposition 187 and its Aftermath.*

2. Increased linguistic and cultural diversity is a phenomenon affecting many countries in addition to the United States. In Canada, for example, more than 50 percent of the student population in Toronto and Vancouver have a first language other than English. In the Netherlands, 40 percent of students in Amsterdam schools are of non-Dutch origin and in the country as a whole close to 20 percent of the population will be of non-Dutch origin by the year 2000.

   In the United States, immigrants' share of total population growth has increased significantly from 11 percent between 1960 and 1970 to 39 percent between 1980 and 1990. Latinos/Latinas will account for more than 40 percent of population growth over the next 60 years and become the nation's largest minority in the year 2013. The Asian American population is expected to increase from 8 million in 1992 to 16 million by 2009, 24 million by 2024, and 32 million by 2038. African Americans are expected to double in number by the year 2050. At current growth rates, the U.S. foreign-born population will probably exceed ten percent by the year 2000 (Hispanic Link Weekly Report, 1995, Vol. 13, No. 31).

   Consistent with these projected growth trends, the proportion of culturally diverse students is rapidly increasing in U.S. urban centers. To illustrate, the National Coalition of Advocates for Students (1988) estimated that by the year 2001, minority enrollment levels will range from 70 to 96 percent in the nation's 15 largest school systems. In California, so-called minority groups (e.g. Latinos/Latinas, African Americans, Asian Americans) already represent a greater proportion of the school population than students from the so-called majority group. By the year 2030, half of all the children in the state are projected to be of Latino/Latina background while Euro-Americans will compose 60 percent of the elderly population, a reality that historian Paul Kennedy terms "a troublesome mismatch" that raises the prospect of "a massive contest over welfare and entitlement priorities between predominantly Caucasian retirees and predominantly nonwhite children, mothers, and unemployed, each with its vocal advocacy organizations" (p. 313).

3. National Clearinghouse for Bilingual Education Internet Newsline, 23 May, 1995. The report entitled *What Employers Expect of College Graduates: International Knowledge and Second Language Skills* can be obtained (free) from the U.S. Department of Education, OERI, 555 New Jersey Ave., NW, Washington, DC 20208. Tel. 800/424-1616.

4. Macedo (1994) reminds readers of the fraud rampant in the military-industrial complex during the 1980s as illustrated in the Pentagon paying $700 for a toilet seat and $350 for a screwdriver. He also illustrates the process of social welfare for the rich with current examples such as a $220 million subsidy paid to bail out McDonnell Douglas in 1990 and military action abroad to protect the interests of U.S. corporations. Among the examples he cites are the following:

- In 1954 the CIA spent millions of dollars to organize the overthrow of the elected president of Guatemala to save the properties of the United Fruit Company.

- In 1973 the U.S. government spent millions of dollars in concert with IT&T Corporation to overthrow the elected socialist leader of Chile, Salvador Allende.

- The average tax rate for the top twelve American military contractors, who made $19 billion in profits in 1981, 1982, and 1983, was 1.5 percent. Middle-class Americans paid 15 percent. (p. 93)

Along the same lines, Chomsky (1995) points out that Newt Gingrich's congressional district, a very wealthy suburb of Atlanta, "gets more federal subsidies — taxpayers' money — than any suburban county in the country, outside the federal system itself... The biggest employer in his district happens to be Lockheed. Well, what's Lockheed? That's a publicly subsidized corporation. Lockheed wouldn't exist for five minutes if it wasn't for the public subsidy under the pretext of defense, but that's just a joke. The United States hasn't faced a threat probably since the War of 1812. Certainly, there's no threat now" (p. 129-130).

5. The debate on Proposition 187, intended to eliminate all services to undocumented immigrants, unleashed a lot of pent-up anti-immigrant emotion in California during 1994. In a presentation to the California Association for Bilingual Education conference in February 1995, I tried to draw out some of the lessons of this debate as follows:

"Proposition 187 represents a turning point in the social history of California and probably in the social history of all of North America. Obviously those who support it intend for it to be a turning point — a first step in reclaiming the nation, reversing direction after 30 years of increasing multicultural fragmentation, increasing crime, increasing economic difficulty — all the social ills of the nation are symbolized within this proposition and the culprit for these social ills has been identified. The cause of the fear and the loathing embodied in this proposition is all around us in everything that we as bilingual educators collectively represent. Proposition 187 expresses the fear of diversity, the fear of difference, the fear of the Other, the fear of strangers — xenophobia.

It is also intended as a statement of identity — a statement of national unity, a statement of who the landlords of this country are and who are the tenants; a warning to the tenants that their lease is close to expiring and if they don't lower their voices, withdraw their demands, become silent and invisible, they will be evicted without ceremony.

Proposition 187 is about power, who has it and who intends to keep it. It is about intimidation and it is about racism and we must recognize these realities if we are to fight against it.

However, if we are to fight it effectively we must understand it better than I think we do. It is not enough to dismiss it as racist because certainly a large proportion of those who supported it do not see themselves as racist and are not racist in the usual sense of the term. If we are to reverse this process and work towards a saner more tolerant society, we must communicate and dialogue with many of those who currently see diversity as a threat. In fact, we must join forces with them to articulate a vision of our society where there is cooperation rather than competition across cultural boundaries, where cultural difference enriches the whole rather than scatters the parts. We have to find those areas where different cultural groups have common vested interests and join forces to achieve these common goals...

The general public, largely white- and blue-collar working people have bought into the message that diversity threatens their way of life. They believe the disinformation that has been transmitted about the costs of immigration, about immigrants taking jobs from residents, about students not learning any English in schools because of bilingual education, about multicultural advocates dismantling the history of this country. These people are afraid not only because of the increase in diversity but also because the media have skillfully associated diversity with increases in crime and economic hardship. Willie Horton may have stopped revolving in the prison door, but George Bush's message lives on: the Other is out there and he's waiting to get you.

Let's look at the realities:

Immigration. *Business Week* (July 13, 1992) reports that at least 11 million immigrants are working and from their earnings of $240 billion are paying more than $90 billion annually in taxes, a great deal more than the $5 billion they are estimated to receive in public assistance. In fact, despite their difficult economic situation as new arrivals, only 8.8% of immigrants receive public assistance, compared with 7.9% of the general population. Furthermore, the average immigrant family pays $2,500 more in tax dollars annually than they receive in public services (New York Times, June 27, 1993, p. A1). The American Council on Civil Liberties (ACLU) has also summarized data regarding the economic impact of immigration; among the information it compiled is the following:

- In a 1990 American Immigration Institute Survey of prominent economists, four out of five said that immigrants had a favorable impact on economic growth. None said that immigrants had an adverse impact on economic growth.

- According to a Los Angeles Times analysis summarizing the best available research, "Immigrants contribute mightily to the economy, by paying billions in annual taxes, by filling low-wage jobs that keep domestic industry competitive, and by spurring investment and job-creation, revitalizing once-decaying communities. Many social scientists conclude that the newcomers, rather than drain government treasuries, contribute overall far more than they utilize in services." (January 6, 1992).

- Studies by the Rand Corporation, the University of Maryland, the Council of Economic Advisors, the National Research Council and the Urban Institute all show that immigrants do not have a negative effect on the earnings and employment opportunities of native-born Americans. A 1989 Department of Labor study found that neither U.S. workers in complementary jobs, nor most minority workers, appear to be adversely affected by immigration (ACLU, Department of Public Education, June 10, 1994).

6. In response to a question about how greed and the pursuit of profit are infused in the histories of the U.S. and other countries, Chomsky discussed how the educational system works to make certain thoughts "unthinkable:"

Well, [the teaching of history is] a little better than it used to be, but not much. Much of history is just wiped out. We just went through a war in Central America in which hundreds of thousands of people were slaughtered, and countries destroyed — huge terror. U.S. operations were condemned by the World Court as international terrorism. It's nevertheless described in this country as an effort to bring democracy to Central America. How do they get away with that? If you have a deeply indoctrinated educated sector, as we do, you're not going to get any dissent there, and among the general population who may not be so deeply indoctrinated, they're marginal. They're supposed to be afraid of welfare mothers and people coming to attack us, and they're busy watching football games and so on, so it doesn't matter what they think. And that's pretty much the way the educational system and the media work. (1995, p. 139)

7. A more elaborated account of the collaborative creation of power (empowerment), and its opposite, can be found in Norwegian peace researcher Johan Galtung's (1980) description of what he calls *autonomy*:

> Autonomy is here seen as power-over-oneself so as to be able to withstand what others might have of power-over-others. I use the distinction between ideological, remunerative and punitive power, depending on whether the influence is based on internal, positive external, or negative external sanctions. Autonomy then is the degree of 'inoculation' against these forms of power. These forms of power, exerted by means of ideas, carrots and sticks, can work only if the power receiver really receives the pressure, which presupposes a certain degree of submissiveness, dependency and fear, respectively. Their antidotes are self-respect, self-sufficiency, and fearlessness... 'self-respect' can be defined as 'confidence in one's own ideas and ability to set one's own goals,' 'self-sufficiency' as the 'possibility of pursuing them with one's own means,' and 'fearlessness,' as 'the possibility of persisting despite threats of destruction. ...
>
> The opposite [of autonomy] is penetration, meaning that the outside has penetrated into one's self to the extent of creating submissiveness to ideas, dependency on 'goods' from the outside, and fear of the outside in terms of 'bads.' (1980, p. 58-59)

8. For example, when the Foundation Center preschools were defunded by the California State Department in June 1995, parents in several centers refused to cooperate with the state until they themselves were granted the contract to operate the center.

References

Abi-Nader, J. (1993). Meeting the needs of multicultural classrooms: Family values and the motivation of minority students. In M.J. O'Hair & S. Odell (Eds.), *Diversity and teaching: Teacher education yearbook I.* (pp. 212-236). Fort Worth, TX: Harcourt Brace Jovanovich.

Abrami, P.C., Chambers, B., Poulson, C., De Simone, C., d'Apollonia, S., & Howden, J. (1995). *Classroom connections: Understanding and using cooperative learning.* Toronto: Harcourt Brace.

Ada, A.F. (1988a). The Pajaro Valley experience: Working with Spanish-speaking parents to develop children's reading and writing skills in the home through the use of children's literature. In T. Skutnabb-Kangas and J. Cummins (Ed.), *Minority education: From shame to struggle.* Clevedon, England: Multilingual Matters.

Ada, A.F. (1988b). Creative reading: A relevant methodology for language minority children. In L.M. Malave (Ed.) *NABE '87. Theory, research and application: Selected Papers.* Buffalo: State University of New York.

American Psychological Association. (1982). Review of Department of Education report entitled "Effectiveness of bilingual education: A review of the literature". Letter to Congressional Hispanic Caucus, April 22.

Artigal, J.M. (1991) *The Catalan Immersion Program. A European point of view.* Norwood, NJ: Ablex.

Association for Supervision and Curriculum Development (ASCD), (1987). *Building an indivisible nation: Bilingual education in context.* Alexandria, Virginia: ASCD.

Auerbach, E.R. (1993). Reexamining English only in the ESL classroom. *TESOL Quarterly, 27,* 9-32.

Baker, C. (1988). *Key issues in bilingualism and bilingual education.* Clevedon, England: Multilingual Matters.

Baker, C. (1993). *Introduction to bilingualism and bilingual education*. Clevedon, England: Multilingual Matters.

Baker, K. (1992a). Comments on Suzanne Irujo's review of Rosalie Pedalino Porter's *Forked tongue: The politics of bilingual education*. A reader reacts ... *TESOL Quarterly, 26*, 397-405.

Baker, K. (1992b). Ramírez et al.: Led by bad theory. *Bilingual Research Journal, 16*(1&2), 91-104.

Baker, K.A. & de Kanter, A.A. (1981). *Effectiveness of Bilingual Education: A Review of the Literature*. Washington, D.C.: Office of Planning and Budget, U.S. Department of Education.

Balderas, V.A. (1995). To be alive in struggle: One teacher's journey. In J. Frederickson (Ed.) *Reclaiming our voices: Bilingual education, critical pedagogy & praxis*. (pp. 260-273). Ontario, CA: California Association for Bilingual Education.

Barlett, D. L. & Steele, J. B. (1992). *America: What went wrong?* Kansas: Andrews & McMeel.

Becker, A. (1990). The role of the school in the maintenance and change of ethnic group affiliation. *Human Organization, 49*, 48-55.

Becker, W., & Gersten, R. (1982). A follow-up of follow through: The later effects of the direct instruction model on children in the fifth and sixth grades. *American Educational Research Journal, 19*, 75-92.

Benton, R.A. (1988). The Maori language in New Zealand education. *Language, Culture and Curriculum, 1*, 75-83.

Berger, T. (1977). *Northern frontier, northern homeland: The report of the Mackenzie Valley Pipeline Inquiry*. Vol. 1. Toronto: James Lorimer and Co.

Berman, P., Chambers, J., Gandara, P., et al. (1992). *Meeting the challenge of linguistic diversity: An evaluation of programs for pupils with limited proficiency in English*. Berkeley: BW Associates.

Bethell, T. (1979). Against bilingual education. *Harper's Magazine*, February.

Beykont, Z.F. (1994). *Academic progress of a nondominant group: A longitudinal study of Puerto Ricans in New York City's late-exit bilingual programs*. Doctoral dissertation presented to the Graduate School of Education of Harvard University.

Bialystok, E. (1991). Metalinguistic dimensions of bilingual language proficiency. In E. Bialystok (Ed.) *Language processing in bilingual children*. (pp. 113-140). Cambridge: Cambridge University Press.

Bialystok, E. & Hakuta, K. (1994). *In other words: The science and psychology of second language acquisition*. New York: Basic Books.

Biber, D. (1986). Spoken and written textual dimensions in English: Resolving the contradictory findings. *Language, 62*, 384-414.

Bigelow, B., Christensen, L., Karp, S., Miner, B., & Peterson, B. (1994). *Rethinking our classrooms: Teaching for equity and justice*. Milwaukee, WI: Rethinking Schools, Ltd.

Blauner, R. (1969). Internal colonialism and ghetto revolt. *Social Problems, 16*, 393-408.

Bracey, G. (1995). Debunking the myth that the U.S. spends more on schools. *Rethinking Schools, 9*(4), p. 7.

Brisk, M.E. (1985). Using the computer to develop literacy. *Equity and Choice, 1*(1), 25-32.

Bruner, J.S. (1975). Language as an instrument of thought. In A. Davies (Ed.) *Problems of language and learning*. London: Heinemann.

Burkheimer, G.J., Jr., Conger, A., Dunteman, G., Elliot, B., & Mowbray, K. (1990). *Effectiveness of services for language minority limited English proficient students*. Raleigh-Durham, NC: Research Triangle Institute.

Buss, M. & Laurén, C. (1995). *Language immersion: Teaching and second language acquisition: From Canada to Europe*. Proceedings of the University of Vaasa Research Papers. Tutkimuksia No. 192. Vaasa: The University of Vaasa.

Byram, M. & Leman. J. (1990). (Eds.) *Bicultural and trilingual education*. Clevedon, England: Multilingual Matters.

California Association for Bilingual Education (CABE). (1991, July/August). Calexico defies odds on dropout rate. *CABE Newsletter*, pp. 1, 20, 23). Reprinted from *California and the West*, June 3, 1991.

California State Department of Education. (1985). *Case studies in bilingual education: First Year Report.* Federal Grant #G008303723.

Campos, J. & Keatinge, R. (1988). The Carpinteria language minority student experience: From theory, to practice, to success. In T. Skutnabb-Kangas and J. Cummins (Ed.), *Minority education: From shame to struggle.* (pp. 299-308). Clevedon, England: Multilingual Matters.

Carson, C.C., Huelskamp, R.M., & Woodall, T. D. (1993). Perspectives on education in America. *Journal of Educational Research*, 86, 257-312.

Cazden, C.B. (1989). Richmond Road: A multilingual/multicultural primary school in Auckland, New Zealand. *Language and Education*, 3, 143-166.

Cazden, C.B. (1995, April). Language, power and development: The significance of doing what comes UNnaturally. Paper presented at the Global Cultural Diversity Conference, Sydney.

Cazden, C.B. & Snow, C.E. (1990). *English Plus: Issues in bilingual education.* The Annals of the American Academy of Political and Social Science. Newbury Park, CA: Sage Publications.

Chamot, A.U., Cummins, J., Kessler, C., O'Malley, M., & Wong Fillmore, L. (1996). *ScottForesman ESL: Accelerating English language learning.* Glenview, Il: Scott Foresman.

Chamot, A.U., & O'Malley, J.M. (1994). *The CALLA handbook: Implementing the cognitive academic language learning approach.* Reading, MA: Addison-Wesley.

Chamot, A.U. (1996). *Accelerating achievement with learning strategies.* Glenview, IL: ScottForesman.

Chang, H.N-L. & Sakai, L. (1993). *Affirming children's roots: Cultural and linguistic diversity in early care and education.* San Francisco: California Tomorrow.

Chomsky, N. (1987). The manufacture of consent. In J. Peck (Ed.) *The Chomsky reader.* (pp. 121-136). New York: Pantheon Books.

Chomsky, N. (1995). A dialogue with Noam Chomsky. *Harvard Educational Review, 65*, 127-144.

Christian, D. & Montone, C. (1994). *Two-way bilingual programs in the United States, 1993-1994 supplement*. Washington, D.C.: National Center for Research on Cultural Diversity and Second Language Learning.

Churchill, S. (1986). *The education of linguistic and cultural minorities in OECD countries*. Clevedon, England: Multilingual Matters.

Clark, R., Fairclough, N., Ivanič, R., & Martin-Jones, M. (1990). Critical language awareness: Part I: A critical review of three content approaches to language awareness. *Language and Education, 4*(4), 249-260.

Clark, R., Fairclough, N., Ivanič, R., & Martin-Jones, M. (1991). Critical language awareness: Part II: Towards critical alternatives. *Language and Education, 5*(1), 41-54.

Clarke, M.A. (1990). Some cautionary observations on liberation education. *Language Arts 67*(4), 388-398.

Cohen, D.K. (1970). Immigrants and the schools. *Review of Educational Research, 40*, 13-27.

Collier, V.P. (1987). Age and rate of acquisition of second language for academic purposes. *TESOL Quarterly, 21*, 617-641.

Collier, V. (1992). A synthesis of studies examining long-term language-minority student data on academic achievement. *Bilingual Research Journal, 16*(1&2), 187-212.

Collier, V.P. & Thomas, W.P. (1988). Acquisition of cognitive-academic second language proficiency: A six-year study. Paper presented at the American Educational Research Association, New Orleans, April.

Comer, J.P. (1980). *School power: Implications of an intervention project*. New York: The Free Press.

Corson, D. (1990). *Language policy across the curriculum*. Clevedon, England: Multilingual Matters.

Corson, D. (1993). *Language, minority education and gender: Linking social justice and power*. Clevedon, England: Multilingual Matters.

Corson, D. (1995). *Using English words.* New York: Kluwer.

Crawford, A.N. (1994). Communicative approaches to second language acquisition: from oral language development into the core curriculum and L2 literacy. In C.F. Leyba (Ed.), *Schooling and language minority students: A theoretical framework. 2nd edition.* Evaluation, Dissemination and Assessment Center, California State University, Los Angeles.

Crawford, J. (Ed.). (1992a). *Language loyalties: A source book on the Offical English controversy.* Chicago: University of Chicago Press.

Crawford, J. (1992b). *Hold your Tongue: Bilingualism and the politics of "English Only."* New York: Addison Wesley.

Crawford, J. (1995). *Bilingual education: History, politics, theory, and practice. Third edition.* Los Angeles: Bilingual Education Services, Inc.

Criddle, J.D. & Mam, T.B. (1987). *To destroy you is no loss: The odyssey of a Cambodian family.* New York: Doubleday.

Cummins, J. (1981a) The role of primary language development in promoting educational success for language minority students. In California State Department of Education (Ed.), *Schooling and language minority students: A theoretical framework.* Evaluation, Dissemination and Assessment Center, California State University, Los Angeles.

Cummins, J. (1981b), Age on arrival and immigrant second language learning in Canada: A reassessment. *Applied Linguistics, 2,* 132-149.

Cummins J. (1984). *Bilingualism and special education: Issues in assessment and pedagogy.* Clevedon, England: Multilingual Matters.

Cummins, J. (1991a). Forked tongue: The politics of bilingual education: A critique. *Canadian Modern Language Review, 47,* 786-793.

Cummins, J. (1991b). The development of bilingual proficiency from home to school: A longitudinal study of Portuguese-speaking children. *Journal of Education, 173,* 85-98.

Cummins, J. (1993). Bilingualism and second language learning. In W. Grabe (Ed.) *Annual Review of Applied Linguistics, 13,* (pp. 51-70). Cambridge: Cambridge Univesity Press.

Cummins, J. (1995a). The European Schools model in relation to French immersion programs in Canada. In T. Skutnabb-Kangas (Ed.) *Multilingualism for all.* (pp. 159-168). Lisse: Swets & Zeitlinger.

Cummins, J. (1995b). Canadian French immersion programs: A comparison with Swedish immersion programs in Finland. In M. Buss & C. Laurén (Eds.) *Language immersion: Teaching and second language acquisition: From Canada to Europe.* (pp. 7-20). Proceedings of the University of Vaasa Research Papers, Tutkimuksia, No. 192. Vaasa: University of Vaasa.

Cummins, J. & Danesi, M. (1990). *Heritage languages: The development and denial of Canada's linguistic resources.* Toronto: Our Schools Ourselves/Garamond.

Cummins, J., Swain, M., Nakajima, K., Handscombe, J., Green, D. & Tran. C. (1984). Linguistic interdependence among Japanese and Vietnamese immigrant students. In C. Rivera (Ed.) *Communicative competence approaches to language proficiency assessment: Research and application.* (pp. 60-81). Clevedon, England: Multilingual Matters.

Cummins, J. & Swain, M. (1986). *Bilingualism in education: Aspects of theory, research and practice.* London: Longman.

Cummins, J., Harley, B., Swain, M. & Allen, P.A. (1990). Social and individual factors in the development of bilingual proficiency. In Harley, B., Allen, P.A., Cummins, J. & Swain, M. (Eds.), *The development of second language proficiency.* (pp. 119-133). Cambridge: Cambridge University Press.

Cummins, J. & Sayers, D. (1995). *Brave new schools: Challenging cultural illiteracy through global learning networks.* New York: St. Martin's Press.

Daiute, C. (1985). *Writing and computers.* Reading, MA: Addison-Wesley.

Danoff, M.V., Coles, G.J., McLaughlin, D.H. & Reynolds, D.J. (1978). *Evaluation of the impact of ESEA Title VII Spanish/English bilingual education program.* Palo Alto, CA: American Institutes for Research.

Darder, A. (1991). *Culture and power in the classroom: A critical foundation for bicultural education.* New York: Bergin & Garvey.

de Kanter, A.A. & Baker, K.A. (1991, October 5). The effectiveness of bilingual education. *Education Times.*

Delgado-Gaitan, C. (1994). Sociocultural change through literacy: Toward the empowerment of families. In B.M. Ferdman, R-M. Weber, & A. Ramírez (Eds.) *Literacy across languages and cultures*. (pp. 143-170). Albany: SUNY Press.

Delpit, L.D. (1988). The silenced dialogue: Power and pedagogy in educating other peoples's children. *Harvard Educational Review, 58,* 280-298.

Delpit, L. D. (1992). Education in a multicultural society: Our future's greatest challenge. *Journal of Negro Education, 61,* 237-249.

DeVillar, R. A., & Faltis, C. J. (1991). *Computers and cultural diversity: Restructuring for school success.* Albany, NY: SUNY Press.

Deyhle, D. (1995). Navajo youth and Anglo racism: Cultural integrity and resistance. *Harvard Educational Review, 65,* 403-444.

Diaz, R.M. (1985). Bilingual cognitive development: Addressing three gaps in current research. *Child Development, 56,* 1376-1388.

Diaz, R.M. and Klinger, C. (1991). Towards an explanatory model of the interaction between bilingualism and cognitive development. In E. Bialystok (ed.) *Language processing in bilingual children.* (pp. 167-192). Cambridge: Cambridge University Press.

Dolson, D. (1985). The effects of Spanish home language use on the scholastic performance of Hispanic pupils. *Journal of Multilingual and Multicultural Development, 6,* 135-156.

Dolson, D. & Lindholm, K. (1995). World class education for children in California: A comparison of the two-way bilingual immersion and European Schools model. In T. Skutnabb-Kangas (Ed.) *Multilingualism for all.* (pp. 69-102). Lisse: Swets & Zeitlinger.

Donaldson, M. (1978). *Children's minds.* Glasgow: Collins.

D'Souza, D. (1991). *Illiberal education: The politics of race and sex on campus.* New York: Vintage Books.

Dunn, L. (1987). *Bilingual Hispanic children on the U.S. mainland: A review of research on their cognitive, linguistic, and scholastic development.* Circle Pines, Minesota: American Guidance Service.

Early, M. (1990). Enabling first and second language learners in the classroom. *Language Arts, 67,* 567-575.

Eccles, F. (1994). How can we get parents to write? (pamphlet). Merced, CA: Merced County Office of Education.

Eccles, F., Kirton, E., & Xiong, B. (1994). *The family connection: Hmong parent education project.* Merced, CA: Merced County Office of Education.

Edelsky, C. (1986). *Writing in a bilingual program: Habia una vez.* Norwood, NJ: Ablex.

Edwards, J. (1994). *Multilingualism.* London: Routledge.

Epstein, N. (1977). *Language, ethnicity and the schools.* Washington, D.C.: Institute for Educational Leadership.

Erickson, F. (1987). Transformation and school success: The politics and culture of educational achievement. *Anthropology & Education Quarterly, 18,* 335-356.

Estrada, H.M. (1986). 'Pajaro experience' teaches parents how to teach kids. *Santa Cruz Sentinel,* Friday October 31, p. A4.

Evans, E. (1978). Welsh (Cymraeg). In C.V. James (Ed.) *The older mother tongues of the United Kingdom.* London: Centre for Information on Language Teaching and Research.

Faltis, C.J. (1993). *Joinfostering: adapting teaching strategies for the multilingual classroom.* New York: Macmillan.

Fielding, L.G. & Pearson, P.D. (1994). Reading comprehension: What works. *Educational Leadership, 51*(5), 62-68.

Fishman, J.A. (1976). *Bilingual education: An international sociological perspective.* Rowley, MA: Newbury House.

Fishman, J.A. (1991). *Reversing language shift.* Clevedon, England: Multilingual Matters.

Fordham, S. (1990). Racelessness as a factor in Black students' school success: Pragmatic strategy or pyrrhic victory? In N.M. Hidalgo, C.L. McDowell, & E.V. Siddle (Eds.) *Facing racism in education.* (pp. 232-262). Reprint series No. 21, Harvard Educational Review.

Foster, J.L. & Swinney, R. (in press). The dual language program of Manhattan's District Three. In D. Sayers (Ed.) *Bilingual education: A curriculum resource handbook*. Ontario, CA: California Association for Bilingual Education.

Foucault, M. (1980). *Power/Knowledge*. Edited by C. Gordon. New York: Pantheon.

Frederickson, J. (Ed.) (1995). *Reclaiming our voices: Bilingual education, critical pedagogy & praxis*. Ontario, CA: California Association for Bilingual Education.

Freeman, D. E., & Freeman, Y. S. (1994). *Between worlds: Access to second language acquisition*. Portsmouth, NH: Heinemann.

Freeman, Y. S., & Freeman, D. E. (1992). *Whole language for second language learners*. Portsmouth, NH: Heinemann.

Freire, P. (1970/1981). *Pedagogy of the oppressed*. New York: Continuum.

Freire, P. (1983). Banking education. In H. Giroux & D. Purpel (Eds.) *The hidden curriculum and moral education: Deception or discovery?* Berkeley, CA: McCutcheon Publishing Corporation.

Freire, P. & Macedo, D. (1987). *Literacy: Reading the word and the world*. South Hadley, MA: Bergin & Garvey.

French, M. (1992). *The war against women*. New York: Summit Books.

Gabina, J.J. et al. (1986). *EIFE. Influence of factors on the learning of Basque*. Gasteiz: Central Publications Service of the Basque Country.

Gale, K., McClay, D., Christie, M., & Harris, S. (1981) Academic achievement in the Milingimbi bilingual education program. *TESOL Quarterly, 15*, 297-314.

Galtung, J. (1980). *The true worlds: A transnational perspective*. New York: The Free Press.

Garcia, E. (1991). *Education of linguistically and culturally diverse students: Effective instructional practices*. Educational Practice report 1. Santa Cruz: The National Center for Research on Cultural Diversity and Second Language Learning.

Genesee, F. (1987). *Learning through two languages: Studies of immersion and bilingual education.* Cambridge, MA: Newbury House.

Gersten, R. (1985). Structured immersion for language minority students: Results of a longitudinal evaluation. *Educational Evaluation and Policy Analysis, 7,* 187-196.

Gersten, R. & Woodward, J. (1985a, September). A case for structured immersion. *Educational Leadership,* 75-79.

Gersten, R. & Woodward, J. (1985b, September). Response to Santiago. *Educational Leadership,* 83-84.

Geva, E. & Ryan, E.B. (1987). Linguistic knowledge and cognitive demands for academic skills in first and second language. Unpublished manuscript, OISE.

Gibbons, J., White, W., & Gibbons, P. (1994). Combatting educational disadvantage among Lebanese Australian children. In T. Skutnabb-Kangas & R. Phillipson (Eds.) *Linguistic human rights: Overcoming linguistic discrimination.* (pp. 253-262). Berlin: Mouton de Gruyter.

Gibbons, P. (1991). *Learning to learn in a second language.* Newtown, Australia: Primary English Teaching Association.

Gibson, M. (1995). Patterns of acculturation & high school performance. *University of California LMRI, 4*(9), 1-3.

Gingrich, N. (1995). English literacy is the coin of the realm. *Los Angeles Times,* August 4.

Giroux, H.A. (1991). Series introduction: Rethinking the pedagogy of voice, difference and cultural struggle. In C.E. Walsh, *Pedagogy and the struggle for voice: Issues of language, power, and schooling for Puerto Ricans.* (pp xv-xxvii). Toronto: OISE Press.

Glazer, N. & Cummins, J. (1985). Viewpoints on bilingual education. *Equity and Choice, 2,* 47-52.

Goldenberg, C. (1991). *Instructional conversations and their classroom application.* Educational Practice Report 2. Santa Cruz: The National Center for Research on Cultural Diversity and Second Language Learning.

Göncz, L. & Kodžopeljić, J. (1991). Exposure to two languages in the preschool period. *Journal of Multilingual and Multicultural Development, 12,* 137-163.

Goodlad, J.I. (1984). *A place called school: Prospects for the future.* New York: McGraw Hill.

Gramsci, A. (1971). *Selections from the prison notebooks.* New York: International Publications.

Graves, D. (1983). *Writing: Teachers and children at work.* Exeter, NH: Heinemann Educational Books.

Gray, T. (1977). *Challenge to USOE final evaluation of the impact of ESEA Title VII Spanish/English bilingual education programs.* Arlington, VA: Center for Applied Linguistics.

Guerra, V. (1984). *Predictors of second language learners' error judgements in written English.* Doctoral dissertation, University of Houston.

Hacker, A. (1995). *Two nations: Black and white, separate, hostile, unequal.* New York: Ballantine Books.

Hakuta, K. (1986). *Mirror of Language: The debate on bilingualism.* New York: Basic Books.

Hakuta, K. & Diaz, R.M. (1985). The relationship between degree of bilingualism and cognitive ability: A critical discussion and some new longitudinal data. In K.E. Nelson (Ed.), *Children's language. Vol. V* Hillsdale, New Jersey: Erlbaum.

Hancin-Bhatt, B., & Nagy, W. (1994). Lexical transfer and second language morphological development. *Applied Psycholinguistics, 15,* 289-310.

Handscombe, J. (1994). Putting it all together. In F. Genesee (Ed.) *Educating second language children children: The whole child, the whole curriculum, the whole community.* (pp. 331-356). Cambridge: Cambridge University Press.

Handscombe, J. & Becker, N. (1994). *A week of school.* North York: North York Board of Education.

Harley, B. (1995). Introduction: The lexicon in second language research. In B. Harley (Ed.) *Lexical issues in language learning*. (pp. 1-28). Philadelphia, PA: John Benjamins.

Harley, B., Allen, P., Cummins, J. & Swain, M. (Eds.). (1990). *The development of second language proficiency*. Cambridge, England: Cambridge University Press.

Harré, R. & Gillett, G. (1994). *The discursive mind*. Thousand Oaks, CA: Sage.

Harris, S. (1990). *Two way Aboriginal schooling: Education and cultural survival*. Canberra: Aboriginal Studies Press.

Harry, B. (1992). *Cultural diversity, families, and the special education system*. New York: Teachers College Press.

Hayes, C.W., Bahruth, R., & Kessler, C. (1991). *Literacy con cariño: A story of migrant children's success*. Portsmouth, NH: Heinemann.

Heath, S.B. (1983). *Ways with words*. Cambridge: Cambridge University Press.

Heath, S.B. (1986). Sociocultural contexts of language development. In California State Department of Education (Ed.), *Beyond language: Social and cultural factors in schooling language minority students*. Los Angeles: Evaluation, Dissemination, and Assessment Center.

Heath, S.B. (1993). Inner city life through drama: Imagining the language classroom. *TESOL Quarterly, 27*(2), 177-192.

Heath, S.B., & Mangiola, L. (1991). *Children of promise: Literate activity in linguistically and culturally diverse classrooms*. Washington, DC: National Education Association.

Hébert, R. et al. (1976). Rendement academique et langue d'enseignement chez les élèves franco-manitobains. Saint-Boniface, Manitoba: Centre de recherches du Collège Universitaire de Saint-Boniface.

Heller, F. & Leone, B. (1995). California's Proposition 187: Moving toward racism and intolerance. *TESOL Matters, 5*(1), pp. 1 & 4.

Henderson, R.W. & Landesman, E.M. (1992). *Mathematics and middle school students of Mexican descent: The effects of thematically integrated instruction*. Research Report 5. Santa Cruz: The National Center for Research on Cultural Diversity and Second Language Learning.

Hirsch, E.D., Jr. (1987). *Cultural literacy: What every American needs to know*. Boston: Houghton Mifflin Co.

Hodgkinson, H. (1991, September). Reform versus reality. *Phi Delta Kappan*, 73, 9-16.

Holt, D. (Ed.). (1993). *Cooperative learning: A response to linguistic and cultural diversity*. Washington, DC: Center for Applied Linguistics.

Hopkins, D.S. (1987). *Improving the quality of schooling*. Lewes, England: The Falmer Press.

Hornblower, M. (1995, November 13). No tolerance for diversity. *TIME*, 44-45.

Houston, M. (1995, Spring). Tell me a story (Then tell it again): Supporting literacy for preschool children from bilingual families. *Interaction*, pp. 32-35.

Hughes, R. (1993). *Culture of complaint: A passionate look into the ailing heart of America*. New York: Warner Books.

Imhoff, G. (1990). *Learning in two languages: From conflict to consensus in the reorganization of schools*. New Brunswick, N.J.: Transaction Publishers.

Imhoff, G. (1990). The position of U.S. English on bilingual education. In C.B. Cazden & C.E. Snow (Eds.) *English Plus: Issues in bilingual education*. (pp. 48-61). The Annals of the American Academy of Political and Social Science. Newbury Park, CA: Sage Publications.

Igoa, C. (1995). *The inner world of the immigrant child*. New York: St. Martin's Press.

Israelite, N., Ewoldt, C., & Hoffmeister, R. (1992). *Bilingual/bicultural education for deaf and hard-of-hearing students: A review of the literature oon the effects of native sign language on majority language acquisition*. Toronto: Ontario Ministry of Education.

Jasso, A., & Jasso, R. (1995). Critical pedagogy: Not a method, but a way of life. In J. Frederickson (Ed.) *Reclaiming our voices: Bilingual education, critical pedagogy & praxis.* (pp. 253-259). Ontario, CA: California Association for Bilingual Education.

Johnson, R., Liddell, S, & Erting, C. (1989). *Unlocking the curriculum: Principles for achieving access in deaf education.* Washington, DC: Gallaudet University. Working Paper 89-3.

Kalantzis, M., & Cope, B. (1993). Histories of pedagogy, cultures of schooling. In B. Cope & M. Kalantzis (Eds.) *The powers of literacy: A genre approach to teaching writing.* (pp. 38-62). London: The Falmer Press.

Kaprielian-Churchill, I. & Churchill, S. (1994). *The pulse of the world: Refugees in our schools.* Toronto: OISE Press.

Kemp, J. (1984). *Native language knowledge as a predictor of success in learning a foreign language with special reference to a disadvantaged population.* Thesis submitted for the M.A. Degree, Tel-Aviv University.

Kennedy, P. (1993). *Preparing for the twenty-first century.* New York: Harper Collins Publishers Ltd.

Kessler, C. (Ed.). (1992). *Cooperative language learning: A teacher's resource book.* Englewood Cliffs, NJ: Prentice-Hall Regents.

Klesmer, H. (1994). Assessment and teacher perceptions of ESL student achievement. *English Quarterly, 26*(3), 8-11.

Kloss, H. (1977). *The American bilingual tradition.* Rowley, MA: Newbury House.

Kozol, J. (1991). *Savage inequalities: Children in America's schools.* New York: Crown Publishers.

Krashen, S. (1981). *Second language acquisition and second language learning.* London: Pergamon Press.

Krashen, S. (1991a). *Bilingual education: A focus on current research.* Occasional Papers in Bilingual Education, Spring 1991, Number 3. Washington, DC: National Clearinghouse for Bilingual Education.

Krashen, S. (1991b, July/August). Review of *Forked Tongue*. *CABE Newsletter*, *14*(1), pp. 16, 22.

Krashen, S. (1993). *The power of reading*. Englewood, CO: Libraries Unlimited.

Krashen, S. & Biber, D. (1987). *Bilingual education in California*. Sacramento: California Association for Bilingual Education.

Labov, W. (1970). *The logic of non-standard English*. Champaign, Illinois: National Council of Teachers of English.

Ladson-Billings, G. (1995). Toward a theory of culturally relevant pedagogy. *American Educational Research Journal*, *32*, 465-491.

Laing, R.D. (1969). *Self and others*. Harmondsworth, England: Penguin Books.

Lambert, W.E. (1975). Culture and language as factors in learning and education. In A. Wolfgang (Ed.), *Education of immigrant students*. Toronto: O.I.S.E.

Lambert, W.E. & Tucker, G.R. (1972). *Bilingual education of children: The St. Lambert Experiment*. Rowley, Mass.: Newbury House.

Landry, R. (1993). Determinisme et determination: Vers une pedagogie de l'excellence en milieu minoritaire. *Canadian Modern Language Review*, *49*, 887-927.

Landry, R. & Allard, R. (1991). Can schools promote additive bilingualism in minority group children? In L. Malavé & G. Duquette (Eds.) *Language, culture, and cognition: A collection of studies in first and second language acquisition*. (pp. 198-231). Clevedon, England: Multilingual Matters.

Laosa, L. (1995). *Longitudinal measurements of English-language proficiency acquisition by children who migrate to the United States from Puerto Rico: Performance and psychometric data on the Language Assessment Battery (LAB) tests*. Princeton, NJ: Educational Testing Service.

Legaretta, D. (1979). The effects of program models on language acquisition by Spanish speaking children. *TESOL Quarterly*, *13*, 521-534.

Levin, H. M. (1988). *Accelerated schools for at-risk students*. New Brunswick, NJ: Center for Policy Research in Education.

Lewis, E.G. (1976). Bilingualism and bilingual education: The ancient world to the renaissance. In J.A. Fishman, *Bilingual education: An international sociological perspective.* (pp. 150-200). Rowley, MA: Newbury House.

Leyba, C. (Ed.) (1994). *Schooling and language minority students: A theoretical framework*, 2nd ed. Los Angeles: Evaluation, Dissemination, and Assessment Center.

Llewellyn, R. (1968). *How green was my valley.* Toronto: Signet.

López, A. (1988, October). The infant-toddler and child development centers and parent education and support. Paper presented at the Workshop on Early Development of Hispanic Infants and Children: Options for Intervention to Improve School Readiness and Long-Term Academic Achievement, New York.

Lucas, I. (1981). Bilingual education and the melting pot: Getting burned. The Illinois Issues Humanities Essays: 5. Illinois Humanities Council, Champaign, Illinois.

Lucas, T., Henze, R., & Donato, R. (1990). Promoting the success of Latino language-minority students: an exploratory study of six high schools. *Harvard Educational Review, 60,* 315-340.

Lucas, T. & Katz, A. (1994). Reframing the debate: The roles of native languages in English-only programs for language minority students. *TESOL Quarterly, 28*(3), 537-562.

Macedo, D.P. (1993). Literacy for stupidification: The pedagogy of big lies. *Harvard Educational Review, 63,* 183-207.

Macedo, D.P. (1994). *Literacies of power: What Americans are not allowed to know.* Boulder, CO: Westview Press.

Mackay, R. (1986). *The role of English in education in an Eastern Arctic school.* Unpublished Ph.D. Thesis, L'Université de Montreal, Montreal, Quebec.

Mackey, W.F. (1970). A typology of bilingual education. *Foreign Language Annals, 3,* 596-608.

Malakoff, M. & Hakuta, K. (1991). Translation skill and metalinguistic awareness in bilinguals. In E. Bialystok (Ed.) *Language processing in bilingual children.* (pp. 141-166). Cambridge: Cambridge University Press.

Malherbe, E.G. (1946). *The bilingual school.* Johannesburg: Bilingual School Association.

Malherbe, E.G. (1969). Introductory remarks. In L.G. Kelly (Ed.) *Description and measurement of bilingualism.* Toronto: Canadian National Commission for UNESCO and University of Toronto Press.

Malherbe, E.G. (1978). Bilingual education in the Republic of South Africa. In B. Spolsky & R.L. Cooper (Eds.) *Case studies in bilingual education.* (pp. 167-202). Rowley, MA: Newbury House.

Mason, D.G. (1994, March). *Bilingual/bicultural deaf education is appropriate.* Occasional Monograph Series, No. 2., Association of Canadian Educators of the Hearing Impaired.

May, S. (1994). *Making multicultural education work.* Clevedon, England: Multilingual Matters.

Mayer, C. & Wells, G. (in press). Can the linguistic interdependence theory support a bilingual-bicultural model of literacy education for deaf students? *Journal of Deaf Studies and Deaf Education.*

McCaleb, S.P. (1994). *Building communities of learners: A collaboration among teachers, students, families and community.* New York: St. Martin's Press.

McCarty, T.L. (1993, March). Language, literacy, and the image of the child in American Indian classrooms. *Language Arts, 70,* 182-192.

McFeatters, D. (1995, March 27). Divided by a common language. *The Globe & Mail,* p. A11.

McLaughlin, B. (1984). Early bilingualism: Methodological and theoretical issues. In M. Paradis and Y. Lebrun (Eds.) *Early bilingualism and child development.* Lisse: Swets & Zeitlinger B.V.

McLaughlin, B. (1986). Multilingual education: Theory east and west. In B. Spolsky (Ed.) *Language and education in multilingual settings.* Clevedon, England: Multilingual Matters.

McLaughlin, B. (1995). *Fostering second language development in young children: Principles and practices.* Santa Cruz: National Center for Research on Cultural Diversity and Second Language Learning.

McLaughlin, D. (1992). Power and the politics of knowledge: Transformative schooling for minority language learners. In D.E. Murray (Ed.) *Diversity as resource: Redefining cultural literacy.* (pp. 235-258). Alexandra, VA: TESOL.

Medina, M. Jr. & Escamilla, K. (1992). Evaluation of transitional and maintenance bilingual programs. *Urban Education, 27,* 263-290.

Mehan, H., Hertweck, A., & Meihls, J.L. (1986). *Handicapping the handicapped: Decision making in students' educational careers.* Palo Alto: Stanford University Press.

Meyer, L. (1994, Fall). Barrio buddies: Learning through letters about kids, cultures, communities, and self-confrontation. *California Perspectives: Special Issue: Community Canons.* Vol. 4, pp. 92-109.

Moffett, J. (1989). Censorship and spiritual education. *English Education, 21,* 70-87.

Mohan, B. (1986). *Language and content.* Reading, MA: Addison-Wesley.

Mohanty, A.K. (1994). *Bilingualism in a multilingual society: Psychological and pedagogical implications.* Mysore: Central Institute of Indian Languages.

Montessori Life. (1990). "To keep the door open"…A conversation with Antonia López. *Montessori Life, 2*(3), 20-22.

Morison, S.H. (1990). A Spanish-English dual-language program in New York City. In C.B. Cazden & C.E. Snow (Eds.) *English Plus: Issues in bilingual education.* The Annals of the American Academy of Political and Social Science. (pp. 160-169). Newbury Park, CA: Sage Publications.

Nagy, W., Garcia, G.E., Durgunoglu, A., & Hancin, B. (1993). Spanish-English bilingual students' use of cognates in English reading. *Journal of Reading Behavior, 25,* 241-259.

National Center for Educational Statistics. (1994). *Mini-digest of educational statistics 1994.* Washington, D.C.: U.S. Department of Education.

National Coalition of Advocates for Students. (1988). *New voices: Immigrant students in U.S. public schools.* Boston: National Coalition of Advocates for Students.

National Commission on Excellence in Education. (1983). *A nation at risk: The imperative for educational reform.* Washington, D.C.: U.S. Government Printing Office.

Newman, D., Griffin, P., & Cole, M. (1989). *The construction zone.* Cambridge: Cambridge University Press.

New Zealand Department of Education. (1988). *New Voices: Second language learning and teaching. A handbook for primary teachers.* Wellington: Department of Education.

Nieto, S. (1996). *Affirming diversity: The sociopolitical context of multicultural education. 2nd edition.* White Plains, NY: Longman.

Oakes, J. (1985). *Keeping track: How high schools structure inequality.* New Haven: Yale University Press.

Ogbu, J. (1978). *Minority education and caste.* New York: Academic Press.

Ogbu, J.U. (1992). Understanding cultural diversity and learning. *Educational Researcher, 21*(8), 5-14 & 24.

Ogle, D. (1986). K-W-L: a teaching model that develops active reading of expository text. *The Reading Teacher, 39*(6), 164-170.

Olsen, L. (1988). *Crossing the schoolhouse border: Immigrant students and the California public schools.* San Francisco: California Tomorrow.

Olsen, L., & Minnicucci, C. (1992, April). Educating limited English proficient students in secondary schools: Critical issues emerging from research in California schools. Paper presented at the American Education Research Association annual conference, San Francisco.

Olsen, L., Chang, H., De La Rosa Salazar, D., Leong, C., McCall Perez, Z., McClain, G., & Raffel, L. (1994). *The unfinished journey: Restructuring schools in a diverse society.* San Francisco: California Tomorrow.

Olson, D.R. (1977). From utterance to text: The bias of language in speech and writing. *Harvard Educational Review, 47,* 257-281.

O'Malley, J.M. (1978). Review of the evaluation of the impact of ESEA Title VII Spanish/English bilingual education program. *Bilingual Resources, 1,* 6-10.

O'Malley, J.M. (1996). *Using authentic assessment in ESL classrooms.* Glenview, IL: ScottForesman.

O'Malley, J.M. & Pierce, L.V. (1996). *Authentic assessment for English language learners: Practical Approaches for the K-12 classroom.* Reading, MA: Addison-Wesley.

Organization for Economic Co-operation and Development (OECD). (1991). *Education and cultural and linguistic pluralism: Synthesis of case studies. Effective strategies and approaches in schools.* Paris: OECD/CERI.

Ortiz, A.A. & Yates, J.R. (1983). Incidence of exceptionality among Hispanics: Implications for manpower planning. *NABE Journal, 7,* 41-54.

Patrick, D. (1994). Minority language education and social context. *Inuit Studies, 18*(1-2), 183-199.

Patthey-Chavez, G.G., Clare, L., & Gallimore, R. (1995). *Creating a community of scholarship with instructional conversations in a transitional bilingual classroom.* Santa Cruz: National Center for Research on Cultural Diversity and Second Language Learning.

Pease-Alvarez, L. (1989). Bilingual education in Healdsburg California: Project Puente and the Healdsburg Two-Way Spanish Immersion Program. Report prepared for the CERI project on Education and Cultural and Linguistic Pluralism.

Peirce, B.N. (1995). Social identity, investment, and language learning. *TESOL Quarterly, 29*(1), 9-31.

Peña-Hughes, E. & Solís, J. (1980). *ABCs* (unpublished report). McAllen, TX: McAllen Independent School District.

Peterson, B. (1994). Teaching for social justice: One teacher's story. In B. Bigelow, L. Christensen, S. Karp, B. Miner, & B. Peterson (Eds.), *Rethinking our classrooms: Teaching for equity and justice.* (pp. 30-33). Milwaukee, WI: Rethinking Schools.

Pierce, L.V., & O'Malley, J.M. (1992). *Performance and portfolio assessment for language minority students.* Washington, DC: National Clearinghouse for Bilingual Education.

Platero, D. (1975). Bilingual education in the Navajo Nation. In R.C. Troike and N. Modiano (Eds.) *Proceedings of the First Inter-American Conference on Bilingual Education.* Arlington Va.: Center for Applied Linguistics.

Poplin, M. & Weeres, J. (1992). *Voices from the inside: A report on schooling from inside the classroom.* Claremont, CA: The Institute for Education in Transformation at the Claremont Graduate School.

Porter, R. P. (1990). *Forked tongue: The politics of bilingual education.* New York: Basic Books.

Porter, R. P. (1991, June 5). The false alarm over early English acquisition. *Education Week,* p. 36.

Pruyn, M. (1994). Confronting ignorance and hate with a pedagogy of empowerment: The U.S. "English Only" movement and critical bilingual education. *Trans/forms: Insurgent Voices in Education, 1*(1), 73-88.

Ramírez, C.M. (1985). *Bilingual education and language interdependence: Cummins and beyond.* Doctoral dissertation, Yeshiva University.

Ramírez, J.D. (1992). Executive summary. *Bilingual Research Journal, 16,* 1-62.

Ratleff, J.E. (1993). *The effects of instructional conversations on the language and concept development of learning handicapped students.* Unpublished doctoral dissertation, University of California, Los Angeles.

Rees, O. (1981). Mother tongue and English project. In Commission for Racial Equality (Ed.), *Mother tongue teaching conference report.* Bradford: U.K.: Bradford College.

Regnier, R. (1988). Indians 'r' us: The experience of a survival school pedagogy. *Our Schools, Ourselves, 1*(1), 22-44.

Rehbein, J. (1984). *Diskurs und Versthen: Zur Role der Muttersprache bei der Textarbeitung in der Zweitsprache.* University of Hamburg.

Reich, R. (1991). *The work of nations: Preparing ourselves for 21st century capitalism.* New York: Knopf.

Reid, E. & Reich, H. (1992). *Breaking the boundaries: Migrant workers' children in the EC.* Clevedon, England: Multilingual Matters.

Rethinking Schools, (1991). *Rethinking Columbus: Teaching about the 500th anniversary of Columbus's arrival in North America.* Madison, WI: Rethinking Schools Ltd.

Reyes, M. de la Luz. (1992). Challenging venerable assumptions: Literacy instruction for linguistically different students. *Harvard Educational Review, 62,* 427-446.

Reynolds, A.G. (1991). The cognitive consequences of bilingualism. In A.G. Reynolds (Ed.) *Bilingualism, multiculturalism, and second language learning.* (pp. 145-182). Hillsdale, NJ: Lawrence Erlbaum Associates.

Ricciardelli, L. (1989). *Childhood bilingualism: Metalinguistic awareness and creativity.* Adelaide: University of Adelaide. Ph.D. dissertation.

Ricciardelli, L. (1992). Bilingualism and cognitive development in relation to threshold theory. *Journal of Psycholinguistic Research, 21,* 301-316.

Rodriguez, R. (1982). *Hunger of memory: The education of Richard Rodriguez.* Boston: David R. Godine.

Rodriguez, R. (1985). Bilingualism, con: Outdated and unrealistic. *The New York Times,* November 10, Section 12, p. 83.

Rogosa, D.R. & Willett, J. (1985). Understanding correlates of change by modelling individual differences in growth. *Psychometrica, 50,* 203-228.

Rosier, P. & Holm, W. (1980). *The Rock Point experience: A longitudinal study of a Navajo school program.* Washington, D.C.: Center for Applied Linguistics.

Rossell, C.H. (1990). The effectiveness of educational alternatives for limited English proficient children. In G. Imhoff (Ed.) *Learning in two languages: From conflict to consensus in the reorganization of schools.* (pp. 71-122). New Brunswick, N.J: Transaction Publishers.

Rossell, C.H. (1992). Nothing matters? A critique of the Ramírez et al. longitudinal study of instructional programs for language-minority children. *Bilingual Research Journal, 16*(1&2), 159-186.

Rossell, C.H. & Ross, J.M. (1986). The social science evidence on bilingual education. *Journal of Law and Education, 15,* 385-418.

Rueda, R. (1989). Defining mild disabilities with language-minority students. *Exceptional Children, 56*, 121-128.

Ruiz, R. (1988). Orientations in language planning. In S.L. McKay & S.C. Wong (Eds.) *Language diversity: Problem or resource?* (pp. 3-25). New York: Newbury House.

Ruiz, R. (1991). The empowerment of language minority students. In C. Sleeter (Ed.) *Empowerment through multicultural education.* Albany: SUNY Press.

Rumbaut, R.G. & Ima, K. (1987). *The adaptation of Southeast Asian refugee youth:A comparative study.* San Diego: Office of Refugee Resettlement.

Ryan, W. (1972). *Blaming the victim.* New York: Vintage.

Sánchez, F. (1992). Integrated thematic exploration process. Unpublished manuscript.

Sánchez, G. 1943, Pachucos in the making. *Common Ground, 4*, 13-20.

San Diego City Schools. (1982). *An exemplary approach to bilingual education:A comprehensive handbook for implementing an elementary-level Spanish-English language immersion program.* San Diego: San Diego City Schools.

Santiago, R.L. (1985, September). Understanding bilingual education — or the sheep in wolf's clothing. *Educational Leadership*, 79-83.

Saville-Troike, M. (1984). What *really* matters in second language learning for academic achievement? *TESOL Quarterly, 18*, 199-219.

Schifini, A. (1994). Language, literacy, and content instruction: Strategies for teachers. In K. Spangfenberg-Urbschat & R. Pritchard (Eds.), *Kids come in all languages: reading instruction for ESL students.* (pp. 158-179). Newark, DE: International Reading Association.

Schlesinger, A. Jr. (1991). *The disuniting of America.* New York: W.W. Norton.

Schlossman, S. (1983). Self-evident remedy? George I Sánchez, segregation, and enduring dilemmas in bilingual education. *Teachers College Record, 84*, 871-907.

Schweinhart, L. J., Weikart, D. P., & Larney, M. B. (1986). Consequences of three preschool curriculum models through age 15. *Early Childhood Research Quarterly, 1,* 15-45.

Shor, I. (1992). *Empowering education: Critical teaching for social change.* Chicago: The University of Chicago Press.

Shuy, R.W. (1977). Problems in assessing language ability in bilingual education programs. In H. Lafontaine, B. Persky, & L. Golubchick (Eds.) *Bilingual education.* (pp. 376-380). Wayne, NJ: Avery Publishing Group Inc.

Siegel, J. (1995, September). Neighborhood as laboratory. *Electronic Learning,* 26-29.

Sierra, J. & Olaziregi, I. (1989). *EIFE 2. Influence of factors on the learning of Basque.* Gasteiz: Central Publications Service of the Basque Country.

Sierra, J. & Olaziregi, I. (199)1. *EIFE 3. Influence of factors on the learning of Basque. Study of the models A, B and D in second year Basic General Education.* Gasteiz: Central Publications Service of the Basque Country.

Sirén, U. 1991. *Minority language transmission in early childhood: Parental intention and language use.* Stockholm: Institute of International Education, Stockholm University.

Sirotnik, K.A. (1983). What you see is what you get - consistency, persistency, and mediocrity in classrooms. *Harvard Educational Review, 53,* 16-31.

Sizer, T. R. (1984). *Horace's compromise: The dilemma of the American high school.* Boston: Houghton Mifflin.

Skutnabb-Kangas, T. (1984). *Bilingualism or not: The education of minorities.* Clevedon, England: Multilingual Matters.

Skutnabb-Kangas, T. (1988). Resource power and autonomy through discourse in conflict - a Finnish migrant school strike in Sweden. In T. Skutnabb-Kangas & J. Cummins (Eds.) *Minority education: From shame to struggle.* (pp. 251-277). Clevedon, England: Multilingual Matters.

Skutnabb-Kangas, T. & Phillipson, R. (1994). *Linguistic human rights.* Berlin: Mouton de Gruyter.

Skutnabb-Kangas, T. & Toukomaa, P. (1976). *Teaching migrant children's mother tongue and learning the language of the host country in the context of the sociocultural situation of the migrant family.* Helsinki: The Finnish National Commission for UNESCO.

Smith, G.H. (1992). Kura Kaupapa Maori: Contesting and reclaiming education in Aotearoa. In D.R. Ray & D.H. Poonwassie (Eds.) *Education and cultural differences: New perspectives.* (pp. 89-108). New York: Garland Publishing Inc.

Snow, C. (1983). Literacy and language: Relationships during the preschool years. *Harvard Educational Review, 53,* 165-189.

Snow, C.E., Cancino, H., De Temple, J., & Schley, S. (1991). Giving formal definitions: A linguistic or metalinguistic skill? In E. Bialystok (ed.) *Language processing in bilingual children.* (pp. 90-112). Cambridge: Cambridge University Press.

Snow, D.E. & Hoefnagel-Höhle, M. The critical period for language acquisition: Evidence from second language learning. *Child Development, 49,* 1114-1128.

Soto, L.D. (in press). *Language, culture, and power: Bilingual families and the struggle for quality education.* New York: SUNY Press.

Spangenberg-Urbschat, K. & Pritchard, R. (Eds.). *Kids come in all languages: reading instruction for ESL students.* Newark, DE: International Reading Association.

Spolsky, B. & Cooper, R.L. (1978). *Case studies in bilingual education.* Rowley, MA: Newbury House.

Stanford Working Group. (1993). *Federal education programs for limited-English-proficient students: A blueprint for the second generation.* Stanford, CA: Report of the Stanford Working Group, Stanford University.

Suárez-Orozco, M. (1987). Towards a psychosocial understanding of Hispanic adaptation to American schooling. In H.T. Trueba (Ed.), *Success or failure? Learning and the language minority student.* (156-168). Cambridge, MA: Newbury House.

Suárez-Orozco, M. (1989). Psychosocial aspects of achievement motivation among recent Hispanic immigrants. In H.T. Trueba, G. Spindler, & L. Spindler (Eds.), *What do anthropologists have to say about dropouts? The first centennial conference on children at risk.* (pp. 99-116). New York: The Falmer Press.

Swain, M. (1979). Bilingual education: Research and its implications. In C.A. Yorio, K. Perkins & J. Schachter (Eds.) *On TESOL '79: The learner in focus.* Washington, D.C.: TESOL.

Swain, M. (in press). Collaborative dialogue: Its contribution to second language learning. *Revista Canaria de Estudios Ingléses, 33.*

Swain, M. & Lapkin, S. (1982). *Evaluating bilingual education.* Clevedon, England: Multilingual Matters.

Swedo, J. (1987, Fall). Effective teaching strategies for handicapped limited English proficient students. *Bilingual Special Education Newsletter, 6,* 1-5.

Taylor, W. L., & Piché, D. M. (1991). *A report on shortchanging children: The impact of fiscal inequality on the education of students at risk.* Washington, DC: U.S. House of Representatives, Committee on Education and Labor.

Terrazas, B. (and Students for Cultural and Linguistic Democracy). (1995). Struggling for power and voice: A high school experience. In J. Frederickson (Ed.) *Reclaiming our voices: Bilingual education, critical pedagogy & praxis.* (pp. 279-310). Ontario, CA: California Association for Bilingual Education.

Tharp, R.G., & Gallimore, R. (1991). *The instructional conversation: Teaching and learning in social activity.* Santa Cruz: National Center for Research on Cultural Diversity and Second Language Learning.

The President's Commission on Foreign Language and International Studies. (1980). A critique of U.S. capability. A report to the President from the President's Commission on Foreign Language and International Studies. *The Modern Language Journal, 64,* 9-57.

Thomas, W. (1992). An analysis of the research methodology of the Ramírez study. *Bilingual Research Journal, 16*(1&2), 213-245.

Thomas, W.P. & Collier, V.P. (1995). *Research summary of study in progress: Language minority student achievement and program effectiveness.* Summary of presentation at the California Association of Bilingual Education, Anaheim, February.

Tikunoff, W.J. (1983). *An emerging description of successful bilingual instruction: An executive summary of Part 1 of the SBIF Descriptive Study.* San Francisco: Far West Laboratory.

Tizard, J., Schofield, W.N. & Hewison, J. (1982). Collaboration between teachers and parents in assisting children's reading. *British Journal of Educational Psychology, 52,* 1-15.

Torres-Guzman, M. (1995). Recasting frames: Latino parent involvement. In O. Garcia & Colin Baker (Eds.), *Policy and practice in bilingual education: Extending the foundations.* (pp. 259-272). Clevedon, England: Multilingual Matters.

Troike, R. (1978). Research evidence for the effectiveness of bilingual education. *NABE Journal, 3,* 13-24.

Trueba, H.T. (1988). Culturally based explanations of minority students' academic achievement. *Anthropology & Education Quarterly, 19,* 270-287.

Tschanz, L. (1980). *Native languages and government policy: An historical examination.* Native Language Research Series No. 2, Centre for Research and Teaching of Canadian Native Languages, The University of Western Ontario.

United States v. State of Texas (1981). *Civil action # 5281 (Bilingual Education) Memorandum Opinion.* January.

U.S. Commission on Civil Rights. (1973). *Teachers and students: Differences in teacher interaction with Mexican-American and Anglo students.* Washington, D.C.: U.S. Government Printing Office.

Vásquez, O.A., Pease-Alvarez, L., & Shannon, S.M. (1994). *Pushing boundaries: Language and culture in a Mexicano community.* New York: Cambridge University Press.

Verhoeven, L. (1991a). Acquisition of biliteracy. In J.H. Hulstijn & J.F. Matter (Eds.) *Reading in two languages.* Amsterdam: AILA. *AILA Review, 8,* 61-74.

Verhoeven, L. (1991b). Predicting minority children's bilingual proficiency: Child, family, and institutional factors. *Language Learning. 41*, 205-233.

Verhoeven, L. (1992). Assessment of bilingual proficiency. In L. Verhoeven & J.H.A.L. De Jong (Eds.) *The construct of language proficiency.* (pp. 124-136). Amsterdam: John Benjamins Publishing Company.

Verhoeven, L. (1994). Transfer in bilingual development: The linguistic interdependence hypothesis revisited. *Language Learning, 44,* 381-415.

Vildomec, V. (1963). *Multilingualism.* Leyden: A.W. Sythoff.

Vygotsky, L.S. (1978). *Mind in society: The development of higher psychological processes.* (Eds. M. Cole, V. John-Steiner, S. Scibner, & E. Souberman). Cambridge, MA: Harvard University Press.

Waite, J. (1992). *Aoteareo: Speaking for ourselves. Part B.: The issues. A discussion on the development of a New Zealand languages policy.* Wellington: Ministry of Education New Zealand.

Walberg, H.J. (1990). Promoting English literacy. In G. Imhoff (Ed.) *Learning in two languages: From conflict to consensus in the reorganization of schools.* (pp. 139-162). New Brunswick, N.J: Transaction Publishers.

Walsh, C.E. (1991). *Pedagogy and the struggle for voice: Issues of language, power, and schooling for Puerto Ricans.* Toronto: OISE Press.

Watt, D.L.E. & Roessingh, H. (1994). Some you win, most you lose: Tracking ESL student drop out in high school (1988-1993). *English Quarterly,* 26:3, 5-7.

Weinstein-Shr, G. & Quintero, E. (Eds.). (1995). *Immigrant learners and their families.* Washington, D.C.: ERIC/CAL.

Wells, G. (1986). *The meaning makers.* Portsmouth, NH: Heinemann.

Willig, A.C. (1981/82). The effectiveness of bilingual education: Review of a report. *NABE Journal, 6,* 1-19.

Willig, A.C. (1985). A meta-analysis of selected studies on the effectiveness of bilingual education. *Review of Educational Research, 55,* 269-317.

Willis, P. (1977). *Learning to labor: How working class kids get working class jobs.* Lexington: D.C. Heath.

Wilson, D. (1991). Native bands demand action on school's abuse of children. *The Globe and Mail*, Wednesday, June 19, 1991, p. A4.

Wirth, A. G. (1993, January). Education and work: The choices we face. *Phi Delta Kappan*, 360-366.

Wong Fillmore, L. (1985). When does teacher talk work as input? In S. Gass & C. Madden (Eds.), *Input in second language acquisition.* (pp. 17-50). Rowley, MA: Newbury House.

Wong Fillmore, L. (1989). Teaching English through content: Instructional reform in programs for language minority students. In J.H. Esling (Ed.), *Multicultural education and policy: ESL in the 1990s. A tribute to Mary Ashworth.* (pp. 125-143). Toronto: OISE Press.

Wong Fillmore, L. (1991a). Second language learning in children: A model of language learning in social context. In E. Bialystok (Ed.) *Language processing in bilingual children.* (pp. 49-69). Cambridge, UK: Cambridge University Press.

Wong Fillmore, L. (1991b). When learning a second language means losing the first. *Early Childhood Research Quarterly, 6,* 323-346.

Wong Fillmore, L. (1991c). A question for early-childhood programs: English first or families first? *Education Week,* June 19, 32 and 34.

Wong Fillmore, L. (1992). Against our best interest: The attempt to sabotage bilingual education. In J. Crawford (Ed.), *Language loyalties: A sourcebook on the Official English controversy.* Chicago: University of Chicago Press.

Wong Fillmore, L., Ammon, P., McLaughlin, B., & Ammon, M.S. (1985). *Learning English through bilingual instruction: Executive summary and conclusions.* (Final Report to the National Institute of Education). Washington, DC: U.S. Department of Education.

Wong Fillmore, L. & Valadez, C. (1986). Teaching bilingual learners. In M.C. Wittrock (Ed.) *Handbook of research on teaching. (3rd ed.)* (pp. 648-685). New York: Macmillan.

Zanger, V.V. (1994). "Not joined in": Intergroup relations and access to English literacy for Hispanic youth. In B.M. Ferdman, R-M. Weber, & A. Ramírez (Eds.) *Literacy across languages and cultures.* (pp. 171-198). Albany:

Subject Index

and language register, 89

and critical literacy, 159, 181-172, 185, 219

affirmation of, 3, 4, 9, 12, 17, 23, 74, 146-147, 149-150, 156, 186, 209

conflict, 144, 188

cultural, 35, 47, 95, 144-147, 167, 209

devaluation of, iii, iv, 3, 11, 12, 13, 30, 169

eradication of, 9, 11, 12, 32, 163

negotiation of, iv, 2, 5, 11-15, 19, 21-22, 35, 72, 78, 93, 137, 139, 144, 193, 236

oppositional, 29, 35, 138, 145

options, 13, 14, 24, 159

social, 26, 29

Immersion

Canadian model of, 39, 48, 100, 103, 105, 123, 131, 197-198, 201-204, 207-209, 212, 214-215, 221

English, 39-40, 48, 102-103, 112-115, 197-198, 203-206, 211

structured, 129-130, 199-203, 208-209, 211-215

two-way bilingual, 100-101, 103, 121-122, 132, 173, 176-180, 182, 200, 205-208, 212, 214-217, 221

Immigrant students, 33, 43, 48, 54, 61-62, 112, 205, 217

Immigration, 42, 49, 229, 232, 238-239

India, 3, 108, 125

Indigenous peoples, 3, 9, 13

Input hypothesis (i+1), 92-93

Instructional conversations, 80, 94

Interdependence principle, 67, 99, 104, 108-123, 125, 127-128, 131-133, 201, 212, 214

Internet, 96

Inuit students, 94, 139, 207

Investment, 26, 73

IQ tests, 33, 54, 104, 140, 142-143, 205

Ireland, 3, 26

K

Khmer language, 149

Kohanga reo, 187-188

Kura kaupapa Maori, 187-188

K-W-L charts, 77, 87

L

Language

awareness, 60, 81, 86-90, 96, 108, 148, 169

cognitively demanding/undemanding, 57-60, 65-66

context-embedded/context-reduced continuum of, 57-60, 65-68, 76, 94

contextualized, 56-60

decontextualized, 56-60, 67, 94

experience approach, 73

home, iv, 2, 35, 47, 69-70, 116, 124, 142-143, 165-166, 173, 186, 190-191

loss, 68, 89, 127, 189

maintenance, 89, 124, 197

New Zealand, 9, 101, 139, 166, 187-189, 191
Native students, iv, 3, 13, 27

O

Office of Civil Rights, 37

P

Pajaro Valley School District, 4-9, 14
Parental involvement, 5, 8, 9, 20, 72, 97, 114, 121, 136, 138, 145-146, 148, 166-169, 177, 186, 223
Pedagogy
    "banking" model of, 138, 152-155, 160, 162
    progressive, 152-157, 169
    traditional, 16-17, 152-156, 196
    transformative, 138, 152-154, 157-160, 176, 196
Peer-tutoring, 73, 83-84, 169
Phonics instruction, 59, 88-89, 154-155
Playground language, 56-57
Power
    coercive relations of, v-vi, 14-20, 45, 164
    collaborative relations of, vi, 14-20, 235-236
    relations, 13, 35, 46, 47, 95, 136, 139, 153-155, 162-163, 197, 211, 228
Preschool, 68, 115, 127, 135, 173-176, 187-191.
Prior experience, 60, 75-79, 83, 93, 155

Proposition 187 (California), 48, 229, 237-239
Puerto Rican students, 64, 68-69, 115-116, 204-205
Punjabi Indian students, 28, 98

Q

Quebec, vii, 38-39, 48, 126

R

Racism, 171, 193, 205, 213, 228, 238
Reading, 69, 75, 77, 80-82, 85, 91, 113-116, 120, 123, 126-130, 135, 151-152, 155, 158, 168, 173, 178-180, 186, 202, 215-216
Relationships between teachers and students, 1, 2, 23, 73-74, 135, 222, 235-236
Resistance, vii, 13, 137-138, 145, 187-188, 228
Role-play, 73, 79

S

Sami, 139
Scaffolding, 60
School failure, v, 3, 20, 64, 123, 135-137, 165, 170, 209, 226-227
Sink-or-swim programs, 46
Social class, 66, 102, 124, 130, 202, 207-208, 212, 215, 217
South Africa, 18, 116
Southeast Asian students, 24, 192
Spain, 3

Notes

Notes 279

Negotiating Identities: Education for Empowerment in a Diverse Society

Notes 281

Negotiating Identities: Education for Empowerment in a Diverse Society

Negotiating Identities: Education for Empowerment in a Diverse Society

Notes 289